WILHELM REICH VERSUS THE FLYING SAUCERS

Fig. 1. Detail from Hieronymus Bosch, *Ship of Fools* (1490–1500)

First published in 2024 by Brainstorm Books
An imprint of punctum books, Earth, Milky Way
https://www.punctumbooks.com

ISBN-13: 978-1-68571-184-9 (print)
ISBN-13: 978-1-68571-185-6 (ePDF)

DOI: 10.53288/0452.1.00

LCCN: 2024940951
Library of Congress Cataloging Data is available from the Library of
Congress

Editing: SAJ and Eileen A. Fradenburg Joy
Book design: Hatim Eujayl
Cover design: Vincent W.J. van Gerven Oei

James Reich

WILHELM REICH
versus
THE FLYING SAUCERS

An American Tragedy

Brainstorm Books
Santa Barbara, California

brainstorm books

Contents

Acknowledgments

I must express my sincere gratitude to Eileen A. Fradenburg Joy and Vincent W.J. van Gerven Oei at punctum books for their commitment to this strange book, perhaps the first to argue for the sanity of Wilhelm Reich in the terms expressed here. Thank you to SAJ for patience and insight in copyediting. Thank you, also, to Laurence A. Rickels and Avital Ronell for both their wit and for not laughing at me. This book was also assisted by the kind cooperation of the Wilhelm Reich Infant Trust and the Wilhelm Reich Archive at Orgonon, Rangeley, Maine, not least Renata Reich Moise, David Silver, and James E. Strick. Bookseller Ken Lopez provided early assistance on the trail of correspondence between Wilhelm Reich and Tuli Kupferberg which led me to the Kupferberg-Topp papers located at the Fales Library at New York University, and I am grateful to the staff there who scanned documents and transmitted them to me during the pandemic. Professors Travis Cox and Stephanie Yuhas oversaw some of my early writing on Reich at Naropa University in Boulder, Colorado, and I would like to acknowledge their generosity and that of all of my colleagues and friends during that period of graduate work and beyond. My publishers at Anti-Oedipus Press and 7.13 Books, D. Harlan Wilson, Kurt Baumeister, and Leland Cheuk have provided invaluable moral and aesthetic support. I have also been fortunate to have the encouragement of my family, particularly Sheila and Leta, with Cayley Bell, Julia Goldberg, and Michael Grodner. Most importantly, my wife Hannah made this work possible by listening to my obsessive ideas over several martinis over the past three years. And thank you, if you are reading this.

A Note on Abbreviations

To thin the bracken of footnotes that might occur with reference to Wilhelm Reich's extensive publications, frequently cited major texts are given inline citations using abbreviations. The abbreviations are as follows:

> [AO] *American Odyssey: Letters and Journals, 1940–1947*
> [BE] *The Bion Experiments on the Origin of Life*
> [BP] *Beyond Psychology: Letters and Journals, 1934–1939*
> [CA] *Character Analysis*
> [CB] *The Discovery of the Orgone,* Vol. II: *The Cancer Biopathy*
> [CO] *CORE* VI, nos. 1–4: *OROP Desert, Part 1: Space Ships, DOR and Drought*
> [CS] *Contact with Space: Oranur Second Report, 1951–1956*
> [EG] *Ether, God and Devil / Cosmic Superimposition,* combined edition
> [EI] *History of the Discovery of the Life Energy (American Period, 1939–1952): The Einstein Affair*
> [FO] *The Discovery of the Orgone,* Vol. I: *Function of the Orgasm*
> [MC] *The Murder of Christ*
> [MP] *The Mass Psychology of Fascism*
> [OE] *The Oranur Experiment: First Report (1947–1951)*
> [PY] *Passion of Youth: An Autobiography, 1897–1922*
> [RS] *Reich Speaks of Freud*

> [WT] *Where's the Truth? Letters and Journals, 1948–1957*

Where Peter Reich's *A Book of Dreams* is considered in detail in Chapter 12, the abbreviation [BD] is used to reduce footnotes.

1

Prefiguration:
Three Skips on the Water

I am neither a "fanatic" nor a "madman." Simply happen to be
involved in work that is destroying me slowly but surely.

—Wilhelm Reich[1]

On March 20, 1956, 10 p.m., a thought of a very remote possibility
entered my mind, which, I fear, will never leave me again:
Am I a Spaceman?

—Wilhelm Reich[2]

Or was this only one of the notorious aberrations of genius, a
kind of wild and lonely abstraction, the ozone of an electrical
intelligence?

—Walter Tevis[3]

On Tuesday, June 24, 1947, an uncanny flash of blue-tinged light
caught the attention of Kenneth Arnold as he piloted his small
agricultural propellor plane over Mineral Lake, Washington.
He was above the red and crystalline arsenic veins and the glit-

1 Wilhelm Reich, *Beyond Psychology: Letters and Journals, 1934–1939,* ed.
   Mary Boyd Higgins (New York: Farrar, Straus and Giroux, 1994), 181.
2 Wilhelm Reich, *Contact with Space: Oranur Second Report, 1951–1956*
   (Haverhill: Haverhill House Publishing, 2018), 1.
3 Walter Tevis, *The Man Who Fell to Earth* (London: Bloomsbury,
   1999), 68.

tering black mines of the town of Mineral, where great Douglas firs flanked the streets. The weather was good, and fishing boats waited on the lake. Arnold, a thirty-two-year-old salesman and amateur aviator, had a sublime view of Mount Rainer to the east, and it was over the pine slopes of the mountain that Arnold saw the formation of bluish unidentified flying objects that were the touchpaper to the explosive post-war "flying saucer" phenomenon. Agitated by what he had seen — perhaps, a Soviet technology — the next day, Arnold told his story to a reporter with the *East Oregonian*. Descriptions of these saucer-like objects would haunt the atomic age. Arnold said that before they raced away at what he estimated to be up to 1,700 miles per hour — Chuck Yeager would not break the sound barrier until October that year — the uncanny objects had a trajectory "like a saucer if you skip it across the water."[4]

The career of Wilhelm Reich might be seen in this analogy, in three parabolic arcs — three skips on the water — each a little shorter and, in certain ways, more intense in character than the last. Reich's four decades of work as a psychoanalyst and as an experimental scientist were haunted by a series of controversies and conspiracies, and much ink has been spilled in the service of defaming Reich, in discovering ways to declare him mad, bad, and dangerous to know. Each of these periods requires some explication, and that is where this work will begin, before turning to my analysis of the Reich fifties. Each preceding period bears vitally upon the period I am concerned with. Chapters 2 and 3 will bring us to the 1950s. The "turmoil" of 1951 which ushered him to the rim of death was a rich harvest of theory, but the same threshing served to expose the "lonely fighting wolf"[5] of Reich's character structure. There were, he would discover, new ways to be wounded. The fifties are shaped by Reich's earlier

---

4   Megan Garber, "The Man Who Introduced the World to Flying Saucers," *The Atlantic*, June 15, 2014, https://www.theatlantic.com/technology/archive/2014/06/the-man-who-introduced-the-world-to-flying-saucers/372732/.

5   Wilhelm Reich, *Where's the Truth? Letters and Journals 1948–1957*, ed. Mary Boyd Higgins (New York: Farrar, Straus and Giroux, 2012), 94.

relationship with Sigmund Freud and its consequences, and by his thwarted overtures toward Albert Einstein.

"There is no trap so deadly," says Raymond Chandler's Philip Marlowe, "as the trap you set for yourself."[6] Marlowe says this in *The Long Goodbye,* published in 1953, the same year that Wilhelm Reich began reading about flying saucers. Reich had said as much about these existential snares in *The Murder of Christ* in 1951. *"The trap,"* Reich says, *"is man's emotional structure, his character structure."*[7] Among many revelatory passages in *The Murder of Christ,* Reich refers to a theory found in Chapter XXII of Ernest Renan's 1927 *The Life of Jesus,* entitled "Machinations of the Enemies of Jesus." Reich reads Renan on the raising of Lazarus at Bethany:

> Some interpreters of Christ believe that the revival of Lazarus was "put over" on Christ by his friends who wanted to help him to fame, to victory over the apathy toward his teachings in Jerusalem (Renan). According to this interpretation, Lazarus, who was reported dead, emerged from a tomb with bandages on his head and body, to meet Christ. Christ was shaken into a tremor, to see his friend alive, and had really nothing whatsoever to do with the whole performance.[8]

As Renan puts it, "Everything, in fact, seems to lead us to believe that the miracle of Bethany contributed sensibly to hasten the death of Jesus."[9] One sees in this passage an ironic prescience, that some of the acts attending Reich in his late years were performative, not least some of those involving flying saucers, UFOS, spaceships, or as Reich would christen them, Ea (Energy Alpha). Renan, followed by D.H. Lawrence, and Wilhelm Reich after him, located the man beneath the Christ. Lawrence's final work of fiction, the novella *The Man Who Died* (1929) was a sig-

6 Raymond Chandler, *The Long Goodbye* (New York: Vintage, 1992), 86.
7 Wilhelm Reich, *The Murder of Christ* (New York: Farrar, Straus and Giroux, 1971), 3. All italics in quotations are present in the original text, unless stated otherwise.
8 Ibid., 118.
9 Ernest Renan, *The Life of Jesus* (London: Trübner & Co., 1871), 252.

nificant influence on *The Murder of Christ*. It had a prodigious effect upon the present writer also, when he encountered it in his teens. Its second part, conflating Christ and Osiris, is indebted to James G. Frazer's *The Golden Bough*. Returning to Lawrence's novella now, one finds an almost orgonomic Jesus in the man who, like Renan's Lazarus, had been mistaken for dead.

> "Don't be afraid," said the man in the shroud. "I am not dead. They took me down too soon. So I have risen up. Yet if they discover me, they will do it all over again..."[10]

Such is Reich's self-conscious thesis in *The Murder of Christ*, that iterations of "Christ" are to be destroyed whenever they arise, for such is the emotional plague of our species, armored against the individual and the flow of the life energy that is Reich's "orgone." To *The Man Who Died*, Lawrence preferred the work's phallic original title *The Escaped Cock*,[11] and one registers something of what Reich must have felt reading Lawrence.

> And the man who had died watched the unsteady, rocking vibration of the bent bird, and it was not the bird he saw, but one wave-tip of life overlapping for a minute another, in the tide of the swaying ocean of life. And the destiny of life seemed more fierce and compulsive to him even than the destiny of death. The doom of death was a shadow compared to the raging destiny of life, the determined surge of life.[12]

Others also experience this familiarity in reading Reich after reading Lawrence, particularly the latter's psychosomatic contra-Freudian works *Psychoanalysis and the Unconscious* and *Fantasia of the Unconscious*, both published in 1923. This was certainly the case for Norman Mailer. Despite their differences, reading Reich after Lawrence reminds one of the obscure mechanisms that intrigued Harold Bloom until the end: *transumption*, or "a trope that revises earlier figurations so as to make them seem belated,

10 D.H. Lawrence, *The Man Who Died* (New York: Ecco, 2002), 11.
11 Ibid., 94.
12 Ibid., 18.

16

and itself possessing priority."[13] Reading Reich has the uncanny effect of transuming Lawrence, as if Lawrence's work did not prefigure Reich's, but was under its influence. Lawrence is one of the trinity invoked by Reich in April 1952, during one of his melancholy hours, remarking upon the resistance to "the discovery of genitality, life, love, such people as Lawrence, or such philosophies as Giordano Bruno's or such great lives as Jesus Christ, and so forth, and so forth. It is a sad, lonely chapter of the human race."[14] Such were the 1950s for Wilhelm Reich.

The present writer who is no relation to Wilhelm Reich, having invoked Philip Marlowe, so admits that this is a psychoanalytic detective story — a mystery, if you will. I am interested in the ways in which Reich unconsciously entered the trap he had set for himself, and interested in those of his remaining intimates who were part of its consolidation. The writer is detective to his own feelings about Reich, his own depressions, also. This will not — it cannot — satisfy everyone. That should be the intention of no writer. It is all right with me. Others have written about the investigations and injunctions against Reich that flourished in the last years of his life, of Reich's trial and his entanglements with the United States Food and Drug Administration (FDA), the FBI, and spectral men in black in their big, black cars. This is not a book about those conspiratorial fogs, but it is about the psychic mechanisms that defended against them: the cinema, the escape personality, art. Reich's relationship with cinema, and the mechanisms of introjection and projection that are discussed in detail in Chapter 6, are not dissimilar — I believe — to those of many readers of this book, even if they are intensified by the specific circumstances of Reich's case. The ways in which this relationship defined his life and career in the 1950s, and how this affected his relationships for better and worse is at the heart of this book.

---

13 Harold Bloom, *Take Arms Against a Sea of Troubles: The Power of the Reader's Mind Over a Universe of Death* (New Haven: Yale University Press, 2020), 20.

14 Anonymous23Skidoo, "Wilhelm Reich – Alone (10 min. home recording) (03.04.1952)," *YouTube,* March 23, 2012, https://www.youtube.com/watch?v=4t5h-93bxOY.

This book was conceived, some years ago, from the writer's own dissatisfaction with the tendency to reduce Reich's last years to psychopathy and paranoia, or to flinch from them. As I regarded the Reich fifties, not least through his admitted cinematic self-identification, I saw someone who was not pathological, but sympathetically "normal" in the way that alienation, atomic-age life, experience, subjectivity — *Dasein*— affected him. There will be those who reject this work as the work, too much, of a novelist, written with a novelist's pattern recognition. A few, I trust, will find something of themselves in my understanding — some will say interpretation — of Reich. The cast of this mystery, this all-too-human American tragedy of Reich and his family and assistants, also includes Sigmund Freud, Albert Einstein, Robert Oppenheimer, punk rocker Patti Smith, avant-pop musician Kate Bush, writers William S. Burroughs and Norman Mailer, poet and performer Tuli Kupferberg, actors Michael Rennie and Spencer Tracy, J. Edgar Hoover, actor and sometime Warhol "Superstar" Jackie Curtis, and the flying saucer investigator and agitator, retired Major Donald Keyhoe.

This book will not substantiate Reich's speculations or beliefs about extraterrestrial interference with the biosphere. Colin Wilson writes of Reich's belief in such influence, "No doubt this conclusion *was* due in part to Reich's paranoia, but it is also necessary to admit that even if he had been completely balanced and unsuspicious, he might still have arrived at the same conclusion."[15] Wilson's last clause is important: one does not have to be paranoid or pathological to believe what Reich believed. In 2019, 41% of American adults, including 37% of college graduates, reported the belief that at least some unidentified flying objects have been of alien origin.[16] *Wilhelm Reich Versus the Flying Saucers* is not written to validate anyone's belief or unbelief in the nature of unidentified flying objects, although

---

15 Colin Wilson, *The Quest for Wilhelm Reich: A Critical Biography* (New York: Anchor Press/Doubleday, 1981), 216.

16 Lydia Saad, "Larger Minority in U.S. Says Some UFOS Are Alien Spacecraft," *Gallup News*, August 20, 2021, https://news.gallup.com/poll/353420/larger-minority-says-ufos-alien-spacecraft.aspx.

perhaps the reader will agree with me about their psychic content.

As I write, yesterday was the anniversary of Reich's birth, March 24. The book resisted me yesterday. Yet, if you are reading this, then it means that I have outdone the legendary English theatre critic Kenneth Tynan on one front: Tynan's book on Reich was never finished. Tynan, a brilliant, laconic sado-masochist, was a force in the promotion of the so-called *angry young men* of British letters who emerged in 1956, including Colin Wilson who published his own critical biography *The Quest for Wilhelm Reich* in 1981. Tynan is right on certain points, not least when he writes, "When one takes a sexual or political line as intransigent as Reich's, one is going to end up without much succor and without many friends. The attack from the outside will be fairly unremitting. The only comfort and fulfillment to be derived from the situation is the knowledge that such situations cannot bring comfort or fulfillment."[17] The entry is from May 12, 1972, exactly one year after Yugoslavian director Dušan Makavejev's *WR: Misterije organizma* (*WR: Mysteries of the Organism*),[18] had shown at the Cannes Film Festival where it won the Luis Buñuel Award before vanishing temporarily under censorship. The film is dismal in terms of representing Reich, and there will be explication of this later. Tynan's emphasis on Reich's "political line" almost certainly reflects the anachronistic and inaccurate Reich myth perpetuated in the film. *WR: Mysteries of the Organism* was shown at Cannes under the auspices of the Director's Fortnight, the *soixante-huitard* wing of the festival to whom the Marxism of the film appealed, despite Reich's actual ambivalence toward Karl Marx, his vehement hostility toward Communism, or "red fascism" as he referred to it, which had been evident since at least 1933 and his early masterpiece *The Mass Psychology of Fascism*. Reich's later politics, such as they were in the fifties, had he lived a little longer, might conceivably have been described as quasi-Birchite, certainly insofar as his loathing for Stalinist totalitarian-

17 Kenneth Tynan, *The Diaries of Kenneth Tynan,* ed. John Lahr (New York: Bloomsbury, 2001), 95.
18 Dušan Makavejev, dir., *WR: Mysteries of the Organism* (Neoplanta Film, 1971).

ism is concerned. In 1947, in preparation for a new edition of *Die Bione* (*The Bion Experiments*), Reich insisted that, given the progress made in orgone research *away* from Marxist dialectics and mechanism, it would be "most important of all, to change the term 'dialectical materialism' to 'energetic functionalism' which it truly and really is. [...] I don't wish anymore to be confused with the Marxist political parties."[19] None of this disturbed Makavejev's mythic agenda, and one suspects that Tynan would have held the Marxist line, also, had his own sensualism and lassitude not intervened. In August of 1953, Tynan was sardonic on the subject:

> Freud says one must forgo sensual pleasure in favor of cultural achievement. Reich says cultural achievement is valueless unless one has sensual pleasure. Following Reich, I refuse to work on my book about Reich for more than four to five hours a day, and devote the rest to pleasure. This inevitably cuts down my achievement. Thus: in order to write a Reichian book about Reich, I must delay writing a book about Reich.[20]

By the end of April 1974, Tynan's book on Reich was "hopelessly blocked: I'm stuck halfway through, and have lost control of my material (as well as interest in it)."[21] There will be more on the effects of Bohemia on Reich's reputation later.

Even prior to his coronary death at sixty within the bitter precincts of Lewisburg Federal Penitentiary, a dark confusion subsumed Reich's life and career, obscuring it beneath a surface of myth and misunderstanding. Inadvertently, Reich seemed to work with increasing intensity toward becoming *persona non grata;* and this was as true with psychoanalysis in the mid-1930s as it was with his experiments with climate, the environment, and "flying saucers" in the mid-1950s. Ironically, Reich "the outsider" has always been popular with countercultures that have both kept his name and work alive, but which have also tended

19 Wilhelm Reich, *The Bion Experiments on the Origin of Life* (New York: Farrar, Straus and Giroux, 1979), v.
20 Tynan, *Diaries of Kenneth Tynan,* 153.
21 Ibid., 175.

to distort both in ways which unwittingly serve Reich's many detractors. In the theatre of sex, Woody Allen's parody of Reich's work in *Sleeper* (1973), the "Orgasmatron," served merely to compound the myth of Reich that always dogged him and had done so particularly since the spring of 1938. During this period at the edge of war — the same in which Freud was arrested by national Socialists in Vienna, before his final exile in London — Reich experienced a series of antisemitic and sex-hysterical attacks in the Norwegian press; Reich had gone to Norway to evade fascism and to continue his bioelectric analysis of libidinal energy, and his experiments concerning the development of cancer cells, the so-called "Bion Experiments." In Reich's words of March 30 of that year, "The extremely stupid smear campaign conducted against the experiments has taken on serious proportions" [BP, 139]. Exiled, and increasingly isolated against the Norwegian scientific establishment, on April 3, Reich wrote: "Once again, I am completely alone in outer space" [BP, 141]. Unconsciously and inexorably, this was his trajectory.

On April 21, 1938, the newspaper *Tidens Tegn* framed Reich thus: "Genius, Dilettante, or Psychopath?" [BP, 146]. A headline in the fascist paper *ABC* offered "Proof That Reich Is a Fraud" [ibid.]. Reich records that the next day *Tidens Tegn* published the "Recommendation that Reich be sent to a concentration camp" [BP, 147]. *Fritt Folk,* the newspaper of the Norwegian fascist party Nasjonal Samling founded by Vidkun Quisling who would become Prime minister of Norway during its Nazi occupation, followed on April 23. Reich's journals paraphrase: "Reich is the slimiest kind of pornographer and he was driven out of Germany." [ibid.]. The article which referred to Reich as a "Jewish pornographer" was written by Quisling's brother Jørgen.[22] Almost a decade later, in the United States, Mildred Edie Brady's 1947 article for *Harper's,* "The New Cult of Sex and Anarchy," reinvigorated the prurient myth of Reich as sex-guru. The moral panic, vitriol, and ridicule Reich attracted always revealed more about the society in which he lived and worked than it did about Reich's work. The essential tragedy of Reich's

22 James E. Strick, *Wilhelm Reich: Biologist* (Cambridge: Harvard University Press, 2015), 231.

life is that he was a scapegoat of reactionary social-political forces, a folk devil for conservatives, subject to the transference of what Reich would call "armored" characters, and brought low by bureaucratic manifestations of what he referred to as "the emotional plague." In the context of ongoing persecutions, Reich not unreasonably envisioned his martyrdom, and this — handing a loaded revolver to his enemies — was turned against him, also.

From June 5 to August 26, 1956, with axes and incinerators, the United States FDA worked to silence Reich by destroying his equipment and burning more than six tons of Reich's literature. This was an event unique in the history of the United States, reminiscent as it was of the Nazi book burnings of May 1933, beginning with the attack on the library of sexologist Magnus Hirschfeld's *Institut für Sexualwissenschaft* and culminating a few days later in the *Bebelplatz* with the burning of works by Freud, Einstein, Marx, and a host of other "subversives." Only, in Wilhelm Reich's case in America, he remains the only victim of this same totalitarian governmental impulse to systematically burn publications and research. It is often argued that Reich did not help his own case, that he was defiant, arrogant, and that his tragedy contains that element of hubris common to all tragedy. To which I say, so what? Deliberately, Reich aligned himself with the scientific martyr Giordano Bruno, burned at the stake by the Inquisition in 1600, and with the incarcerated Galileo; to be a man of convictions, however controversial, and to be willing to test one's convictions and to risk error in the service of understanding, were essential to Reich's character. Giordano Bruno is one of the martyrs in Reich's *The Murder of Christ.* The martyr should not, he insisted, be a matter for legislation or punishment where they contradicted consensus. The martyr's convictions would become, in every sense, his convictions.

To the extent it is known today, Reich's name is synonymous with two misunderstood concepts in his work: orgasm, or the orgasm formula, and orgone, or orgone energy. The former informed the latter. Reich's theory of orgasm, sometimes also referred to as the orgasm reflex or the orgasm mechanism, is expressed in his 1948 account of his work from 1919–1939, *The Function of the Orgasm.*

MECHANICAL TENSION → BIOELECTRIC CHARGE → BIO-
ELECTRIC DISCHARGE → MECHANICAL RELAXATION. This
proved to be the formula for living functioning as such. It led
to the experimental investigation of the organization of living
from non-living matter, to experimental bion research, and
more recently to the discovery of orgone radiation.[23]

Reich developed Freud's theory of a conservative libidinal energy
and observed sexual repression, neuroses, and psychoses were
manifest and expressed in rigidity and other instances of what
he called "character armor." Reich believed that orgasm in the
genital embrace could unblock and release biopsychic or biopathic disease, but he *never* asserted "orgastic potency" or that
"the capacity to surrender to the flow of biological energy, free
of any inhibitions; the capacity to discharge completely the
damned-up sexual excitation through involuntary, pleasurable
convulsions of the body" [FO, 102] was merely a matter of *quan-
tity,* of *more* sex, and *more* orgasms. This misconception, perpetuated by establishment and countercultural actors in aligned
confusion — frequently deliberate and self-serving — damaged
Reich's reputation significantly, and set in motion all of the
mechanisms of persecution that exaggerated his downfall. The
problem for Reich was that his certainty about the orgasm and
his shifting ambivalence on the subject of UFOS, his attempts
to understand the phenomena, formed similar reactions in his
allies and detractors, this sometimes genuine and sometimes will-
ful confusion. Yet, Reich was no more of a "free love" advocate
than was Freud, or Carl Jung. What Reich achieved in his theory
of the orgasm was an extension, implicit in Freud's "Beyond
the Pleasure Principle" (1920), of the contraction and release of
unpleasure and pleasure, to what Reich called a "*common functioning principle*"[24] in nature. This, he observed in all living sys-

23 Wilhelm Reich, *The Discovery of the Orgone,* Vol. I: *The Function of the
    Orgasm: Sex-Economic Problems of Biological Energy,* trans. Vincent R.
    Carfango (New York: Farrar, Straus and Giroux, 1973), 9 and 275.
24 Wilhelm Reich, *Ether, God and Devil/Cosmic Superimposition* (New
    York: Farrar, Straus and Giroux, 1973), 167.

tems, from the most microscopic and, eventually, to a flourishing cosmology.

Orgone (OR) is Reich's term for pre-atomic, mass-free life energy that is both atmospheric and present within organic matter. As will become clear, Reich stressed the importance of orgone energy as primordial, *before matter,* versus nuclear energy as an *after matter.* For Reich, within the Cold War, there was even a *moral* distinction between the "good" life energy of orgone and the "evil" destructive energy released in atomic physics. In his experiments, the bluish lumination of orgone was perceptible as a fog on photographic plates, in the aurora borealis, in the intensifications of blue in the sky, in thunderclouds, and in the blue of the ocean and of deep mountain lakes. It was also visible in vacuum tubes and could be intensified and made more perceptible within an orgone accumulator — that "orgasm box" of myth and slander. Although he did not systematically describe orgone energy as such until 1939, Reich's interest in the origins of life and of vitalism — and orgonomy is not vitalism — emerged concurrent with his nascent studies in sexology and psychoanalysis in 1919. In his readings of Hans Dreisch, Reich was unconvinced by the German's reliance upon Aristotelian entelechy, concluding "I couldn't quite accept the transcendentalism of the life principle" [FO, 23]. Henri Bergson influenced Reich: "My present theory of the identity and unity of psychophysical functioning originated in Bergsonian thinking, and has become a new theory of the functional relationship between body and mind," but, Reich says, "his 'élan vital' reminded me very much of Dreisch's 'entelechy'" [FO, 23–24]. Thus neither was satisfactory, nor were teleological intrusions into biology. Reich attended lectures by Paul Kammerer and was impressed by this "champion of the natural organization of life from inorganic matter and of the existence of a specific biological energy" [FO, 26]. Reich's meeting with Freud provided the necessary synthesis: "Freud's 'libido' is and can be nothing other than the energy of the sexual instinct" [FO, 30]. Orgone is pulsatory, consistent with the mechanism of tension and release in the orgasm; indeed, the mechanism is recapitulated from orgone, which is to say the orgasm reflex, that is all life, evidences orgonomic, or orgonotic functionalism. "Orgonotic functions of attraction, penetration, pulsation, and lumination had already been observed in the period between 1936 and 1939, and had been subjected to investigation in a variety of bion preparations. However, I had no presentiment that I was working with manifestations of a specific biological energy."[25] Of the bion, Reich explains, "The term 'bion' refers to the vesicles into which all matter disintegrates if made to swell. The vesicles represent transitional forms between non-living and living matter. *The bion is the elemental functioning unit of all living matter.* At the same time it is the bearer of a quantum of orgone energy and, as such, functions in a specifically biological way" [CB, 15]. From observation and experimentation, Reich named orgone and orgonicity in the spring of 1939. It would be his theoretical ground until the end of his life. Reich observed the evidence for orgone energy in atmospheric luminescence and as an energetic field surrounding inorganic forms. The fullest account is given in Reich's *The Cancer Biopathy: Volume II of the Discovery of the Orgone,* and is described in the theoretical context of the history of biogenesis in James E. Strick's *Wilhelm Reich, Biologist* (2015). Reich understood immediately that his thesis could only be elucidated at great cost.

And there is no doubt that Reich's work can be difficult, to Kenneth Tynan's point about losing control of the material. The greater difficulty is that his work at times asks questions from which polite minds have recoiled. The lesser, but not insubstantial difficulty one encounters in reading Reich is in his elliptical exposition. There are instances in his retrospective reports of the 1950s, not least his writing in *The Oranur Experiment: First Report (1947–1951), CORE* VI, nos. 1–4: *OROP Desert, Part 1: Space Ships, DOR and Drought,* and *Contact with Space: Oranur Second Report, 1951–1956* that will be elucidated here, where Reich's chronological reportage is confounded by the force of his energies, the simultaneity of his various turmoils. Indeed, not only reading, but also writing about Reich can be difficult due to his searching, mercurial, autodidactic disposition which led to a vertiginous output of theory and experimentation, even as he

25 Wilhelm Reich, *The Discovery of the Orgone,* Vol. II: *The Cancer Biopathy,* trans. Andrew White, Mary Higgins, and Chester M. Raphael (New York: Farrar, Straus and Giroux, 1973), 14.

was increasingly involved in personal and legal struggles. Reich possessed, to an extraordinary degree, the ability to sustain and separate several competing fronts, and yet this had its limits, and arguably this relentlessness and passion exhausted his heart.

Reich's published letters and journals reveal withering depressions and ecstatic convictions. Resolutely within the human sciences, Reich's temperament nonetheless fits our heroic yet melancholic image of the artist, as much as, or more than it does the conventional image of the scientist. This cycle of tension, charge, discharge, and relaxation, this pulsation in Reich's life that was its restless motion is its own kind of continuity; it was as Reich saw it, describing what he would call the orgasm formula, "the formula of living functioning as such" [FO, 9]. As a result, Myron Sharaf, a patient and intimate who attempted the first comprehensive biography of Reich, threw in the towel, and produced an equally elliptical biography where, for example, the events of 1940–1950 are covered in overlapping cubist chapters, sequentially: "Getting Settled in America: 1939–41," "The Discovery of the Orgone: 1940," "The Medical Effects of the Orgone Accumulator, 1940–1948," "Psychiatric, Sociological, and Education Developments: 1940–1950," "Personal Life and Relations with Colleagues: 1941–1950," and "The American Campaign against Orgonomy — The Beginnings: 1947–1948."[26] It is my intention to avoid this cubism here, as far as is possible.

What to make of this man who fled Nazism, only to have his writing and research incinerated by the government of the United States? What to make of this man so constant in the vicissitudes of "the sexual revolution" from the 1930s through the 1960s, and who toiled to vindicate and further Freud's theories of libido where Jung and others could not stand to; of this man who perceived the totalitarian impulses of the right and left and delineated their psychologies; of this of man who declared a planetary emergency far in advance of the modern environmental movement; of this man who was immersed in atomic age and Cold War preoccupations and anxieties — radiation, movies, flying saucers, Communism, morality, youth, religion,

26 Myron R. Sharaf, *Fury on Earth: A Biography of Wilhelm Reich* (New York: Da Capo, 1994).

freedom — and whose sincere pursuit of knowledge, of an episte-
mology, an ontology, and a cosmology, destroyed him?

The third and final plangent skim and skip of Reich's career
was the arc that began in 1950, when he turned his experiments
with orgone energy to immunization from the effects of radiation sickness, to weather control with the iconic cloudbuster
device, and then to interventions against UFOS using the cloudbuster now recast as a space gun. Herbert Marcuse deigned to
call these "the wild and fantastic hobbies of Reich's later years."[27]
This book takes issue with that condescension. This is a book
about, among other things, how a life of meaning is constructed,
and I trust the reader will understand that this is neither hatchet
nor hagiography, but an interpretation of Reich in the fifties that
does not diagnose to dismiss, nor analyze away Wilhelm Reich's
last seven years as merely a series of psychotic symptoms.

Throughout this final arc of his career, Reich was engaged
with the US government on two losing fronts: to have his ideas
taken seriously as contributions to the Cold War effort against
"red fascism," and to defend his work — specifically the orgone
accumulator — against ongoing litigation from the FDA. The
latter would lead to his imprisonment in Lewisburg Federal
Penitentiary where he was admitted on March 19, 1957, almost
precisely one year after he posed the question of cosmic identity that opened this book, and where he died as an inmate on
November 3.

It was during this period of emergencies in the fifties that
Reich saw his first flying saucer, or spaceship. Writing in 1954,
he dates this experience to a day in August 1952. The moment is
recalled with striking nonchalance. Indeed, the object is *heard*
more than seen, "crossing the sky from horizon to horizon in
a few seconds with a speed unknown on earth. I knew it was a
space ship."[28] Recalling how he had been standing on his terrace,
outside his laboratory, Reich goes on, "There was no undue surprise connected with this observation; it was not even written

27 Herbert Marcuse, *Eros and Civilization: A Philosophical Inquiry into
     Freud* (Boston: Beacon Press, 1974), 239.
28 Wilhelm Reich, *CORE (Cosmic Orgone Engineering)* VI, nos. 1–4:
     OROP Desert, Part 1: Space Ships, DOR and Drought (1954): 19.

down in the Log book. Several people had reported seeing *fly-ing saucers'* near Orgonon [Reich's laboratory, observatory, and home] in 1952" [COE, 19–20]. In 1954, Reich was engaged in vari-ous struggles with these flying saucers, and by 1956 he was able to speculate on the ontological problem, that of a cosmic identity, that opened this book.

Reich's placement of his encounter in the fall of 1952 sets it prior to his reading of either of the two most influential fly-ing saucer books of the early fifties, Donald Keyhoe's *Flying Saucers from Outer Space* which Reich read in the fall of 1953, and Keyhoe's first saucer book from 1950, *The Flying Saucers Are Real* which Reich did not read until 1954 [CO, 19n]. Not only was it not recorded in the lab's Log Book, but there is no mention of this event in the three August entries for 1952 in Reich's pub-lished letters and journals. There, as elsewhere, Reich does not mention UFOS, flying saucers, or spaceships until the late spring of 1954. It would be irresponsible to ignore the possibility that Reich engaged in some careful revisionism regarding the 1952 encounter. But in any case, before 1954, Reich had been through a series of emergencies and introjections that informed his fly-ing saucer experiences that will be explored later: the Oranur emergency, Reich's fateful encounter with Robert Wise's film *The Day the Earth Stood Still* (1951), and the uncanny return of Freud. The flying saucer work emerges, very specifically, from these. Reich had good reasons for his "unreasonable" behavior.

Retired Major Donald E. Keyhoe's *Flying Saucers from Outer Space* was published in August 1953. It was thirty years since Keyhoe's retirement, and this was his second influential book on the subject of UFOS. Since the mid-1920s he had been freelanc-ing as a writer of pulp fiction for *Weird Tales,* then more consis-tently for the Fu Manchu rip-off *Dr. Yen Sin,* and a series of para-normal aviation war stories for *Flying Aces* magazine. Keyhoe's first contribution to flying saucer mythology was an eight-page article entitled "The Flying Saucers Are Real," written for *True* magazine, published in December 1949. On the basis of its noto-riety and magazine sales, the article was expanded and published as a book in 1950. Keyhoe's article and first book popularized and standardized many aspects of flying saucer or UFO mythol-ogy in the 1950s. In his Author's Note to the book-length *The*

Flying Saucers Are Real, Keyhoe quotes a secret Air Force report, Project "Saucer." A significant theory that receives only glancing speculation in the original article is now fully developed. Of these strange visitors, Project "Saucer" says: "Such a civilization might observe that on Earth we now have atomic bombs and are fast developing rockets. In view of the past history of mankind, they should be alarmed. We should therefore expect at this time above all to behold such visitations."[29] This is precisely the premise of the 1951 science fiction film and Cold War parable *The Day the Earth Stood Still*[30] that so affected Reich, his cinematic sense of self, and his relationship with his son, Peter.

A review of Keyhoe's second saucer book, *Flying Saucers from Outer Space,* appeared in the *New York Times Book Review* on November 22, 1953, framed with advertisements for Bibles, textbooks on Hinduism and Judaism, and *Audubon Magazine's* 'Killer...Welcome' announcing the rehabilitated reputation of the coyote. Jonathan N. Leonard's review does not stoop to flatter but lacerates Keyhoe's account of an Air Force conspiracy of silence. In Leonard's most biting line, "It contains abundant evidence that the major is no expert in the field of physics."[31] This is the kind of accusation that haunted Reich almost from the moment he turned from psychoanalysis to experimental biology and physics.

In researching *Flying Saucers from Outer Space,* Keyhoe was briefly returned to active duty in order to conduct interviews and receive the classified material that underpins the book. Among the many real-life figures encountered in Keyhoe's interactions with the Air Technical Intelligence Center are Captain Edward J. Ruppelt, director of Project Blue Book, the UFO investigative contingent of the US Air Force from 1952 until 1969, and journalist Frank Scully, whose name appears in homage in the television series *The X-Files.* Keyhoe's terse investigative writing

29 Donald E. Keyhoe, *The Flying Saucers Are Real,* illust. Frank Tinsley (New York: Fawcett Publications, 1950), np.

30 Robert Wise, dir., *The Day the Earth Stood Still* (20th Century Fox, 1951).

31 Jonathan N. Leonard, "Flying Sky-High," *The New York Times Book Review,* November 22, 1953, 50.

and the television show's enigmatic, pulpy atmosphere are kin-
dred styles. My own 1954 paperback copy of *Flying Saucers from
Outer Space* depicts six yellowish flying saucers streaking over
Manhattan. This follow-up is a hard-boiled memoir disclosing
Keyhoe's meetings with military and intelligence witnesses to
UFO phenomena "to prepare all Americans, whether skeptics or
believers, for the final act of the saucer drama — an act that will
have an impact on the lives of all of us."[32] Reich would use similar language in his assessment of *The Day the Earth Stood Still*:
"It tended to prepare the population for extraordinary events
to come" [CS, 2]. This saucer drama played out in the last act
of the life of Wilhelm Reich, and Keyhoe's book would inform
elements of Reich's late theory, with its reports of flying saucers
emitting light with a "queer blue tinge,"[33] suggestive of Reich's
observations of orgone energy.

Reich was not alone in being one of Freud's original circle
who was influenced by flying saucer phenomena. *Flying Saucers
from Outer Space,* among other conspiratorial works by Keyhoe,
informed Jung's *Flying Saucers: A Modern Myth of Things Seen
in the Sky,* which was first published in 1958,[34] a year after Reich's
death, and was published in English the following year. Our
cause necessitates a brief flyby of Jung's shifting positions on flying saucer incidents and observations. This was Jung's twilight,
after the imposing alchemical *Mysterium Coniunctionis.* Jung's
short book on flying saucers is concerned with UFOS as "visionary rumors"[35] or projections. After a brief panic that occurred to
Jung in 1950, his aim was to reclaim the flying saucer as mandala,
and to reintegrate these aberrant forms as a psychosomatic technology within his gnostic, alchemical *weltanschauung.* In some
anticipation of protest that Jung always and ever considered fly-

32 Donald E. Keyhoe, *Flying Saucers from Outer Space* (Hutchinson:
    Doubleday, 1954), 7.

33 Ibid., 24.

34 Carl Jung, *Flying Saucers: A Modern Myth of Things Seen in the Sky*
    (Oxford: Routledge, 2002). The term "flying saucers" does not appear
    in Jung's original German title: *Ein moderner Mythus: Von Dingen, die
    am Himmel gesehen werden.*

35 Ibid., 1–19.

ing saucers as *psychic* phenomena, and thus he should not be compared with Reich, let us not forget an entry from the diaries of Mircea Eliade. The subject of flying saucers came up during the 1950 Eranos Conference on the banks of Lake Maggiore, Ascona-Moscia, southern Switzerland. On August 22, Eliade watched Jung reclining on a terrace at Casa Eranos, apparently attending a lecture by Gershom Scholem by listening through the open window. At the conference, Jung smuggled food into his room to sustain himself against the meagre catering of Eranos's Mme. Frobe-Kapetyn. Mircea Eliade records an encounter between Jung and his colleague, the French philosopher Henry Corbin.

> Jung told Corbin that he is grief-stricken over the real existence of "flying saucers." Always he believed in the symbolic significance of the circle and the circular; now that "the circle" seems actually to be "realized," it no longer interests him. It seemed infinitely more real to him in dreams and myths.[36]

Jung's grief in the fall of 1950 upon finding, like Donald Keyhoe's title, that the flying saucers are real, and his — petulant, was it? — abandonment of the circular motif needed treatment, and some analysis to recover his core ideas. The material reality of flying saucers briefly threatened the integrity of Jung's system, and there is something of an existential crisis, a grasping, in Jung's book. Jung seems, briefly, to bring the flying saucer within his domain, only to have it confound him again. I describe Jung's experience not least to illustrate the way in which Reich's reputation suffered as a result of his engagement with UFO phenomena where Jung's did not, even when Jung asked equally cinematic questions, including the idea that his being was a figment of alien imagination. The simplest explanation for Jung's escape of the saucer stigmata is that Jung avoided the stigmatization of sexology, took a diffuse view of libidinal energies, and thus was not victim of orchestrated slanders and libels. In October of 1958, after publication of his flying saucer book, Jung had a dream of two UFOS, both saucer-shaped lenses, "metallically gleaming disks,

36 Mircea Eliade, *Journal I, 1945–1955,* trans. Mac Linscott Ricketts (Chicago: University of Chicago Press, 1990), 113.

which hurtled in a narrow arc over the house and down to the lake."[37] Jung recounts: "I awoke with a feeling of astonishment. Still half in the dream, the thought passed through my head: 'We always think that the UFOS are projections of ours. Now it turns out that we are their projections.' I am projected by the magic lantern as C.G. Jung. But who manipulates the apparatus?"[38]

Now, is Reich's probing of his cosmic identity any more radical than Jung's? Certainly, it is not. Lastly, Jung was also more explicit than Reich in his endorsement of Donald Keyhoe. Jung wanted to "call attention to Keyhoe's books, which are based on official material and studiously avoid the wild speculation, *naïveté* or prejudice of other publications."[39] Perhaps that is an extravagant claim. Jung incorporated the perspective of Project "Saucer" and Keyhoe in his summary of the saucer literature: "It also seems that airfields and atomic installations held a particular attraction for them, from which it was concluded that the dangerous development of atomic physics and nuclear fission had caused a certain disquiet on our neighboring planets and necessitated a more accurate survey from the air."[40] In his early pages, Jung follows Reich in evoking versions of H.G. Wells's Martian invasion. Reich says that he saw "the Wells film 'The War Between (sic) the Worlds'" [CS, 6] in early January 1954. He is, of course, referring to the George Pal version of *The War of the Worlds*[41] directed by Byron Haskin, released in August 1953, simultaneous with Keyhoe's *Flying Saucers from Outer Space.*

With each skip on the water, Reich's "official" reputation diminished, exacerbated by rejections. Each subsequent parabolic arc brought him closer to both the entropic forces of a countercultural audience that misunderstood and distorted his work, and suspicious agencies in psychoanalysis, biology, physics, and at last within the US government. With the three major

---

37 Carl Jung, *Memories, Dreams, Reflections,* ed. Aniela Jaffé, trans. Richard Winston and Clara Winston (New York: Vintage, 1989), 323.

38 Ibid., 323.

39 Jung, *Flying Saucers,* xiii.

40 Ibid., 3.

41 Byron Haskin, dir., *H.G. Wells' The War of the Worlds* (Paramount, 1953).

arcs of Reich's theoretical trajectory, with each shortened parabola, so did his work deal with more extraordinary questions, and so did his theoretical positions come to be regarded as more eccentric. In 2005, Christopher Turner, author of *Adventures in the Orgasmatron*, put the idea directly to Reich's son Peter that, "in every biography of Reich there seems to be a cut-off point, an eye-rolling threshold after which the biographer considers Reich to be mad. For the psychoanalysts, it was Lucerne; for others it was one of his odd inventions, be it the orgone box, the cloudbuster, or the space gun."[42] So, I want to go beyond the conventional cut-off points and chronicle the last years of Reich's life and work without eye-rolling, and without any obstruction of self-interest.

How does one come to ask extraordinary questions, perhaps to believe extraordinary things? Wilhelm Reich did both. This book is about how those questions arose, how a psychoanalyst and scientist — heir to Sigmund Freud — came to be regarded as psychotic, how he has been mythologized and misunderstood, and how this might happen to any of us, depending on the constellation of our experiences.

At the outset, I should say that I do not regard Reich or his work after the initial psychoanalytic period as "mad," nor as Paul Robinson, author of *The Freudian Left*, has it, "insane."[43] Nor do I agree with Colin Wilson's initial assessment in *The Quest for Wilhelm Reich* that Reich was "more or less insane"[44] and quite deserving of imprisonment. Reich was not mad. Even if he was, to steal Norman Mailer's self-identity, a figure of "monumental disproportions," Reich was a man of prodigious intelligence and intuitions, and he was never sick in the way that, say, Friedrich Nietzsche was sick. One does not need to share Reich's analysis and response to the flying saucer contagion of the atomic age or accept Reich's accounts of the eccentric battles he and his son

42 Christopher Turner, *Adventures in the Orgasmatron: How the Sexual Revolution Came to America* (New York: Farrar, Straus and Giroux, 2011), 375–76.

43 Paul A. Robinson, *The Freudian Left: Wilhelm Reich, Geza Roheim, Herbert Marcuse* (New York: Harper, 1969), 59.

44 Wilson, *The Quest for Wilhelm Reich*, 2.

Peter, and others of his assistants, waged with spaceships in the deserts of the American southwest, in order to grant him some dignity. And perhaps they are not that eccentric, or unusual, once the Reich myth and experimental devices like the cloud-buster are placed in a position where their novelty and strange-ness no longer overshadow the man, the intelligent and suffer-ing human being at the controls. An examined life reveals any number of what might be considered strange, unreasonable, eccentric, bizarre, irrational, or neurotic beliefs. That we do not always register these in ourselves as such — or that we can some-times perceive them thus, and yet sustain them — is testament to the complex psychological structures and mechanisms that support them and that seem to render them all but unassailable from within. We will examine these. This is not to say that the vicissitudes of Reich's life were inevitable, but that in certain per-sonalities, the unconscious takes grandiose advantage of what in others is barely visible.

2

Beyond the Catastrophe:
Psychology, Cancer, and Orgone

The first arc of Wilhelm Reich's career can be measured from 1919–1939, within which Reich began his psychoanalytic work in Vienna and gradually elucidated his theories of the libido and the orgasm before turning toward experimental biology and cancer research. This period culminated in Reich's discovery of orgone energy in March of 1939, and his escape from Nazism to the United States in August that same year.

Reich developed an unorthodox line of Freudian theory; Reich would later argue that he never abandoned Sigmund Freud, but rather that Freud and his acolytes were disturbed by Reich's more determined experimental pursuit of Freud's speculations. Reich produced two major works in the crisis year of 1933 with the ascent of Hitler, *Character Analysis* and *The Mass Psychology of Fascism,* before his unorthodox practice of analysis and theories of orgasm and orgastic potency led to a conspiracy at the 1934 conference of the International Psychoanalytic Association in Lucerne, Switzerland, to force him out. In Norway, Reich continued working toward empirical observation and verification of libidinal energy, before the so-called Bion experiments concerned with the genesis of cells led him to investigations into the origin of cancer. None of this was without controversy, scandal, and defamation.

In January 1919, when Reich was twenty-two and a medical student at the University of Vienna, a handbill promoting the new Seminar for Sexology landed on his desk. Reich attended without being impressed with the approach of the small group of medical students. The subject was certainly neglected at the university, but the inaugural meetings of the seminar left Reich frustrated, and this was true also of the visit of a senior psychoanalyst. "He spoke well and what he said was interesting, but I had an instinctive dislike for the manner in which he treated the subject. I heard a great deal that was new, and I was very much interested, but somehow the lecturer was not worthy of the subject. I would not have been able to say why this was so."[1] What Reich needed was meaningful contact, a certain energy, a natural and charismatic force. Among the readings he undertook around that time in Vienna were Freud's *Three Contributions to the Theory of Sex* and *Introductory Lectures to Psychoanalysis*. This initial encounter with Freud's work was "a tremendous intellectual experience" [FO, 22]. In *Passion of Youth: An Autobiography, 1897–1922*, Reich describes beginning to benefit from Freud's theories in March, 1919.[2]

Freud's work bore directly upon Reich's ambivalent memories of what had been his own quintessentially Oedipal puberty, and what Reich referred to as The Catastrophe [PY, 18–50]. When Reich was twelve, his mother, Cecilia, began an affair with his tutor. For several nights, with his father Leon Reich away, Wilhelm Reich played voyeur.

> Slowly I made my way to the door of his room. It was ajar. I stood there and listened. Oh, the frightful memories that drag each recollection of my mother down into the dust, that soil my image of her with muck and filth! Must I go into details? [...] I heard them kissing, whispering, and the horrible creaking of the bed in which my mother lay. Ten feet away stood her own child a witness to her disgrace. [...] With a head full

1   Wilhelm Reich, *The Discovery of the Orgone,* Vol. I: *The Function of the Orgasm: Sex-Economic Problems of Biological Energy,* trans. Vincent R. Carfango (New York: Farrar, Straus and Giroux, 1973), 21.

2   Wilhelm Reich, *Passion of Youth: An Autobiography, 1897–1922,* ed. Mary Boyd Higgins, trans. Philip Schmitz and Jerri Tompkins (New York: Farrar, Straus and Giroux, 1988), 84.

of bizarre fantasies I crept back to bed, without hope of consolation, my youthful spirit broken! For the first time a deep feeling of misfortune and of having been abandoned overcame me. [PY, 28–29]

This experience of abandonment, of alienation and isolation, would be one of the recurrent motifs of Reich's life and work. The years 1950–1957 that I analyze in this book resonate with painful depressions and wild enthusiasms, which are often characteristic of intense creativity. Arguably these experiences got worse, but they have their origin at that open bedroom door. Reich could not tear himself away from the adulterous primal scene.

Gradually, I became accustomed to it! My horror gave way to erotic feelings. Once I even considered breaking in on them and demanding that she have intercourse with me too (shame!), threatening that otherwise I would tell father. [PY, 29]

Reich's father was violent. Even as the secret was forced from Reich by his livid father, who suspected a *different* affair, his mother was drinking Lysol in the bedroom; later, another suicide attempt by poison would begin the hemorrhaging that would end her life in October 1910. Reich believed always that he had betrayed his mother. He drew back the sheet of her deathbed, exposing her corpse to the stricken mourners. The stillness of her breasts appalled and fascinated him.

Leon Reich died of tuberculosis in 1914. The father's illness is thought to have developed from pneumonia in what might have been a painfully drawn-out suicide. According to Reich's second wife, Ilse Ollendorff-Reich, "He insured his life heavily and afterward contracted pneumonia, standing for hours in cold weather in a pond, ostensibly fishing."[3] The insurance money was never paid, but this image of a man "severed" by the surface of water

3   Ilse Ollendorff Reich, *Wilhelm Reich: A Personal Biography* (New York: Avon Books, 1970), 25.

would become part of Reichian unconscious, surfacing as it did even in the dreams of Reich's son, discussed in Chapter 12.

In 1915, Reich entered the First World War in the 18th Infantry Regiment of the Austrian Army, where Ilse Ollendorff said he became a "dashing young officer... He wore a small mustache and was a very handsome young man, indeed."[4] At the Italian front, Reich endured days of shelling, the mud of the trenches exacerbating the psoriasis that he was afraid developed as a psychosomatic consequence of The Catastrophe, the incestuous fantasies, and the terrible deaths that followed his witness and confession.

When Reich entered the University of Vienna in 1918, he was poor, hungry, and neurotic. Writing in December 1919, Reich was conscious of his pathology. "Twice I masturbated while consciously fantasizing about my mother — saw and felt only her abdomen, never her face" [PY, 102]. Reich used verbatim his earlier journal entries regarding his desire to break in on his mother and the tutor in his paper "A Case of Pubertal Breaching of the Incest Taboo."[5]

Around that time, Reich was elected chairman of the Vienna Seminar on Sexology and it was under these auspices that his fateful personal meeting with Freud took place in 1920.[6] Despite Reich's apprehension, Freud was unpretentious and generous. One imagines Reich's relief, to meet the diagnostician of one's intimate and terrifying complexes and to be welcomed by the patriarch.

4   Ibid., 26.
5   Wilhelm Reich, "A Case of Pubertal Breaching of the Incest Taboo," in *Early Writings: Volume 1*, trans. Philip Schmitz (New York: Farrar, Straus and Giroux, 1975), 65–72.
6   Reich describes the meeting in *The Function of the Orgasm* in the context of the seminar's work in 1920 (34–35). Reich's patient and assistant Myron Sharaf's *Fury on Earth: A Biography of Wilhelm Reich* describes this as occurring in 1919. In *Reich Speaks of Freud* (1967), Reich says that he analyzed his first patient in March 1919, but he is uncertain, and this is not borne out in his *Passion of Youth* diaries of 1919. Reich's chronology contains many inconsistencies. The published diaries are unfortunately silent on the meeting with Freud.

Freud did not put on any airs. He spoke with me like a completely ordinary person. He had bright, intelligent eyes, which did not seek to penetrate another person's eyes in some sort of mantic pose, but simply looked at the world in an honest and truthful way. [FO, 35]

This was the contact Reich needed. At their first meeting, Freud presented Reich with several important volumes of his work, including *The Vicissitudes of the Instincts, The Unconscious, The Interpretation of Dreams,* and *The Psychopathology of Everyday Life.* Freud had interrupted work on "Beyond the Pleasure Principle" and completed "The Uncanny," publishing the latter in 1919 and the former in 1920. Both of these would have important conscious and unconscious bearing on Reich's development as a psychoanalyst and as a theorist, as well as on the development of orgonomy, the science of orgone energy. Reich became a member of the Vienna Psychoanalytic Circle in October 1920, a week after delivering his paper "Libidinal Conflicts and Delusions in Ibsen's *Peer Gynt*"; of this, more in Chapter 6. Freud recognized Reich's brilliance immediately and began sending him patients for analysis in the same year. Something like "to tell the truth at all costs" would become Reich's *raison d'être,* and he believed this was significant in his affinity with Freud. He had faith in Freud. Freud's work rendered The Catastrophe intelligible. Of his first encounter with Freud, Reich would recall:

Freud spoke rapidly, objectively, and animatedly. The movements of his hands were natural. There was a hint of irony in everything he said. I had been apprehensive in going to him — I went away cheerful and happy. From that day on, I spent fourteen years of intensive work in and for psychoanalysis. In the end, I was severely disappointed in Freud. Fortunately, this disappointment did not lead to hatred and rejection. Quite the contrary; today I can appreciate Freud's achievement in a far better and deeper way than I could in those days of youthful enthusiasm. I am happy to have been his student for such a long time, without having criticized him prematurely, and with complete devotion to his cause. [FO, 35]

Wilhelm Reich could not have met Sigmund Freud at a more auspicious time than 1920. Freud was sixty-four, and Reich twenty-three. The work that would affect Reich so potently was just completed, and although there were important works ahead, not least *The Future of an Illusion* (1927) and *Civilization and its Discontents* (1930), one sees Freud at his theoretical zenith. But in three years, he would discover the cancer in his mouth that would spread to his jaw, and ultimately end his life in 1939. The image of this — of Freud's illness and despair, the cancer latent beneath the skin — haunted Reich. He would see it in the photograph of Freud that he kept always in his library. Freud presented Reich with the photograph in March 1925. It was with him — watching over him — at Orgonon in Maine when, after decades of isolation from the inner circle of Freudians, the wily and yet transparent Secretary of the Freud Archive Dr. Kurt Eissler reached out to Reich again in 1952. This was two months after the August in which Reich saw his first spaceship but none of this is apparent in the interview with Eissler.[7] Freud inscribed the photograph "To Dr. Wilh. Reich as a kind remembrance of Sigm. Freud. March 1925."[8] The photograph had a particular place in Reich's life. In its specific constellation it would come to function on Reich's unconscious like the trigger activation of identity in the Cold War film *The Manchurian Candidate*. This photograph, more than any other factor, inaugurated Reich's "flying saucer" period, as will become clear.

At the time of their meeting, Freud had developed his theory of the psychosexual economy of the drives. In "Beyond the Pleasure Principle" he explained, "these processes are invariably triggered by an unpleasurable tension, and then follow a path such that their ultimate outcome represents a diminution of this tension, and hence a propensity to avoid unpleasure or to generate pleasure."[9] Freud was at pains to note that "Beyond the

7   Wilhelm Reich, *CORE (Cosmic Orgone Engineering)* VI, nos. 1–4: *OROP Desert, Part 1: Space Ships, DOR and Drought* (1954): 19

8   The photograph is reproduced in Wilhelm Reich, *Reich Speaks of Freud,* eds. Mary Higgins and Chester M. Raphael, trans. Therese Pol (New York: Farrar, Straus and Giroux, 1967), 141.

9   Sigmund Freud, "Beyond the Pleasure Principle," in *Beyond the*

Pleasure Principle" was speculative, and yet, it was a vital turning point for Freud, and the conservative view of sexual energy would impel Reich toward his first major developments. Freud saw, in the libidinal economy of tension and release, unpleasure and pleasure, a repetition that is observable in all of the organic world. Reich would take this further than anyone in psychoanalysis, beyond psychology. Freud wrote:

> At this point, we cannot help thinking that we have managed to identify a universal attribute of drives — and perhaps all organic life — that has not hitherto been clearly recognized, or at any rate not explicitly emphasized. A drive might accordingly be seen as *a powerful tendency inherent in every living organism to restore a prior state,* which prior state the organism was compelled to relinquish due to the disruptive influence of external forces; we can see it as a kind of organic elasticity, or, if we prefer, as a manifestation of the inertia of all organic life.[10]

"Beyond the Pleasure Principle" would have a profound effect on Reich, and those familiar with his work will recognize the origins of his "orgasm formula" in Freud's "expression of the *conservative* nature or organic life."[11] Reich's innovation was to seek an empirical, experimental verification for the libidinal drives. Reich held that the nonmaterial force of libido, this biological energy present in nature, should yield itself to laboratory observation. Where the pleasure principle in Freud gave rise to what has become known, unfortunately, as the death instinct — "the goal of all life is death"[12] — or reversion from the organic to the inorganic, Reich developed the view that the libidinal economy was conservative as a life energy, with no drive "toward" or "instinct for" death. So, a vital aspect of the first arc of Reich's career was the development, from Freud's pleasure principle, of the "orgasm

Pleasure Principle and Other Writings, trans. John Reddick (London: Penguin, 2003), 45.
10 Ibid., 76.
11 Ibid., 77.
12 Ibid., 78.

formula." "At issue," Reich said, "was more than the elaboration of known material; essentially, it was a matter of discovering the biological basis of the libido theory through experimentation."[13] As he would write to Albert Einstein in February 1941, "My own biological work is only the experimental continuation of Freud's research into the psychic energy ('libido') in the biological foundation of psychic apparatus."[14] Outside of Reich's own writing on the subject, the best account of the experimental biology evolving from Reich's encounter with Freud is given by James E. Strick in *Wilhelm Reich: Biologist.* Strick describes the process:

> Over time, as he pondered how widespread his "orgasm formula" was in the living world, Reich said he began to think about bioelectric experiments on human subjects but also about studying worms, starfish, and jellyfish — in which their pulsatory movements could be seen clearly — and even protozoa.[15]

It was in the course of these experiments as well as those on cancer cells that Reich observed first impressions of what would become his theory of orgone energy.

13 Reich, *The Function of the Orgasm,* 36.
14 Wilhelm Reich, *American Odyssey: Letters and Journals, 1940–1947,* ed. Mary Boyd Higgins (New York: Farrar, Straus and Giroux, 1999), 79.
15 James E. Strick, *Wilhelm Reich: Biologist* (Cambridge: Harvard University Press, 2015), 59.

3

The Beginning and the End:
Orgone and Einstein

28 March 1939
Courage and caution!
Dangerous conclusion:
Orgone is a type of energy that is the opposite of electricity; it is
the specific form of biological energy. In keeping with the orgasm
theory, which equates the sexual and the vegetative, it must at the
same time be the specific sexual energy, orgasm energy.

Concepts: "Orgone," "orgonicity" as a state, "orgonomic" as an
adjective.

— Wilhelm Reich[1]

The second arc of Reich's career can be drawn from 1939–1950
with the second splash and skip of stone or saucer occurring
with the discovery of orgone energy just before he left Europe
for good. In October 1939, Reich fell in love with Ilse Ollendorff,
who would become his second wife. With Ollendorff, he would
have a third child, Peter. Reich's first children were his daugh-
ters — Eva and Lore — with Annie Reich (neé Pink), a former
patient who became an analyst in her own right and trained with
Anna Freud. In the United States on December 12, 1941, not
quite a week after the Japanese attack on Pearl Harbor, Reich
was arrested "as a 'dangerous enemy alien.' Taken to Ellis Island.

1 Wilhelm Reich, *Beyond Psychology: Letters and Journals, 1934–1939,* ed.
Mary Boyd Higgins (New York: Farrar, Straus and Giroux, 1994), 199.

Fingerprinted, photographed, put behind bars."[2] Under nebulous suspicions, he was held until January 5, 1942. As Myron Sharaf writes, "Since his credentials as an anti-Nazi and anti-Stalinist were impeccable, it was hard to understand why he was being held."[3] Reich's journal on the date of his release reads, in part: "I looked up every day from behind the bars to the Statue of Liberty in New York Harbor. Her light shone brightly into a dark night" [AO, 138]. A few days later, he raged defiantly, "Nobody really understands what I am doing, and since they don't, I appear suspect, the agent of a foreign political power, not the person I really am: *the discoverer of life energy and destroyer of every brand of mysticism!*" [AO, 139]. This period of 1939–1950 also saw the construction of Orgonon, Reich's laboratory, observatory, and finally his home in Rangeley, Maine.

When Reich began to describe "orgonicity" and "orgone" in March 1939 [BP, 194–96], it was during his last months in Norway before leaving for the United States to escape Nazism, and to a lesser extent, to escape the hostility to his work of the Norwegian scientific community.

Securing a berth on the last ship to leave for America before the Nazi invasion, Reich would take up a professorship at The New School in New York. In September, having established a home in Forest Hills, Reich was already being referred to as Freud's heir in New York, something which he found "a heavy burden!" [BP, 240]. This second parabola also includes his attempts to reach Albert Einstein and convince him of orgone theory. These are documented in the third volume of Reich's autobiography in letters and journal entries, *American Odyssey,* and in papers published by the Orgone Institute Press and known as "The Einstein Affair."[4] We will see that not only Freud, but Einstein also is cru-

2   Wilhelm Reich, *American Odyssey: Letters and Journals, 1940–1947,* ed. Mary Boyd Higgins, trans. Derek Jordan, Inge Jordan, and Philip Schmitz (New York: Farrar, Straus and Giroux, 1999), 128.

3   Myron R. Sharaf, *Fury on Earth: A Biography of Wilhelm Reich* (New York: Da Capo, 1994), 371.

4   Wilhelm Reich, *History of the Discovery of the Life Energy (American Period, 1939–1952): The Einstein Affair* (Rangeley: Orgone Institute Press, 1953).

cial to the constellation of Reich's psyche and work in its "flying saucer" phase.

In March 1939, Reich wrote to W.F. Bon, a Dutch physicist with whom he had been corresponding since November 1938 after Bon expressed interest in Reich's research into cancer. Reich's letter concerns his observation of a "mysterious 'something'" that did not "appear to be ordinary electricity or ordinary magnetism" [BP, 194]. Continuing with a brief parenthesis, Reich says of this something, "(let us provisionally call it 'orgonicity')." This aside does not suggest the definitive importance of this provisional coinage and definition for Reich's career, but Reich would come to see that he had discovered the bio-energetic basis for Freud's libidinal theory, a basis that Freud himself had balked at trying to establish scientifically.

At the end of April, Reich was more aware of its portents. He wrote, "Read a book on Galileo. Could only read it very slowly. Was afraid of coming to the end." In language that prefigures that of his 1951 manuscript *The Murder of Christ,* he continued:

I have just experienced Galileo's death — almost physically. This is the way the great have died, are dying now, will always die. And the clergy will rule the world as long as human consciousness does not tear unarmored life away from the clutches of the church. I once wrote; "The church thrives on the life it destroys." It will die when life awakens, but this requires experimental control of the process of consciousness. The church will not die before that happens. The discovery of the orgone, life-giving solar radiation, was the final step in that direction. [...] But I do not, do not want to die like Galileo. I will be cautious. If I succeed in solving the problem of prolonging life, then...I am not far from it. All I need is peace, a little money, and some sort of a life. [...] The invention of an orgone accumulator...a final solution to the problem of cancer is at hand. [BP, 206]

Orgone, Reich theorized, was the point at which "the investigation of the living organism went beyond the boundaries of depth psychology and physiology; it entered unexplored biological territory."[5] He discovered the charge of orgone to be present "visually, thermally, and electroscopically, in the soil, in the atmosphere, and in plant and animal organisms" [FO, 383–84]. This blue energy could be concentrated or accumulated in devices built by Reich and his assistants — the notorious orgone accumulator box or booth, hand-held chambers or room-sized arrangements, with their layers of organic and inorganic materials creating a resonant insulation of the energy. Not only did Reich find himself in the position of having, in a sense, fulfilled the promise of Freud's theories of a conservative libidinal economy, but he had also discovered the "life energy" — something more than Henri Bergson's *élan vital,* and that preceded atomic radiation in the order of the cosmos. It was in the blood, it was in chlorophyll, and it filled in the desolation of a universe emptied by physics, for which Reich would bear some of his later resentment toward Einstein; and it could, some of Reich's experiments suggested, cure cancer cells. Reich envisioned profound possibilities for orgonomy, but he lacked the resources to pursue his experiments at scale. As Reich would concede syllogistically:

1. I am famous as a psychiatrist.
2. I am doubted as a biologist.
3. As a physicist, I am regarded as nothing. Therefore I am going to Einstein.[6]

Reich wrote to Einstein on December 30, 1940, about what he called a "scientifically difficult and urgent matter" introducing himself as Freud's assistant at the Vienna Polyclinic in the 1920s, and through his own position at The New School. Reich paraphrases,

All I can say now in a few words is that this energy, which I called "Orgone" has definitely been proven as existent in the living organism as well as in the soil and the atmosphere,

5   Wilhelm Reich, *The Discovery of the Orgone,* Vol. I: *The Function of the Orgasm: Sex-Economic Problems of Biological Energy,* trans. Vincent R. Carfango (New York: Farrar, Straus and Giroux, 1973), 383.

6   Reich, *American Odyssey,* 54.

by making it visible, by concentrating it and by temperature measurements. I am also operating with this energy with some success in research of cancer therapy.

The matter is growing factually as well as economically far above my forces and needs cooperation on a large scale. There are a few points which make it seem possible that it could be used in the fight against the Fascist pestilence. [EI, n.p.]

Einstein was intrigued enough to propose that Reich visit him. Einstein's secretary confirmed their appointment for January 9, at 4pm. Their initial meeting went well, and Reich ordered appa-ratus — first an "orgonoscope" of the type Reich had used to demonstrate the presence of orgone in Einstein's study, and later a small orgone accumulator — that he would deliver to Einstein in early February. During their meeting at Einstein's Princeton home, the physicist acknowledged that orgone was visible to him in Reich's apparatus and experienced the change of room temperature in proximity to the orgone accumulator [EI, n.p.]. On February 7, 1941, Einstein wrote that he could not replicate Reich's experimental findings: "Through these experiments I regard the matter as completely solved" [EI, n.p.]. Einstein's let-ter describes the intervention of his assistant in the experiment, and here Reich was suspicious. In his journal entry of February 9, Reich wrote, "There has been mischief in the business with Einstein — personified by an 'assistant'" [AO, 63]. Reich refuted the assistant's work as based on improper measurement tech-nique. It seems to my reading that Reich did not believe there was an assistant at all, but that Einstein was screening himself; the assistant was a shadow. Yet, Einstein's single-page dismissal struck Reich hard, and it took him the better part of two weeks to effect a written response. When it came it was 26 typed pages of detailed explanation of Reich's past experimentation and what factors might have resulted in non-replication in Einstein's tests. On the twenty-third page, Reich referred sneeringly to the assis-tant, regarding this shadow as an obtuse saboteur of the experi-ment. Nevertheless, Reich found his way to be hopeful, trust-ing that his detailed account would cause Einstein to reconsider and to support orgonomy. Reich did not receive a reply. Indeed,

Reich wrote several other letters to Einstein, until October 1941, when he reached the end of his tether.

> You will understand that I cannot regard your letter of February 7th as a final step in this matter, because the phenomenon of the temperature difference was confirmed; and it was now only a question of the wrong interpretation of your assistant, which was definitely refuted through measurements in the open air. Furthermore, I cannot presume that you regard my earnest information as not to be taken seriously or as a swindle; otherwise you would not have listened to me for 4-1/2 hours with such interest and understanding; You would not have been willing to take an apparatus and make your own observations and to give the promise of help in the matter, should the difference in temperature be a fact. [...] I cannot concede, either, that you keep in suspense, a matter of such serious and far-reaching consequences as some people suspect who know academic behavior. [...] But your silence is unpleasant and strange. [EI, n.p.]

As Reich wrote to his friend, the educator and founder of the alternative Summerhill school, A.S. Neill, that the experience with Einstein "shattered my confidence not only in practical knowledge but also in the ability of physicists to think, act, and behave correctly where 'bombs' in physics are concerned" [AO, 201]. One sees in the Einstein Affair a second disappointment, after Freud.

4

The Oranur Experiment:
Emergency, Isolation, and
Emergence

1951 was a year of extreme turmoil for Wilhelm Reich. The Oranur Experiment, with its origins in the fall of 1950, designed to demonstrate the palliative effects of orgone energy upon radiation sickness, would run amok, producing biopathic sickness in Reich and his assistants, including his twenty-six-year-old daughter Eva, culminating in her near-death in an accumulator accident on February 19. Yet, even this turmoil Reich was able to reframe as necessary stages in his evolving analysis of climate and planetary emergency, into which, even with his doubts, the "flying saucers" would seem to fit.

Where Reich abbreviated orgone as OR, nuclear radiation was abbreviated NR. Thus, the Oranur Experiment was a test of OR against NR, or the ORgone Anti-NUcleaR Experiment. During this spring turmoil, Myron Sharaf, the assistant who Reich said was "closest to my level of thinking,"[1] was moved by Reich's "rapid and profound"[2] reactions to the emergency as he passed through the shock of failure, transformation, and something

1 Wilhelm Reich, *Where's the Truth? Letters and Journals, 1948–1957,* ed. Mary Boyd Higgins, trans. Derek Jordan and Inge Jordan (New York: Farrar, Straus and Giroux, 2012), 85.

2 Myron R. Sharaf, *Fury on Earth: A Biography of Wilhelm Reich* (New York: Da Capo, 1994), 376.

like recapitulation of his hypothesis in the space of four months. Reich's urgency, and an anxiety and ambivalence of confidence, led to mistakes affecting not only himself and his family, but also his assistants: Lois Wyvell who managed the Orgone Institute Press, the surgeon Dr. Simeon Tropp, Myron Sharaf, physician H. Lee Wylie, and biologist Helen MacDonald. Six-year-old Peter Reich suffered physically and emotionally in ways that reverberated from his memoir into popular culture.

Reich's original intent had been to discover: "CAN ARTIFI-CIALLY PRODUCED RADIATION SICKNESS BE TREATED or PRE-VENTED WITH OR ENERGY?"[3] Orgone, Reich would discover, reacted with ferocity to the presence of forms of nuclear radiation. Orgone agitated in this way would become Deadly Orgone Radiation (DOR), producing dangerous atmospheric and organismic effects that persisted even after the nuclear materials were removed and shielded. The emergency resulted from the volatile interaction of nuclear materials and concentrated orgone energy in various accumulators, and would lead to the temporary dismantling of the laboratory at Orgonon, and the necessity of its evacuation. At its most volatile, the reactions of the antithetical energies meant that the presence of even a "tiny amount" of radioactive material "was sufficient to cause a DOR reaction in the total building, to such an extent that my wife and my son, 7 years old, developed severe symptoms of blood disintegration and had to be evacuated" [OE, 302]. Reich's most detailed account is published and available from the Wilhelm Reich Museum as *The Oranur Experiment, First Report (1947–1951)* in a comb bound edition with a yellow paper cover.

During the meeting of the Board of Trustees of the Wilhelm Reich Foundation at the end of August 1950, Reich proposed "the *anti-nuclear* possibilities of OR energy" [OE, 272]. Prior to the meeting, his journal entries are explicit in their concerns. On June 18 he writes, "The atom physicists are in a mess. They created a bomb and nothing else. No peacetime uses!! They are finished—orgone provides the answer: Protection against atomic energy" [WT, 62]. Ten days later, he writes, "The Russian fas-

3   Wilhelm Reich, *The Oranur Experiment, First Report (1947–1951)*
    (Rangeley: Orgone Institute Press, 1951), 273.

cists are marching in Korea. World War III?" [ibid.]. In the *First Report,* Reich recalls his critical need to begin the experiment, addressing practicing orgonomists in New York:

> We made it clear, to begin with, that there is at present no remedy known to medicine in cases of decline of organismic functioning, except OR energy as applied in the cancer biopathy. This, naturally, constituted a heavy responsibility which fell on *our* shoulders. We alone were able to find out whether or not OR energy contained any hope in the treatment of NR radiation sickness. The USA faced a dangerous situation in the first days of 1950, when the disaster in Korea had struck with the evil attack of the Chinese communists; with the hands of the USA bound by the pledge not to bomb their hinterland in Manchuria; with the English allies still doing business with the red dictators; with the helplessness in the face of the tactics of the red fascists who were far superior in the use of all the most refined methods of the emotional plague, and with the terrible experience of the Chinese aggressors MAKING propaganda through the UN right in the middle of the USA, while their forces marched in Korea. The USA was left holding the bag. [OE, 272]

Reich wrote to Peter Mills, attorney for the Wilhelm Reich Foundation on September 6, 1950, describing August's Board of Trustees meeting and the potential for the application of orgone to a range of biopathic symptoms, from tissue damage to the effects of shock, that, taken together, suggested that orgone energy might "suffice to indicate what tremendous benefits could be derived from a general application of orgone energy in cases of emergencies such as atomic warfare, epidemics, etc." [WT, 65]. Reich believed that orgone energy preceded nuclear radiation in the cosmos, referring to them as "before matter" and "after matter" respectively. At Reich's request, Mills forwarded his letter to the Atomic Energy Commission. The Commission demurred.

Nevertheless, having procured paperwork from the Atomic Energy Commission on December 15, 1950, Reich applied to obtain 20 millicurie of the radioactive isotope Phosphorus P-32 to be delivered in 4 millicurie samples at two-week intervals, lay-ing out the injection schedule of the isotope into one hundred mice, a number of which would receive orgone treatment. Reich also ordered a sample of radioactive cobalt CO-60 for use in the calibration of Orgonon's selection of Geiger-Müller counters, to establish background radiation levels in the laboratory and across the property where radioactive material and the carcasses of the experiment's irradiated mice were to be buried. He wrote to President Truman announcing that he and other orgonomists were "preparing to join the national effort in this national emergency." He told Truman,

> It is our sincere belief, based on many years of working with cosmic orgone energy, that at the present time this energy constitutes the only available measure containing some hope for coping with the damaging nuclear radiation effects in atomic bombing. This we say in full responsibility and awareness for the implications. We are scientists and physicians who wish to help make the USA ready should a disaster strike. [WT, 73]

And yet, Reich was not without doubts about whether he and his assistants could meet the moment. The CO-60 arrived at Orgonon December 28. On January 4, 1951, Reich studied the dial of his wristwatch with its atomic-age radium glow. He had worn it for years in the presence of concentrated orgone energy from accumulators charging the atmosphere in the laboratory and surrounds. He noted that at 40,000–45,000 cpm, the counts per minute intensity of the radiation was "ten times the count of a newly arrived wristwatch. This was striking" [OE, 278]. It might have been a warning. In his discussion of mistakes in *The Psychopathology of Everyday Life,* Freud had written,

> I think we may wonder whether we should extend the same ideas to assessing those much more important *errors of judgement* made by people in their daily lives and in scientific studies. Only the most unusual and well-balanced minds seem able to preserve the perceived image of outward reality from

the distortion it usually suffers by being filtered through the psychic individuality of the subject perceiving it.[4]

The Oranur errors of January 5, 1951 should be seen through the dominant personality of Reich — including the mistake made by an unnamed "assistant" (shades of the Einstein Affair) — and with Freud and Freud's cancer in the background. These inadvertent but, finally, fortuitous mistakes are detailed in the *First Report* as "Orgone Energy Runs Amok (DOR): The 'Oranur Sickness'" [OE, 278–87]. The turmoil of January 1951 was the irruption of subjectivity inside his ostensibly objective scientific work, the stirrings of unconscious creative errors.

The experiment was to be conducted using mice. This would involve the manual injection of the mice. Reich made a decision that opened the experiment to error. "In order to save time, we decided to order two milligrams of *pure radium*, and, instead of injecting fluid radioisotopes, to irradiate some of our mice with radium" [OE, 278]. No longer needing to individually inject one hundred mice, the experiment continued with one milligram of radium reserved away from the laboratory as a control (No. I), approximately 150 feet away, in a garage close to Orgonon's hilltop observatory. The other milligram (No. II) or needle of radium was placed inside a small "one-fold"[5] orgone charger. There is a diagram in the *First Report,* reproduced in *Where's the Truth,* but in absence of this, the arrangement of the experiment is perhaps best visualized like nesting layers or a matryoshka doll: the No. II sample of radium inside the one-fold charger, inside the 5ft 20-fold orgone accumulator, inside the 18x18ft orgone energy room with its layered sheet iron and organic walls, encompassed by the outer workspace or hall of the laboratory of 60x70ft.

The first error of January 5 was Reich's. He measured the background radiation count in the large outer hall before the

4   Sigmund Freud, *The Psychopathology of Everyday Life,* trans. Anthea Bell (London: Penguin, 2003), 218.
5   The description of the charger as "one-fold" in Reich, *The Oranur Experiment,* shows that Reich's reference to a "10x charger" in his journals (*Where's the Truth,* 79) contains an extra, erroneous zero.

needle was placed in the charger and found it normal at 11:30 a.m. But he neglected to measure the background count immediately *after* the radium needle was placed in the charger. Had Reich taken that routine measurement, he "would have found a very high count in the hall," containing the orgone energy room, the accumulator, and the charger. Reich admits, "I would have immediately taken the Ra needle out of the charger and the hall and would have missed the whole Oranur effect" [OE, 280]. In other words, the error itself was essential to the outcome of the experiment. And yet, given his long-observed wristwatch with its glowing dial of radium-infused paint, Reich must have suspected that there would be a potentially dramatic effect of orgone on pure radium needle, particularly inside a potent accumulator. Reich would not have had to search for long for an unconscious desire to see Oranur run amok; it would determine the remaining years of his life, defining his final theoretical period from psychoanalysis, to biology, to ecology and cosmology. Reich's more cavalier moments, those slips of recklessness, and his overconfidence were necessary precursors. They were the critical and creative errors of judgement made by scientists that had interested Freud.

At 1 p.m. the same day, January 5, one of Reich's assistants took readings that showed an elevation in the background radiation count, but almost inexplicably, this measurement was not reported to Reich. This second mistake was not discovered until 4:30 p.m. By this time, workers at Orgonon had begun to feel the effects of what Reich would term Oranur sickness. The radium needle had been left unshielded in the orgone charger for five hours, with the background count in the hall of the laboratory steadily increasing during that time. Reich evacuated his assistants. "The inside of the OR room was unbearably charged. The walls felt 'glowing' 10 to 16 feet away from where the Ra needle was located" [OE, 281]. The needle was removed. When he attempted to read the atmosphere at the laboratory, Reich's Geiger-Müller counter jammed. At H. Lee Wylie's insistence, they checked the battery, but this was not at fault. Reich and his assistants worked to ventilate the room, only to find that some malignancy remained even without the radium needle. Those who had been inside suffered a range of symptoms from nausea, enervation, conjunctivitis, loss of balance, and headaches, to skin mottling on their palms, shivers, and a strange pulling sensation above the abdomen. Reich concluded, "THE OR ENERGY ITSELF SEEMED TO HAVE BEEN CHANGED INTO A DANGEROUS, DEADLY POWER. We came to call this effect 'DOR' (Deadly ORgone)" [OE, 282]. Wrestle with the experiment as Reich would, Sharaf wrote that the possibilities later suggested by orgone's interaction with nuclear radiation "paled in comparison to his surprise at finding a deadly quality in orgone energy, hitherto seen as entirely benign."[6]

Reich's journal and the *First Report* appear slightly asynchronous with regard to what happened next. The *First Report* recounts that "We repeated the same experiment from January 5–12, daily, for one hour. On Friday, the 12th of January, we undertook the last in this series of daily Oranur experimentation" [OE, 283]. Once the radium was situated, Reich, Tropp, and another assistant retreated outside. They waited, pacing in the grass, outside the laboratory.

A few minutes later, we could clearly see through the large windows that the atmosphere in the laboratory had become "clouded"; it was moving visibly, and shined blue to purple though the glass. As we walked up and down some 100 to 250 feet OUTSIDE the laboratory, all three of us had the same experience but no one at first dared to mention it. I felt severe nausea, a slight sensation of fainting, loss of equilibrium, clouding of consciousness, and had to make an effort to keep erect on my feet. I saw Dr. S. Tropp, who was with me, getting very pale. He had not said anything, and I had not told him how I felt. Then I asked him how he felt, whether he felt what I felt. He immediately admitted to feeling very ill and faint, with pressure in the forehead, nauseated, cramped the stomach, and weak. [OE, 283]

Reich's earlier journal entry at the approach of midnight on Wednesday, January 10 describes the same atmospheric flashing, but seen and felt at 40 feet. "OR in the hall severely excited;

6   Sharaf, *Fury on Earth,* 376.

flashing; blue through window" [WT, 80]. Note the use of *severe* that is echoed in the October *First Report's* "severe" results. The *First Report* does not contain reference to the blue flashing atmosphere prior to the events of Friday, January 12. This is surprising for such an otherwise meticulous account. Did Reich omit his observations made on Wednesday, selecting only the more dramatic experience on Friday? Did he simply neglect to consult his journal about the date of the observation when writing the report? It matters to the extent that if Reich observed effects at 40 feet on January 10, then it would indicate that he was, based on his own empirical experience, forcing the issue to greater intensity, to greater danger in terms of Oranur sickness on January 12, consciously or unconsciously precipitating the crisis. Through Tropp, Reich wrote to the Oak Ridge Institute of Nuclear Studies and the Atomic Energy Commission that day, explaining: "The reaction of orgone energy to nuclear energy (1 mg radium) was so extreme and penetrating that any kind of attempt at protection in the dual routine sense became meaningless" [WT, 81]. Reich's determination was that the initial catastrophe, sickness, evacuation of the laboratory, etc. were caused by the agitation of orgone by nuclear radiation. Because orgone is ubiquitous, there seemed no way to protect against the penetration of DOR through lead aprons or walls. The experiment had unleashed an energy of unprecedented danger.

Two days later, on Sunday, one finds an almost revisionist clarity in Reich. His journal entry that day begins, *"Theoretical harvest of turmoil is very rich"* [WT, 82]. Perhaps, he had been pushing for a breakthrough in crisis; perhaps his vital mistakes are best seen in Freudian terms, as unconscious desires. His entry draws on what literary critics and analysts of Romanticism would call pathetic fallacy, that attribution of emotion to the elements: "The physical orgone reacts to the poison of nuclear radiation exactly as a healthy living organism reacts to the Emotional Plague: It fights the plague off with withdrawal and death or with rage, *consuming itself;* it conquers only if it is *strong* enough to cope with evil" [ibid.]. Through Tropp, Reich wrote again to the Atomic Energy Commission on the 19th, describing the recovery of the Oranur participants from its worst effects, and altering the initial 20 millicurie request for Phosphorus P-32 to have far less — 10 microcuries — delivered as a solution, diluting the violence of the first reactions. In the last week of January, Reich's journal records a change of perception and of attitude, as the shock of the original Oranur "mistakes" and the effects of the reaction are transformed. Reich was finally able to consider whether the effects of exposure to regulated doses of radiation-contaminated orgone might have inoculating effects. Orgonomy may yet prevail against the atomic nightmare, and Reich suddenly discovered further unexpected creativity: "I began to *paint* yesterday. The form and color streams right out of my fingers on to the canvas" [ibid.]. The oils had languished in their tubes for the year since Reich's daughter Eva presented them to him for Christmas 1950. Now, six paintings were done in six days as Reich gave form to his subjectivity, to the slips in his experimentation that would generate breakthroughs.

At first, Oranur had dealt Reich a bitter blow; some carelessness, some arrogance in his method required integration. In *Totem and Taboo,* Freud describes our evolution from our earliest animistic psyche to the religious condition, to the modern scientific viewpoint. During the earliest phase, "the principle of magic, the technique of the animistic mode of thinking is the principle of the 'omnipotence of thought.'"[7] Freud continues:

> At the animistic stage men ascribe omnipotence to *themselves.* At the religious stage they transfer it to the gods but do not seriously abandon it themselves, for they reserve the power of influencing the gods in a variety of ways according to their wishes. The scientific view of the universe no longer affords any room for human omnipotence; men have acknowledged their smallness and submitted resignedly to death and the other necessities of nature. None the less some of the primitive belief in omnipotence still survives in men's faith in the power of the human mind, taking account, as it does, the laws of reality.[8]

7   Sigmund Freud, *Totem and Taboo: Some Points of Agreement between the Mental Lives of Savages and Neurotics,* trans. James Strachey (New York: W.W. Norton, 1950), 107.
8   Ibid., 110.

It was that residual sense of the omnipotence of his own thoughts that Oranur disturbed in Reich, and which provoked the paintings. As Freud remarks, "Only in art does it still happen that man who is consumed by desires performs something resembling the accomplishment of those desires [...]. It worked originally in the service of impulses which are for the most part extinct to-day."[9] In other words, painting emerged in Reich at the moment when he required that residual omnipotence that had been almost overturned when Oranur ran amok. The blow was partially integrated by its displacement in compensatory environmental paintings and self-portraiture.

At the beginning of February, Reich understood his painting against a backdrop of loneliness, the isolation at the core of Orgonon. By February 11, he had integrated it as scientific method, spontaneous recording, and outpouring. It may even have eclipsed writing in the depiction of orgone phenomena, with practice. Reich was energized by painting, and it opened for him the study of orgone as it affects the qualities of light. The appearance and diminishment of points of light defined his last years, watching the sky for spaceships.

> Emotionally, painting became a major experience. I am discovering my 'seeing,' so to speak. I can find out now what I see *true* and what *false,* and whether I see things correctly at all. And I love to paint. It is something so visible. [WT, 86]

Reich even considered that painting might replace writing detailing orgone phenomena. Carl Jung's use of painting in expressing mandalas, archetypes, etc., in *Liber Novus,* the famous Red Book, are of like matter. I don't wish to suggest that Reich's orgone is reducible — if that would be the word — to an analog of Jung's esotericism, with both men undergoing significant "creative illness" or "spiritual emergency," but it is curious that Reich would indulge such a radically subjective idea.[10] Jung's work,

9   Ibid., 113.

10 For an introduction to the parallels between the lives and works of Wilhelm Reich and Carl Jung, see John P. Conger's *Jung & Reich: The Body as Shadow* (Berkeley: North Atlantic Books, 2005).

particularly in its later alchemical phase follows in the footsteps of another of the Freud circle, Herbert Silberer. Silberer's interest in alchemy, hermeticism, and the paranormal led to his own painful break with Freud in 1914. Silberer died by suicide in 1923. Jung's esoteric work *Aion* was published in 1951, while Reich was painting. In it, Jung quotes Silberer, "I would almost prefer to surrender entirely to picture-language, and to call the deepest subconscious *our internal heaven of fixed stars.*"[11]

The paintings signed WR51 have a naive amateurism, a gauche "outsider art" quality. They share this with some of D.H. Lawrence's oils. And then there is a latent thread of return to Freud when Reich notes: "I must inevitably, think of Leonardo da Vinci" [WT, 86]. Freud's "Leonardo da Vinci and A Memory of His Childhood" was published in 1910. Certainly, in da Vinci, Reich observes a fellow traveler, a peer of genius traversing the mountains of art and science. Reich must have sensed the uncanny presence of Freud haunting his thoughts of da Vinci. In one year from the turmoil of the January 1951 Oranur experiments, the advertisement that would explicitly return Reich's thinking to Freud, with Eissler, would be posted. The photograph of Freud that Reich would discuss with him was hanging there in the library all through the Oranur episodes; Freud with his cancer and his irony.

On February 6, the atmosphere at Orgonon, particularly in the observatory building's experimental hall, remained dangerously active, despite the NR materials having been removed on February 3. Reich records that after removing the No. II radium needle from the 10-fold charger they had used in January, it and the other control needle, both "within lead shielding, were still placed half-a-mile away from any building" [OE, 295]. It was determined that the source of agitation was the shielded fraction of a microgram of radium that was present in Reich's scintilloscope, which had been left inside a small orgone accumulator. Even it was sufficient to generate an OR reaction. With this removed, Geiger-Müller readings showed that the CPM returning to the base 30–40 count.

11 Carl Jung, *Aion: Researches into the Phenomenology of the Self,* ed. R.F.C. Hull (Princeton: Princeton University Press, 1979), 164n43.

Meanwhile, the mice were dying. On Sunday, February 11, dozens of experimental mice that had been in the proximity of Oranur were discovered decayed and in grotesque conditions of distention, with blackened blood and indications of leukemia. The Oranur Experiment was halted temporarily to allow for blood tests to be carried out on the affected workers. Suffering the effects of Oranur sickness, Ilse and Peter Reich left Orgonon to stay with Tropp in Rangeley. Later, Reich would discover that mice that had been exposed to higher levels of orgone accumulation prior to encountering Oranur had far greater survival rates, and this would, by April of 1951, lead him back to his hypothesis that orgone could defeat the effects of radiation.

Yet, on February 19 Eva Reich was close to death. It is not obvious from the account in *The Oranur Experiment, First Report* that "A Close Call for One Physician" refers to Reich's daughter, but this is made clear in both Reich's journals and in Ilse Ollendorff's biography of Reich. Eva had previously used an orgone accumulator to alleviate the effects of diphtheria that had lingered more than 20 years after she contracted the illness as a child, and for bradycardia. Orgone treatment had improved her low pulse rate, from 50 to 70 beats per minute. Reich recounts that at 11 a.m. that day, he was interrupted in his library by a physician "slightly wavering and very pale, with a livid discoloration around her mouth and chin. She was visibly in shock, frightened and in distress" [OE, 305].

Eva Reich's account describes her searching for sources of DOR that she suspected might account for the oppressive atmosphere in the students' laboratory, opening windows to ventilate it, and checking for any small accumulators that they might have missed and not disassembled. She found they had indeed missed a one-fold accumulator, neglected among various glassware at the back of the laboratory.

> I very quickly removed all the contents onto a shelf, just putting my arms inside, and when I had finished, *I tested the accumulator with my head which is my most sensitive area. I put my head inside it for a moment, and felt suddenly as if hit by a sledgehammer on my head.* [...] A sense of total stoppage, localized in my brain, sandlike around the ocular segment

and in my arms. Also, weakness, and disassociation of the rest of my body. I was semi-conscious, could not see clearly, there was a buzzing in my ears, and I could not hear clearly. I found it difficult to swallow, my pulse was very weak and slow, between 45 and 48. I had a hard time breathing, and I had to support myself against the wall because I was so dizzy. [...] I felt as if I were going to die, just simply stop. [OE, 307]

Reich recounts a two-hour fight to save his daughter's life. "She had nearly no pulse, only 44 beats, was livid in lips, felt paralyzed in arms" [WT, 87]. Ilse Ollendorff Reich recalls:

I think that by the end of that year every one of us who had been involved in that experiment had reacted not only with physical symptoms, but with equally strong emotional upsets. A few of the assistants had to leave Orgonon early in the spring of 1951, among them Eva who suffered a severe attack of radiation sickness and could not stand the atmosphere at Orgonon either physically or emotionally.[12]

Reich was in no doubt of the overwhelming dangers of the Oranur experiment and discontinued it while he and others attempted to recover from the effects of the sickness. With the near-death of Eva, Reich was more confident than ever that the agitated OR energy tended to strike at the weakest parts of the body. In late February, Reich ordered that no one work in the vicinity of the original Oranur reaction for more than a few minutes. All orgone accumulators were to be dismantled and their panels stored carefully to avoid the layering that might inadvertently generate a charging effect. The sheet metal lining of the OR room was removed, and the walls washed. Ventilation of the buildings was carried out regularly, particularly at any sign of the heavy, oppressive atmospheric evidence of Oranur or DOR. At a cabin Reich used in the summer, "all NR material was put half a mile away, enclosed in a safe with heavy four-inch walls of steel and cement; this of course, was not done because the NR material

12 Ilse Ollendorff Reich, *Wilhelm Reich: A Personal Biography* (New York: Avon Books, 1970), 139.

was dangerous, but because it excited OR into Oranur action" [OE, 310]. The measures taken did bring down the background counts, but "the walls of the OR room were still 'glowing,' even after dismantling of their metal lining, as late as May 1951" [ibid.], when *The Oranur Report* was produced.

Throughout this period, Reich attempted to alert and inform the Atomic Energy Commission about his remarkable findings. Robert Oppenheimer, however, believed the Oranur Experiment to be a hoax and wrote to Eleanor Roosevelt to that effect. Reich dismissed Oppenheimer as a conventional relativist after Einstein; Reich's theory of orgone was in contradiction with Einstein's conclusion that space was empty. Reich was indignant at being dismissed again by another preeminent physicist, ten years after his deleterious encounters with Einstein. In the context of the near-death of his daughter, and with Reich's sincere belief that he was contributing to the Cold War fight against "red fascism," Reich was both bitter and bewildered.

The breakthrough came on April 12, 1951. Finally, it was the mice — the original subjects of the Oranur Experiment before it ran amok and occupied Reich with its effects on the human organism — that brought the initial work to a resolution. April saw snow in Rangeley and it settled at Orgonon, covering the location where the radium needles had been sequestered in the steel and concrete safe. The snow melted on the half-mile of road to the cabin where the safe was housed. When Reich was able to access it, he reported:

> There were no OR accumulating arrangements in the summer dwelling except: THE STEEL CONCRETE SAFE ITSELF. This I had overlooked, and thus I committed a grave mistake, which under slightly different conditions could have caused much harm. *The safe itself which housed the NR source acted as an OR accumulator.* [OE, 317]

Reich and his assistants discovered that — in this unobserved place — "the Oranur experiment had actually gone on all the while since February" [ibid.]. If their previous experience with Oranur had convinced them of anything, it was that the presence of the *two* radium needles inside an accumulator, where one had been dangerous enough, should have generated a terrible DOR reaction in the vicinity, and that it would have contaminated the building and its surrounds, radiating outwards for a great distance. Reich and his assistant felt the effects immediately, such as the sensation of pressure and nausea. Reich was shocked; here was another error that he might have anticipated. Now, the caretaker who lived nearby would have an explanation for the chest pains he had felt in the weeks prior when he had gone to collect provisions from another building, thirty feet from the cabin and the safe. It was with no little trepidation that measurements were taken the following day. The exterior surfaces of the safe radiated at 20,000 cpm. Its room in the cabin read 6,000 cpm. On April 13, a box of mice was placed in the room, close to the wall of the safe. These same vigorous mice had been present when the experiment began but had not succumbed to the rapid onset of leukemia-like symptoms that had killed the others. Mice that had been exposed to accumulated orgone energy before exposure to radiation seemed to have some resistance, and Reich felt that in himself. Eva Reich had felt it also, after DOR had almost killed her. She reported a kind of rejuvenation. Nevertheless, with the prodigious counts recorded by Reich's Tracerlab SU-5 Beta Gamma Survey Meter, it could be expected that they would all be dead the following day. Yet, when Reich examined them, they were all healthy. On Sunday, April 15, the mice remained unaffected by the NR radiation of the safe walls.

> It was only the fact that the mice remained healthy after 56 hours close to this safe which made us stop and think. WERE WE HERE DEALING WITH NR ACTIVITY AT ALL? HAD OR ENERGY PERHAPS DONE ITS JOB OF KILLING THE NR COMPLETELY? How otherwise could the good health status of the mice be explained? [OE, 319]

Examining the mice again on April 23, they were unaffected by their experience in the cabin. It struck Reich that they had returned to the original impetus of the experiment, and now he could formulate or dramatize three phases in the Oranur conflict. It is worth recalling that Reich regarded nuclear energy as a secondary, later, or *after matter* in relation to the primordial omnipresence of orgone energy.

In the first phase, OR is damaged by the usurpation, the insurgency of NR brought into an accumulator reaction. Reich explains, *"The organismic and atmospheric OR energy reacts to sudden, unexpected NR action with prostration, decline, helplessness, as it were, psychologically speaking"* [OE, 320].

In the second phase, OR "FIGHTS BACK *ferociously. It goes mad, runs berserk, as it were. It becomes a killer itself, attempting to kill the irritating NR"* [ibid.]. This part of the Oranur reaction is most inimical to life, reminiscent in Reich's analogies of the force of love becoming its destructive antithesis in the process of fighting it.

In the third phase, provided that the orgone energy can be reinforced with a greater accumulation of fresh atmospheric orgone energy, given time, "IT WILL FINALLY SUCCEED IN RENDERING NR RADIATION HARMLESS" [ibid.]. Reich proceeds to his radical theory, the primary intent of the Oranur Experiment:

> *It will replace the noxious* SECONDARY ACTIVITY OF THE NR BY PENETRATION OF THE NR MATTER, AND WILL PUT IT AT ITS OWN SERVICE. WHAT WE ARE DEALING WITH HERE IN THIS THIRD PHASE IS NO LONGER NR BUT OR ENERGY WITHIN THE FORMERLY NOXIOUS MATERIAL. IN THIS FORM, THE PROPERTIES OF THE CHANGED NR MATERIAL WILL SHOW ALL THE SIGNS OF OR ENERGY: PENETRATION OF ALL WALLS NO MATTER OF WHAT KIND OR THICKNESS, HIGH COUNTS, BUT NO ILL EFFECTS UPON ORGANISMS. [...] *But such* IMMUNITY *to Oranur, most likely required having gone through and suffered the life-dangerous phases One and Two.* [ibid.]

One wonders what Reich might have made of the resurgence of the biosphere around Chernobyl. The writer here recalls the words of Will Self from his essay on the Chernobyl Sarcophagus and its attendant Zone of Alienation.

> As for the rampant wildlife of the Zone — the wolves, the wild boar, the lynxes and reintroduced Przewalski horses — well, in

an area twice as big as Rhode Island it would take more than a couple of days to run them to ground. Instead, there was birdsong of a strength and intensity only heard — one imagines — before the Industrial Revolution.[13]

A replacement for noxious activity, indeed. At this same time, Reich's journals reveal that experimentation with Oranur had, by April 23–26, precipitated greater feelings of abandonment, and Reich descended into and was struggling to escape from "another deep crisis of my whole existence: Oranur has touched the very *bottom* of the universe" just as he would find that summer in the writing of *The Murder of Christ* he had reached "rock bottom of human sociology" [WT, 99]. His marriage to Ilse was ending. Peter contracted scarlet fever. Eva was absent. His painting lost its initial momentum. For Reich, Oranur had the effect of stripping away the masks that had been worn by all of his intimates. It was a biopathy that exposed aspects of the emotional plague, attacked his family and colleagues at their weakest point, and alienated him from them as they gradually distanced themselves, not least from the dangers of the experiment.

One year later, on April 3, 1952, after contact with the Sigmund Freud Archives but preceding the Eissler interview, Reich made a tape recording of his own from his pine cabin now known as Tamarack, close to Dodge Pond. Without using the terms, Reich described cultural armoring, the emotional plague, and the structural resistance to his work that had left him isolated. He did not blame his colleagues for this abandonment but attributed his alienation to the same structures that produced resistance to Lawrence, Giordano Bruno, and Christ.

I shall not go into the great strain, into the details, into the worries, the sleepless nights, the tears, the expenditures of money and effort, the patience which I had to have with all my workers and with all my students. I would like only to mention the fact that there is nobody around, there is not a single soul either here at Orgonon or down in New York who would

---

13 Will Self, "Chernobyl," in *Why Read: Selected Writings, 2001–2021* (New York: Grove Atlantic, 2023), 65.

fully and really, from the bottom of his existence, understand what I'm doing, and be with me in what I'm doing. They are all very good people. They are decent, honest hardworking. I trust them. They are very good friends, all of them, or most of them. But, this does not alter the fact that they *all,* without any exception, are against, I say, are *against* what I am doing. Every single one of them spites me, *interferes* with my effort, crosses it out, blocks out, flattens out, there's one thing or another thing, whatever it may be, to diminish my effort — No, to diminish the *effects* of my effort — to block out the sharpness and acuity of my thoughts, to reduce to rubble and nothing, or nothingness, what I have elaborated in about now thirty-three or thirty-four years of systematic thinking, and in about forty years of human suffering, since about 1912, or rather 1910 when my mother died. There is not a single soul around who would fully understand, or would not say 'no' to it all. This 'no' is identical with 'I don't want it,' 'I don't like it,' 'I loathe it,' 'Why is it here?' 'Why does he have to exist?' 'Why does he — Why doesn't he sit down and take it easy?' 'Why did he have to start this ORANUR experiment which gives us so much trouble?' They see only the trouble. They don't see, or they don't want to realize what it means for medicine, biology and science in general, as well as philosophy, to have this oranur going. To them, it is mostly a bother, an inducer of sickness, suffering and, at times, I have the distinct feeling that they believe — though they do not dare quite to admit their own thoughts — that I may have gone haywire.[14]

The effects of the experiment on the atmosphere at Orgonon persisted into the early summer of 1951. In June, Reich began work on *The Murder of Christ,* which would become cross-referenced in the flying saucer complex. Despite the outpouring of writing that saw this, *Cosmic Superimposition* and *The Oranur*

14 Reich used the same term two weeks earlier, on March 22, 1952: "Orgonon atmosphere begins to go haywire" (*Where's the Truth?,* 107), and it is almost as if Reich and the atmosphere at Orgonon are mirror archetypes or projections.

Experiment: First Report (1947–1951), all completed that year, Reich had come to doubt the persuasive power and reach of his writing. In September, he was burned out, but Oranur had its volta, as he committed to his journal on September 27: "I believe that I have found a powerful weapon to strengthen life energy in plants and animals. Now I feel 'empty,' hanging once more in the clouds, useless" [WT, 97]. There is, in reference to hanging in the clouds, something of the emptied messianic figure and a prefiguration of Reich's turn toward weather experiments. The strain of the Oranur disaster and its reconstruction as a benefit was too much. One thing Oranur unmasked in Reich was the condition of his heart where he had developed a systolic murmur. On October 25, Reich's journal entry reads:

Am I dying
   I was and am seriously ill: "Heart break" — "Heart anorgonia"
   It is *deadly* serious. My heart can stop any minute. I am somehow giving up. There is no point going on. *For what?*
   After another rapid heart attack on Friday the 19th, a pain set in the heart. To cure the pain, I used Oranur funnel — this knocked me out
   [...]
   I feel weak, as if giving up, *nothing to live for.* [WT, 99]

Reich almost killed himself in the application of the Oranur funnel, as Eva had almost been killed by the one-fold accumulator that had been contaminated in the experiment. It was an almost suicidal gesture; one of atonement, perhaps. The rest of the journal entry anticipates the tape recording of April 1952, six months later. Reich would be bedridden for four weeks — "with 'heartbreak' What a smash up!" — and he had experienced a prefiguration of the cardiac event that would result in his death six years later.

My first anorgonia heart attack will most likely repeat itself and it will kill me one day — When?
   I am dying because I realized and gave up:
   My belief in people

Their "sin," emotional plague, is boundless, not to be managed with books or courses on sex.

There is no one doing anything in Orgonomy, basically, besides myself.

Between the conviction that man is at fault himself, and no grant, on the one hand, and the utter inability to do anything about it, there is DEATH if one remains alive and emotionally involved in human fate.

With *The Murder of Christ* written, I reached rock bottom of human sociology.

One must, under all events, be for the American way and against the Russian because of the great aliveness which is in the American way, bad and ugly as it often is. [ibid.]

Convalescent, Reich was erratic in November, sometimes depressed, at other times feeling life energy and creativity returned to him. He managed to leave his bed properly on the 19th. During his illness, he kept track of radio reports of atrocities in Korea, but also found himself at a distance. "I have truly discovered God, and have lost contact with Man, without losing my sanity" [WT, 100]. He believed that he had come to understand his reluctance to acknowledge his genius and difference: because of his profound fear of the loneliness this would admit. He describes himself as if waking from an Edenic dream at Orgonon, only to find himself "forsaken by all who remained far behind. And here my heart began to break, *months ago,* long before I put the Oranur funnel on my heart" [ibid.]. Reich's heart was broken as soon as the experimental radiation attacked the community at Orgonon, as his family was fragmenting, as the second giant of physics, Oppenheimer, called him a fraud. This was a coda to the disappointment with Einstein in 1940, and the disappointment of Freud earlier, and led to the despair that Reich saw in the photograph of Freud at that same time.

During the period of Reich's 1951 depression and just preceding his October heart attack, September 18 of that year saw the release of the science fiction film *The Day the Earth Stood Still,* one more turn of the screw that would have the most profound effects on Reich's sense of self and the direction of his work. It is not clear precisely when Reich saw it, but I will explain my belief that certain uncanny constellations in the film proved irresistible to Reich's unconscious. The haunting photograph of Freud will have its role to play in this, also. We will need to return to its tragic imprint. In some sympathy with Reich, my position is that the force of the arrangement of uncanny elements in *The Day the Earth Stood Still* directed him, quite reasonably, toward the unreasonable. Throughout the 1950s, Reich would become increasingly cinematic, and he was not — and is not — alone in this.

5

Freud's Ghost:
The Eissler Tapes

Reich wrote a poignant journal entry on January 14, 1952. It is poignant not only because it concerns his melancholy relationship with Freud—new overtures presaging a return to the vicissitudes of the past—but also because of Reich's concern for the future of his own seven-year-old son Peter whose 1973 bildungsroman *A Book of Dreams* would contribute so profoundly and inadvertently to the flying saucer mythology of Reich. The entry is poignant also as a false dawn following the darkness of 1951, deepened as it was by the radioactive fallout and health crises of the Oranur Experiment at Orgonon, described in the next chapter.

I'm looking at the photograph of Reich from a first edition of *The Murder of Christ* from later in 1952. Before me, Reich at fifty-five is almost expressionless. With his short-back-and-sides haircut, he is heavy-set in a suit that seems oversized, and he seems haunted, joyless. Earlier portraits capture a more expansive Reich. Experience has bitten down upon him, and in the moment captured there is a quality of duress; his gaze does not meet the lens. The international nuclear tensions that would be partially released ten years later in the 1962 Cuban Missile Crisis, after Reich's death, preoccupied him throughout the fifties. It was in fighting these tensions, and in the catastrophe of the Oranur experiments against radiation sickness that what many—including many who are "with" Reich in his earlier work—regard as his most extravagant, even pathological, formulations would emerge. But the first journal entry for 1952 published in *Where's the Truth: Letters and Journals, 1948–1957* begins with great optimism and assurance: "I feel Life pulsing again fully, strongly, unbeatably."[1]

Reich also makes four resolutions re-asserting his commitment to vitality and honesty, to the urgency of communicating his work. The first of Reich's resolutions of January 1952 is a refusal of stagnation, to "not ever permit my bioenergetic system to go stale or sluggish or filled with DOR" [WT, 106]. DOR refers to Deadly Orgone Radiation, an accidental discovery made during the Oranur Experiment discussed in the previous chapter. The second resolution is to "further sharpen my weapon of truth and to use it wisely and bluntly." The third concerns his son: "Third, I must not ever abandon Peter who needs me. I would suffer from it more than he would, but to guide this boy through puberty, through all the pitfalls of a crazy world is crucial to me and to him." The fourth is to "let myself go freely in the new contacts which will come my way over the coming years, freely, honestly, without lament or false aspirations" [ibid.].

The resolutions follow Reich's recording of a synchronicity: while preparing material for his own archive, he had discovered an advertisement in *Psychiatric Quarterly* from the nascent Sigmund Freud Archives, founded by Dr. Kurt R. Eissler, seeking to gather and bind the internationally scattered ephemera from Freud's intimates and associates. At the point of first contact with the Sigmund Freud Archive, almost two decades had passed since some of these same intimates conspired in Reich's defamatory expulsion from the International Psychoanalytic Society in August 1934. Reich warned, "I have plenty to give, alright, but will they want it, really?" In other words, be careful what you wish for, Dr. Eissler.

> Involved are peoples' highly private affairs, love affairs, cheat affairs, and other affairs; Freud's personal tragedy, scientific tragedy, historic tragedy, his hopes in me and his later disap-

1   Wilhelm Reich, *Where's the Truth? Letters and Journals, 1948–1957,* ed. Mary Boyd Higgins, trans. Derek Jordan and Inge Jordan (New York: Farrar, Straus and Giroux, 2012) 105.

pointment since my work made a turn he feared. Involved are, too, the fates of future generations of newborn infants, whether they should grow the *sublimating* way or the way of *natural self-regulation*. Great responsible things. Do the heirs of Freud know it? Are they ready to take what is in store for them? [WT, 105]

It was in this spirit that Reich met with Eissler and his reels of tape, on October 18 and 19 of 1952, in the library at Orgonon beneath the inscribed photograph of Freud that Reich had treasured for more than twenty-five years. The transcripts of the interview were published as *Reich Speaks of Freud*,[2] a decade after Reich's death. In his biography of Reich, Myron Sharaf says that Reich was "misled by Eissler's interviewing technique, his 'fascinatings,' and 'go ons.'"[3] It's a vivid image, but there is no evidence in the published transcript that Reich is in any sense the victim of Eissler's guile. Sharaf's characterization risks amplifying the myth that Reich's openness was itself a symptom of naïveté or guilelessness. Eissler uses the word "fascinating" only once, close to the end of the first session when they have been talking for some time, and Reich isn't certain how much Eissler needs, and Eissler replies somewhat sardonically, "I mean it's your fault that you are speaking in such a fascinating way that I don't notice the time, really" [RS, 60]. Eissler never uses the insinuating "go on." A reader would be forgiven for imagining, from Sharaf's account, that Eissler scatters this come-on throughout the interview, but this is not at all the case. Yet, this is not to vindicate Eissler entirely.

Contra Sharaf's view of Reich as victim of the Eissler interview, the transcript shows Eissler struggling often to contain the intensity of Reich's exposition. Eissler would later recall to Sharaf seeing Reich speaking in Vienna in the 1920s. According to Sharaf, Eissler "found him to be a 'marvelous' speaker, elo-

---

2 Wilhelm Reich, *Reich Speaks of Freud,* eds. Mary Higgins and Chester M. Raphael, trans. Therese Pol (New York: Farrar, Straus and Giroux, 1967).

3 Myron R. Sharaf, *Fury on Earth: A Biography of Wilhelm Reich* (New York: Da Capo, 1994), 401.

quent and forceful."[4] Now, in the Orgonon library, comparing himself with the Freud of his primary recollections and of their first encounter, Reich asserted:

> There was an immediate contact. Oh, yes! You see me now. I am quite alive, am I not? I am sparkling, yes? He had the same quality. He had an aliveness which the usual human being didn't have, you know. His hands, their movements were very graceful. His eyes were good. He looked straight at you. He didn't have any pose. [RS, 37]

This is in contrast to the tragic image of Freud's later life, which Reich wanted Eissler to understand from the beginning of the interview. It is also uncannily close to the account given in *The Function of the Orgasm* a few years earlier of Freud's gaze, his affect, the movements of his hands, and his lack of "mantic pose."[5] Reich does not seem to have deteriorated; his articulation of his memories and perceptions is consistent. All of this is remarkable given his urgent preoccupations, and at times, his despair and isolation.

The first thing Eissler asks Reich for his recording of October 18 is a sardonically expressed "simple" question: "I would like to know everything you know about Freud, everything you observed and everything you thought" [RS, 3]. Reich gives a very brief exposition of his technique of character analysis which expanded the conventional field of psychoanalytic observation from the spoken language of the analysis and to the musculature, posture, facial expression, and the resistant character armor; in short, Reich's innovation was to approach neurosis through the totality of the organism. He explains to Eissler that, "Freud told me what he was through his facial expression" [RS, 5]. One imagines Reich glancing at the photograph above them. He wanted Eissler to understand that the vital Freud of 1919 underwent a change, and that this alteration in Freud was, in the most inti-

4 Ibid., 131.
5 Wilhelm Reich, *The Discovery of the Orgone,* Vol. I: *The Function of the Orgasm: Sex-Economic Problems of Biological Energy,* trans. Vincent R. Carfango (New York: Farrar, Straus and Giroux, 1973), 35.

mate sense, essential to the nature of their relationship and what Reich would refer to as Freud's final disappointment in him. Reich invites Eissler to examine the photograph.

> Would you look at this picture of Freud. Please go and look at it. I don't know whether you will see what's in that picture. I didn't see it when I received it from him in 1925. Can you see what's in that picture? [RS, 5]

Eissler equivocates. It's clear that he is unsure about Reich's ominous "what" and "it," and given his acknowledgement of Reich's charisma and force of personality, Eissler could be forgiven for not being certain of himself when Reich calls for a character analysis of Freud's image within minutes of the interview's opening. Reich explains:

> It's a very sad expression, true despair. I began to see the despair in Freud's face some time around 1940.[6] Although he was dead, he had a great influence upon the direction of my further search in the realm of human emotions. *What was his despair about?* Now, if I am right, if I read the emotional expression correctly, the problem is why he was in such despair. And why didn't I see it before, in 1925 or 1930?
>
> When I met Freud in 1919, he was a very alive person. I described him a bit in the first volume of *The Discovery of the Orgone.* He was alive. He was outgoing. He was hopeful. He was full of zest and zeal. Then, around 1924, something happened. I don't know whether you know that he withdrew from all meetings and congresses in 1924. And he developed cancer of the jaw at that time. Are you following me? [RS, 5–6]

The patriarch haunts with his cancer the prodigal who will turn libido theory into a search for a cure for the same disease. Reich tells Eissler that the cancer emerged from Freud's resignation, the first stirrings of conflict with Reich to his terminal disappointment. The uncanny return of this haunted and haunting image

6   December 30, 1940 is the date of Reich's first overture in correspondence with Albert Einstein.

of Freud would have profound effects on Reich in the 1950s. The photograph needs to be viewed through the lens of a series of events in 1951. It is important that this is the first thing Reich uses to explain Freud, and to explain himself, after all that is done.

Early in the transcript from October 18, Reich senses, correctly, that Eissler is being disingenuous, feigning ignorance of the nature of the slanders against him. Reich presses Eissler three times: "You don't know that rumor of schizophrenia? [...] I doubt that you never heard I'm paranoiac, schizophrenic." Eissler denies this. Reich pushes him: "Sure?" [RS, 10]. It is obvious that Reich knows he is being lied to, whether this is because Eissler is holding back as a manipulation or because he feels it would be improper to admit to Reich that he has come to the interview in full possession of the slanders. Perhaps he is trying to avoid embarrassing his subject. On another occasion, shortly after Reich has described his last meeting with Freud, Reich notices immediately that Eissler is putting words in his mouth, either as a conscious or unconscious distortion. Eissler suggests, "Before, you mentioned Freud's meanness. That would be important." Reich replies "Meanness? Did I say that word? Did I use that word?" Eissler thinks so. Reich corrects him: "Not meanness. Irony, a biting irony" [RS, 66–67]. Indeed, Reich has not referred to meanness at all.

When discussing the history of the Archive, Freud biographer Peter Gay laments Eissler's "addiction to secrecy" to which he was "so passionately committed." Debating Eissler, Gay articulated "the palpable contradiction of a discipline devoted to the greatest possible candor, psychoanalysis, showing itself before the world as secretive, not to say devious."[7] Ironically, Gay omits Reich from the early history of psychoanalysis. At issue for Gay with regard to Eissler has been the fact that, having amassed a wealth of donated material for the Sigmund Freud Archives, Eissler kept significant sections away from scholars, refusing access or publication. In 1982, for different reasons, the Archive was the subject of a thirteen-million-dollar lawsuit, brought by Jeffrey Moussaieff Masson whom Eissler asked to serve as

7   Peter Gay, *Freud: A Life for Our Time* (New York: W.W. Norton, 1998), 784–85.

Projects Director of the Archives, to succeed him as Secretary in 1981, and, after her death, to live in Anna Freud's home, which had been purchased by the Archive and turned into the Sigmund Freud Museum, at 20 Maresfield Gardens, Hampstead, London. This, the scandal around and expulsion of Masson, and—on Eissler's part—some of the psychopathology of everyday life, were exposed in "Trouble in the Archives," Janet Malcolm's two-part interview for *The New Yorker* that became the book *In the Freud Archives*[8] in 1984. Eissler says,

> I search myself for ambivalence toward Freud. To have put someone like Masson in a position where he might become Secretary of the Archives! To have made such a blunder at the end of the game! I wouldn't listen to anybody. Even my own secretary warned me about him.[9]

Malcolm pressed Eissler on this point, the poor judgment that would end in the lawsuit. Was there another explanation than an ineffable ambivalance toward Freud for promoting Masson? "'The homosexual explanation, Eissler said.'" Eissler went on to admit to Malcolm that Masson had "great homosexual appeal, strong appeal," but denied any specific sexual fantasies. "But," he says, "I find the homosexual explanation even worse. I prefer the other explanation."[10] It was material secreted within the Archive that turned Masson from an acolyte to an adversary of psychoanalysis, and with Eissler's project as the repository for his

8 Janet Malcolm, *In the Freud Archives* (New York: New York Review of Books, 1997). On pages 69–70, Malcolm notes, "On October 17, 1980, Eissler formally offered Masson the job of Projects Director. In his letter, he was a little untruthful. He wrote, 'At its meeting on October 15th, the Board of Directors of the Sigmund Freud Archives instructed me to inquire whether you would be willing to serve for at least one year as Projects Director of the Archives.' As the minutes of the meeting reveal, Eissler was instructed to offer Masson the job for *at most* one year. We are all perpetually smoothing and rearranging reality to conform to our wishes; we lie to others and to ourselves constantly, unthinkingly."

9 Ibid., 73.

10 Ibid.

bitterness, he concluded that Freud was a sell-out and a "moral coward,"[11] and proclaimed his disillusionment with psychoanalysis.[12] This "ambivalence toward Freud" on Eissler's part is telling. One could argue for its presence in Eissler's passionate secrecy with the Archive, and his handling of the two-part interview with Reich. During the second recording session, Reich discusses this fundamental ambivalence in nature, of the kind that Eissler sought in himself and that he had sought to resolve by simply preferring one to the other.

> What [Freud] did not do, and I do not know why, was to see that *these two opposite forces were actually one in the depth because everything opposed in nature is ultimately a unit.* Yes, a unit. Do I make myself clear? [...] *Out of a unitary force a splitting, an antithesis develops.* That is my way of thinking about natural scientific things.[13]

Reich explains that this is the meaning of the symbol of orgonomic functionalism or the common functioning principle that hangs at his observatory door (and that appears on all of Reich's publications today).

With important and ironic differences, one thinks of F. Scott Fitzgerald, three years after Reich's original insight into what would become orgonomic functionalism and the orgasm formula, composing "The Crack-Up" in February 1936 from the lows of his alcoholism—"the test of a first-rate intelligence is the ability to hold two opposed ideas in the mind at the same time and still function."[14] This is Eissler's dilemma as he searches for signs of his own ambivalence toward Freud, for something unnatural; whereas Reich takes that ambivalence—or simulta-

11 Ibid., 68.

12 Prior to this, in 1981, Peter Swales, a former associate, wrote to Masson: "It really must be some perverted twist of fate that you are in such reverence of Freud, rather than, say, of Otto Gross or even Wilhelm Reich." Malcolm, *In the Freud Archives,* 104n.

13 Reich, *Reich Speaks of Freud,* 92.

14 F. Scott Fitzgerald, *The Crack-Up* (New York: New Directions, 1993), 69.

neous identity and antithesis—as natural and innate. If Eissler struggled with his own instincts, those instincts and his affect were similarly vexing to Janet Malcolm who spoke both of his great intelligence and his "maddening guilelessness."[15] In lying to Reich about his knowledge of the slanders against him, Eissler was certainly not being guileless. Jeffrey Moussaieff Masson told Janet Malcolm that Eissler and Anna Freud "loved to hear from me what creeps and dolts analysts are."[16] Arguably, Eissler wanted to hear some of Reich's account of other analysts for the same reason—his own pleasure—rather than to mislead Reich. When Reich asks if Eissler wants more intimate details, one senses that Eissler can't help himself; and yet, who would refuse? Reich isn't just unburdening himself, he's submitting his criticisms, a rebuttal of defamations, to the Sigmund Freud Archive and the Library of Congress. Eissler is forty-four years old; Reich is fifty-five; Eissler has all of his significant work ahead of him in terms of the Archive and publications. Reich, despite the oscillations of his mood throughout 1952, had been anticipating that tape recorder, the release of his potency for it, and its entry into the posterity of the Archive for ten months. Reich speaks as he resolved in his January journal entry. As much as he speaks of Freud, he necessarily speaks of himself, issuing his theories and correctives for Eissler's tapes. I explain all this to demonstrate Reich's grasp on reality, his sharpness. Given the events of the previous twelve months, Reich's composure and focus on the subject at hand are remarkable.

15 Malcolm, *In the Freud Archives,* 14.
16 Ibid., 41.

6

The Day the Earth Stood Still: Introjection

In 1951, I believe, Hollywood introduced a new film with the title "The Day the Earth Stood Still." [...] The film was excellent. It tended to prepare the population for extraordinary events to come. It had the right, and not the wrong, ideas about the functioning of cosmic energy used in the propulsion of spaceships. It pictured the spaceman as being akin to earthmen, but different in his attitude to women, in his behavior with a small boy, etc. It conceded that insoluble problems of mathematics were easily solved with his knowledge of Life Energy. There was no doubt that the Life Energy was meant: Lights went on in the spaceship when fingers moved across certain switches; lamination of vacuum tubes can actually be achieved by approaching strong bodily energy fields. All through the film show I had the distinct impression that it was a bit of my story which was depicted there; even the actor's expression and looks reminded me and others of myself as I had appeared 15 to 20 years ago.

— Wilhelm Reich[1]

Wilhelm Reich is writing retrospectively, from the vantage of 1956. This chapter relates the first of two hermit crab conclusions that I have reached regarding Reich in the fifties, specifically the uncanny science fiction aspects of *The Day the Earth*

1   Wilhelm Reich, *Contact with Space: Oranur Second Report, 1951–1956* (Haverhill: Haverhill House Publishing, 2018), 1–2.

Stood Still.[2] Reich, as Myron Sharaf observed regarding the Oranur Experiment turned emergency in Chapter 4, was able to revise and reframe his hypotheses rapidly and profoundly. He did so throughout the fifties. Reich's own revisions lead me to the second, functionally identical conclusion elucidated in the final chapters of this book with regard to Reich and his intimate associates and his family.

One imagines Reich watching *The Day the Earth Stood Still* with increasing restlessness, the red velvet upholstery of his movie theater seat tilting on its metal axis, ashen clouds of cigarette smoke drifting through the flickering the projector beam, Reich likely somewhat unkempt, dressed perhaps in a plaid shirt. In certain ways, Reich was the same as any other audience member for any work of art: sometimes, the work leaves us cold and we find it mute, impenetrable, or hostile; at other times, it seems — to use the cliche deliberately — to "speak to" us ineffably, or by allegory; and in more certain powerful instances, the motifs of our lives are re-presented to us and we experience them as uncanny. And it is natural, also, to want to see ourselves somehow, to seek an idealized self, or for the work to express that which we keep silent. But Reich was more than that. He was a trained analyst, one of the foremost of his generation. Furthermore, his technique of character analysis stressed attention to the complete affect of the patient. Reich was then, an intense observer of nuance, and the unconscious background of being, the performance of armoring and neurosis. Therefore, I have no sympathy for the potential objection that we cannot know how Reich appraised *The Day the Earth Stood Still.* It would be a decidedly poor analyst or critic who did not register what I believe can be said with confidence that Reich observed, because Reich was not so impoverished an analyst. From a perspective of character analysis, he was most uniquely placed to apprehend the conscious and unconscious content of film. Reich describes the content with which he consciously identified: the Reich doppelgänger, as he saw it, the passion narrative of the dying and resurrected spaceman, his conflicts with bureaucracy, and the orgone-like energy. Certainly,

2   Robert Wise, dir., *The Day the Earth Stood Still* (Twentieth Century Fox, 1951).

as he writes, Reich was conscious of the allegory within which he found himself implicated. Then, there are the more potent images about which Reich was not explicit, and which follow. As Reich put it, "Without my intention, somehow a ball of history started rolling, putting me in the center of space problems: I made actual contact by way of the cloud buster on May 12, 1954, between 9:40 and 10:45 p.m." [CS, 2].

One could suggest that if some demon or malign power had sought to make Wilhelm Reich 'mad,' it might have made *The Day the Earth Stood Still.* That is not my position, although arguably the case for neurosis is the more facile case to make. No, instead I will show that the work of Sándor Ferenczi on the process of introjection will permit us to see Reich as he always was: unrelentingly curious, concerned, at times grandiose, but tragically normal.

Reich was 30 years old when *The Jazz Singer* starring Al Jolson was released, ushering in, as is generally acknowledged, the age of sound cinema and the "talkies." He is of the generation that came of age with and within cinema. The power of cinema is such that there is no modern psyche exposed to it that does not enter, to some extent, into the process of introjection and projection that is evident in Reich to a great and self-conscious extent. Reich's consciousness of what I call his own "cinematic self" evolving from his earlier Peer Gyntish self is crucial to understanding the Reich fifties.

The Day the Earth Stood Still would exert an intense influence over Wilhelm Reich in the last years of his life, over his family, and his assistants in ways that were sometimes conscious and sometimes unconscious, reflecting what I call the unconscious of the film. This symbolic plexus, once taken in, exerted a powerful gravity upon Reich's unconscious drives, and their presence in the external world of conscious action. To say that Reich's cinematic self was conscious and highly developed — given what he saw and how this related to his subjective experience — is not to pathologize or patronize. It is to say that a botanist or a physicist, an artist or an analyst, have particular perceptions of experience, and that some of this is instinct and some of this is trained.

In *The Day the Earth Stood Still,* directed by Robert Wise, and based on Harry Bates's story *Farewell to the Master* (1940), a flying saucer lands on the Washington, DC National Mall, between the baseball diamonds on the Ellipse, just beyond the South Lawn of The White House. There is a conscious design in the appearance of the saucer on the Ellipse, and the circles of men, women and children surrounding it, suggesting the orbits of planets, or perhaps consequential ripples on a pond from a skimmed stone. As for the baseball diamonds — diamonds are the currency of the visitor from space. The film begins with a view of Earth from space. This stylized science fiction environment shows space as cloudy, not the emptied space of Einstein that Reich found false. Reich may or may not have thought of the cloudiness of DOR at Orgonon. But soon, he would find himself inhabiting the film fully. First, the spaceship is detected by radar, traveling at 4,000 mph, prompting a British observer to exclaim "Holy Christmas!"[3] This is the first in a series of allusions to the figure of Christ that the film makes and which appealed to Reich, who had completed his book on the same subject earlier that year. The superior scientist, the genius, the great individual, the bringer of peace — here, the spaceman is such a figure — is always murdered in Reich's book. Over the capitol, the spaceship glows brightly in the daylight. *The Day the Earth Stood Still* uses real-life reporters Elmer Davis and Drew Pearson in its exposition, and the kind of global montages that are part of the UFO film genre, evident in more contemporary movies like Steven Spielberg's *Close Encounters of the Third Kind* (1977), and Denis Villeneuve's *Arrival* (2016). Elmer Davis urges, "This is *not* another flying saucer scare,"[4] and Drew Pearson warns against rumors of mass invasion, in language predicting Jung's use of "visionary rumors" to describe flying saucers. The reporters are referring to the scare of October 1938 produced by the radio broadcast of Orson Welles's Mercury Theatre production of H.G. Wells's *The War of the Worlds,* from Howard Koch's adaptation.[5]

3   Wise, *The Day the Earth Stood Still,* 0:02:18.

4   Ibid., 0:03:16.

5   "The War of the Worlds," *The Mercury Theatre on the Air* (New York: CBS Radio Network, October 30, 1938).

On the Ellipse, the spaceship is surrounded by troops and armaments from Fort Myer, and a crowd of onlookers. From the apparently seamless saucer, a ramp extends, and a door opens. The spaceman with whom Reich identifies, Klaatu, played by Michael Rennie, emerges. He declares that he is on a mission of peace and good will and reaches inside his suit to retrieve a device he intends to present. A nervous soldier shoots Klaatu, and he collapses, destroying the device. Gort, the film's iconic robot, descends the ramp and uses an energy weapon from his visor to destroy the several of the carbine rifles, tanks, and artillery that have been massed against them. The film's reworking of the original name for the robot from Gnut to Gort permits a pun on "God," for it is Gort that is the Master, the policeman, and the superego of the film. After explaining that the device was a gift for the President, to aid in the study of other planets, Klaatu is taken to Walter Reed Hospital. Visited by Harley, a Secretary to the President, Klaatu attempts to impress on him the necessity of a meeting of representatives from all of the nations of Earth. Harley returns with bad news. Cold War tensions will make this impossible, Harley explains. Klaatu, in a moment Reich might well have appreciated, declares "I am impatient with stupidity."[6] The rapid healing of Klaatu's bullet wound, as well as his disclosure that he is 78 years old (with a life expectancy of 130), despite appearing to be only in his late thirties, astound the physicians. He is held under guard at the hospital. Meanwhile, metallurgists work in vain to penetrate the flying saucer.

In the second allusion to the figure of Christ, Klaatu escapes the hospital, disguised in the stolen suit of a Major Carpenter, and goes seeking lodgings to conceal himself in his new identity. Klaatu, disguised as Carpenter, finds a room at a boarding house. He meets several characters, most importantly a young boy named Bobby Benson who takes Carpenter for a new father-figure, and Bobby's widowed mother Helen. The boy with the spaceman father would become the constellation of Peter and Wilhelm Reich; they would play out this relationship consciously and unconsciously. The landlady of the boarding house, Mrs. Crockett, identifies Carpenter as alien to Washington, DC

---

6 Wise, *The Day the Earth Stood Still*, 0:20:19.

DC by his New England accent; Reich's Orgonon was in New England, of course.

In August 1955, during a conference at Orgonon, Reich met a medical researcher with the appropriately science fiction name Aurora Karrer with whom he would have an affair, and who he would refer to as his wife in his last years, although they never married. Aurora Karrer was thirty-three, and Reich was fifty-eight at the time of the conference, which concerned the use of the cloud buster, turned space gun. Aurora Karrer resembled Patricia Neal's on-screen Helen Benson and Reich resembled Michael Rennie as Klaatu. When Reich moved to Washington in November ahead of his trial, he too moved through the city under a pseudonym, adopting the name Walter Roner. In *Adventures in the Orgasmatron: How the Sexual Revolution Came to America,* Christopher Turner suggests incorrectly that the name might be "a reference to his mother's maiden name, Roninger."[7] I think he picks up this error from Myron Sharaf's *Fury on Earth.* No, it is this: In addition to retaining his initials W.R., Reich is continuing the wordplay he employs in his science. Roner (R-on-er) is a pun on Oranur, and Walter is used with its German meaning of "one who wields power." Thus, Reich asserts himself as master, the one who has mastered Oranur. Peter Reich remembers visiting him there. "He lived at Alban Towers, a big hotel, and used another name, Walter Roner. It was good to sleep close to him and smell his oil and sometimes we talked in the dark and I watched car lights move around on the ceiling. Actually, I liked going to Washington because we went to see things and went to movies a lot."[8] It would be with Karrer that Peter Reich would visit his father at the penitentiary, the father dressed in the blue uniform not of a spaceman, but of a prisoner.

Returning to the plot of the film, the following day, Cold War tensions are evident at breakfast with the other tenants at the boarding house. Carpenter reads in the newspaper that a certain "savant," Professor Barnhardt, intends to convene a

7 Christopher Turner, *Adventures in the Orgasmatron: How the Sexual Revolution Came to America* (New York: Farrar, Straus and Giroux, 2011), 400.

8 Peter Reich, *A Book of Dreams* (London: John Blake, 2019), 73.

meeting of international scientists to discuss the significance of the arrival of the flying saucer. Carpenter and Bobby spend the day exploring the capital's monuments together, while Helen Benson has a date with her suitor Tom Stevens. At Arlington Cemetery, we learn that Bobby's father was killed at Anzio in 1944. Incidentally or not, the first allied battle force at Anzio was codenamed "Peter." We might also recall that it was in Italy that Reich suffered beneath artillery during the Great War, albeit in the more Alpine theater of that front. After a visit to the Lincoln Memorial, Carpenter asks Bobby who he thinks the greatest thinker on Earth is, and Bobby confirms that this must be Professor Barnhardt. Bobby wants to see the spaceship and is curious about its propulsion system. Klaatu's disguise slips a little as he explains that is a form of atomic power. Bobby thinks that such radioactive power is reserved for bombs, but Carpenter explains, "No, no. It's for lots of other things, too."[9] We have to imagine Reich watching and experiencing all of this in the context of the Oranur experiments with radiation and biology, his own attempts to avert atomic catastrophe, his analysis of Christ, and his disappointments with Einstein and Freud. Carpenter proposes a visit to Professor Barnhardt. He and Bobby find that Barnhardt is not at home, but Carpenter opens the locked French doors to Barnhardt's study. The next few minutes of *The Day the Earth Stood Still* — the uncanny arrangement of certain potent elements that impacted Reich's psyche — must have hit him with profound force. It is remarkable that it has not been appreciated until now.

Barnhardt — the Einstein figure — has a large blackboard in his study, filled with an extensive, but incomplete equation. Carpenter tells Bobby that Barnhardt is working on an apparent problem of "celestial mechanics,"[10] but that he is on the wrong track. The endpoint of the equation, in the bottom right of the blackboard is chalked:

"O! "O!! "O!!!!?"[11]

9 Wise, *The Day the Earth Stood Still*, 0:31:06.
10 Ibid., 0:35:48.
11 Ibid., 0:35:40.

Consciously or unconsciously, the irony that the Einstein figure's equation ends in orgasm, or in orgone energy as the solution to celestial mechanics, impressed itself upon Reich. Carpenter opens the locked doors and invades Barnhardt's study. Precisely at that moment, we glimpse something more dangerous, or of greater consequence for Reich's psyche: It is the appearance of a certain portrait on the wall of Bernhardt's study. As Carpenter moves toward the blackboard, he is, as it were watched by an enlarged and cropped reproduction of *the same photograph of Freud that haunts Reich.*[12]

This photograph of Freud that was present at Orgonon for the Oranur catastrophe and for the interview with Kurt Eissler is placed very deliberately so that we — almost as if so that Reich — would get the message. The Reichian spaceman steps forward and marks the correct elements of the celestial equation with chalk ticks of approval. The first thing he ticks is the O formula.[13] Reich had utilized that capital O so frequently in his abbreviations by now that he must have registered it, at some level. The O is also the form of the mandala that Jung conflates with the saucer shape. Carpenter adds a series of corrections to the formula for Barnhardt when he returns.

When Carpenter and Bobby are interrupted by the return of Barnhardt's secretary, the photograph of Freud is in shot again, behind her. It remains in shot — except for a brief cutaway to the note Carpenter writes for Barnhardt — for the rest of the scene, and the editing means that it lingers in our sight for a moment after Carpenter and Bobby exit again through the French windows. I do not think it is possible that this failed to make an impression on Reich.

The next day, Carpenter returns to Bernhardt's study and meets him in person. The photograph of Freud is over Carpenter's shoulder, slightly out of focus, when he says of the formula, "I find it works well enough to get from one planet to another," and reveals his identity as the spaceman to Barnhardt, "I am Klaatu."[14] Thus, symbolically, we have Freud at Carpenter/

12 Ibid., 0:36:14.
13 Ibid., 0:36:21.
14 Ibid., 0:41:36.

Reich's back, as he corrects Einstein. Freud is his past, and Reich announces himself to Einstein as the future. Klaatu says,

> We know, from scientific observations, that your planet has discovered a rudimentary kind of atomic energy. [...] Soon one of your nations will apply atomic energy to spaceships. That will create a threat to the peace and security of other planets. That, of course, we cannot tolerate. [...] I came here to warn you that you that by threatening danger, your planet faces danger. Very grave danger. I am prepared, however, to offer a solution.[15]

Again, it is impossible that the irony for Reich of Barnhardt's response that, "We scientists are too often ignored, or misunderstood,"[16] was lost on Reich. At one point, Klaatu picks up Barnhardt's pipe, examines it, and puts it aside again, and one cannot help but feel that this is a cuckolding of the Einstein substitute that would have struck Reich.

At this point, around 45 minutes into *The Day the Earth Stood Still,* we can understand Reich's comment that, "All through the film show I had the distinct impression that it was a bit of *my story* which was depicted there; even the actor's expression and looks reminded me and others of myself as I had appeared 15 to 20 years ago" [CS, 2].

I believe the fact that Reich's published work makes no mention of this uncanny synchronicity, this constellation of the Reich and Einstein doppelgängers with Freud's photograph, is evidence of the force of its registration, and how the cinematic analogy would come to bear on Reich's future. In those moments in the dark of the cinema, with the projection hanging enlarged and numinous in the smoke of the auditorium, Reich, orgonomy, and Oranur were all vindicated. And there is Bobby watching his father-figure enter the spaceship, as Peter Reich would dream his real father did in his *A Book of Dreams.* When

15 Ibid., 0:42:38–0:43:21.
16 Ibid., 0:44:22.

89

Bobby tells his mother what he has seen, she says, "Oh, Bobby, you've been dreaming, again."[17]

After Klaatu is shot a second time, and killed, Gort takes his body to the spaceship. First, Gort uses his energy beam to—as it were—roll away the stone of his tomb, breaking through the wall where Klaatu is confined. On the spaceship, a halo of healing energy resurrects him before the ascension. Klaatu delivers on final message to the multitudes assembled on the Ellipse, the ripples of consequence from atomic experiments rippling outward into the orbits of the universe. He describes "an organization for the mutual protection of all planets, and for the complete elimination of aggression." As we will see, with Peter and others, Wilhelm Reich will establish a group called CORE (Cosmic Orgone Engineering) or CORE Men organized to use orgone energy in such a manner.

Even as he observes himself in *The Day the Earth Stood Still,* Reich does not mention the spectral presence of the photograph of Freud. It occupies a deliberate and prominent position in the film. Reich's silence alone is extraordinary and suggestive. Why did Reich's attention to the film "miss" the picture of Freud? It did not. No artist worth his or her salt could miss it. No psychoanalyst could miss it, particularly not one with Reich's relationship to Freud, and with the same photograph, an iconic presence for more than twenty-five years.

Sándor Ferenczi's essential paper "Introjection and Transference"[18] was published in the *Jarbuch der Psychoanalyse* in 1909. If Reich did not know it from preserved copies of the yearbook, he certainly knew of it through Freud who drew on it in "The Instincts and their Vicissitudes,"[19] one of the texts that Freud gave Reich during their first meeting in 1920. The mechanisms were not unfamiliar to Reich, even if—as Maria Torok

17 Ibid., 0:57:20.

18 Sándor Ferenczi, "Introjection and Transference," in *First Contributions to Psycho-analysis,* ed. and trans. Ernest Jones (London: Routledge, 2018), 35–93.

19 Sigmund Freud, "Instincts and Their Vicissitudes," in *On the History of the Psycho-Analytic Movement: Papers on Metapsychology and Other Works,* trans. James Strachey (London: Vintage, 2001), 109–40.

concludes — Freud's application of the term clouded Ferenczi's original usage.[20] Some explication of this is necessary, since both Freud and Karl Abraham managed to fuse the mechanism of introjection with that of incorporation, a point made by Torok in a necessary restatement of Ferenczi's original. Indeed, Ferenczi's references to Freud's work contribute to the idea that Ferenczi's introjection is synonymous with incorporation, compensation, and so forth, when it was quite distinct. Every analyst has experience of projection and transference, from the patient upon the analyst. "The neurotic," Ferenczi explains, "is constantly seeking for objects with whom he can identify himself, to whom he can transfer feelings, whom he can thus draw into his circle of interest, i.e. introject."[21] Yet, always Ferenczi is at pains to stress that, "paranoiac projection and neurotic introjection are merely extreme cases of psychical processes the primary forms of which are to be demonstrated in every normal being."[22] The object of introjection, the introject, becomes part of the more or less conscious and unconscious structuring of experience. As Laurence A. Rickels writes in *I Think I Am Philip K. Dick,* "introjection must be recognized as the alternate mechanism without which our projections cannot be made or followed."[23] As an aside, if the reader perceives parallels between Reich's experiences and those of Philip K. Dick which produced his visionary *Exegesis,*[24] those perceptions might not be unreasonable. Ferenczi continues: "Freud's discoveries in the field of psychopathology of everyday life convince us that the capacity for projection and displacement is present also in normal human being, and often overshoots the

20 Maria Torok, "The Illness of Mourning and the Fantasy of the Exquisite Corpse," in Maria Torok and Nicholas Abraham, *The Shell and the Kernel: Renewals of Psychoanalysis,* Vol. 1, ed. and trans. Nicholas T. Rand (Chicago: University of Chicago Press, 1994), 107–24.

21 Ferenczi, "Introjection and Transference," 47–48.

22 Ibid.

23 Laurence A. Rickels, *I Think I Am Philip K. Dick* (Minneapolis: University of Minnesota Press, 2010), 3.

24 Philip K. Dick, *The Exegesis of Philip K. Dick,* eds. Pamela Jackson, Jonathan Lethem, and Erik Davis (New York: Houghton Mifflin Harcourt, 2011).

mark."[25] The difference in the so-called normal person and the neurotic is that, "the healthy person is conscious of the greater part of his introjection, whereas with the neurotic this remains for the most part repressed, finds expression in *unconscious* phantasies, and becomes manifest to the expert only indirectly, symbolically."[26] Note that Ferenczi does not state that the healthy person is conscious of all of his introjection, but the greater part. We should say that every introjection includes conscious and unconscious material. In *Contact with Space,* Reich describes the conscious introjects of *The Day the Earth Stood Still,* that is, its broad generalities with which his ego could identify consciously and recount without struggle. Yet, the process of introjection is intensified and made durable by the unconscious material. This, precisely, is what cinema exploits most successfully. Cinema is a psychic technology, which is to say, it is psyche's analog and extension: occasioning the introjection and projection of desires both auto- and hetero-erotic. Cinema presents symptomatic, confirmatory evidence of psychoanalytic theory. In Ferenczi's paper: "What we describe as introjections and other symptoms are really — in Freud's opinion, with which I fully agree — self-taught attempts on the patient's part to cure himself."[27]

It has been found that in the "unconscious" (in Freud's sense) all the impulses are pent up that have been repressed in the course of the individual development, and that their unsatisfied, stimulus-hungry affects are constantly ready to "transfer" on to the persons and objects of the outer world, to bring these unconsciously into connection with the ego, to "introject."[28]

Again, this is how and why cinema works. And we might regard introjection not only as a process, but as a capacity. The capacity to introject was well-developed in Reich, as we will see. The

25 Ferenczi, "Introjection and Transference," 49.
26 Ibid., 52–53.
27 Ibid., 55.
28 Ibid., 60.

mechanism of introjection is further explicated in Ferenczi's 1912 paper "On the Definition of Introjection."

> I described introjection as an extension to the external world of the original autoerotic interests, by including its objects in the ego. I put the emphasis on this 'including' and wanted to show thereby that I considered *every sort of object love* (or *transference*) both in normal and in neurotic people (and of course also in paranoiacs as far as they are capable of loving) as an extension of the ego, that is, of introjection.[29]

Ferenczi's mechanism of introjection is "an extension to the external world of the autoerotic interests, by including its objects in the ego."[30] It is as a result of autoerotic or narcissistic interests that an object becomes desired and is "included," in the ego, as extension, a "growing onto," a prosthetic growth toward which unconscious orients. In Torok's words:

> Like transference (that is, like its mode of action in therapy), introjection is defined as the process of including the Unconscious in the ego through objects contacts. The loss of the object will halt this process. Introjection does not tend toward compensation, but growth. By broadening and enriching the ego, introjection seeks to introduce into it the unconscious, nameless, or repressed libido. Thus, it is not a matter at all of introjection of the object, as is all too commonly stated, but of introjection the sum total of the drives, and their vicissitudes as occasioned by the mediated object... Moving back and forth between the "narcissistic and objectal realms," between auto- and hetero-eroticism, introjection transforms instinctual promptings into desires and fantasies

29 Sándor Ferenczi, "On the Definition of Introjection," in *Final Contributions to the Problems and Methods of Psycho-analysis,* ed. Michael Balint, trans. Eric Mosbacher et al. (Oxford: Routledge, 2018), 316.
30 Ibid.

of desire, making them fit to receive a name and the right to exist and to unfold in the object sphere.[31]

To be explicit, *The Day the Earth Stood Still* was the object of and for introjection in Reich's case. Reich was conscious of his psychic relation and reaction to the film, in the way that any of us might experience that uncanny sense of resonance that cinema exploits. The simple truth is that cinema begins with projection and transference: we seem to recognize a part of our own being on screen, and we see our antagonists there, also. With introjection, more or less consciously, the structure of the film is taken in and becomes part of the reality structure, particularly, of the neurotic, but also of the healthy person. The contingencies of the introjects become a kind of psychic overlay, functionally identical with the introjected object that retains original contingency in the external world.

Recall that Wilhelm Reich entered the Vienna Psychoanalytic Society under Sigmund Freud in 1920 with the presentation of a paper entitled "Libidinal Conflicts and Delusions in Ibsen's *Peer Gynt.*" In his recollections of delivering the paper, including his attempt to speak extemporaneously as Freud wished, but losing his thread and returning to reading from the manuscript, Reich describes repeated readings of Henrik Ibsen's play even until the 1940s when the "Peer Gynt" chapter of *The Function of the Orgasm* was published.

Everything was seething and whirling within me when I read and understood Peer Gynt and when I met and comprehended Freud. I was ostensibly like Peer Gynt. I felt his fate to be the most likely outcome if one ventured to tear oneself loose from the closed ranks of acknowledged science and traditional thinking.[32]

31 Torok, "The Illness of Mourning," 113.
32 Wilhelm Reich, *The Discovery of the Orgone,* Vol. I: *The Function of the Orgasm: Sex-Economic Problems of Biological Energy,* trans. Vincent R. Carfango (New York: Farrar, Straus and Giroux, 1973), 39.

Reich's paper also draws on Ferenczi, although ironically his reference is not to the mechanism of introjection. What is clear, however, is that Reich had already begun the process of introjection of a dramatic archetype long before the culminating introjection in the case of *The Day the Earth Stood Still*. The opening introjection of Henrik Ibsen's *Peer Gynt* served him through his psychoanalytic and biological work from 1919 until the crisis year of 1951 when another introjection became necessary, and the arrangement of that second introjection has been the subject of this chapter, and in many ways, of this book. The second introjection will undergo an important revision later.

As *Peer Gynt* opens, a young man, twenty-years old, crawls through the snow on a high mountain slope. Somewhere below, where the snow gives way to the green pulse of summer, his mother struggles to maintain the farm, alone. A month has passed since the young man abandoned her to stalk reindeer, and now a magnificent buck emerges from the frozen alder trees. While the animal is scratching with his antlers at the snow to uncover lichens, silently, the young man takes aim. His shot fells the buck. He rushes to it, straddling its back to finish it with his hunting knife. He raises the blade, to plunge it into the base of the buck's skull. But the buck throws its head back, its antlers pinning the young man's thighs to its body, the knife and its sheath cast in shock and pain into the snow. With the young man's thighs trapped, the buck stands and gallops away, carrying its helpless adversary, the gun that wounded it lost in the snow. When, at last, the young man returns to his mother, she is furious and accuses him of lying. In his absence, the girl the young man had dreamed of marrying has chosen another. The young man takes his mother upon his back: he will be the buck, and she will be him, and he will take his mother to the wedding.

The buck fantasy is the first of a series of Gynt's dreams in which Reich identifies the Oedipal drama of Freudian psychoanalysis. The buck fantasy is also an image of man crucified upon Nature, upon his own nature, of the dream object that turns back upon him and abducts him, of the hunter captured by the game. In retrospect these all have their oscillations between the narcissistic and objectal realms: Reich's introjection of Peer Gynt, his own Oedipal crisis, the desire to become a man of science, the dream of reversing desertification, the encounter with the Sphinx, the figure of the psychic father Freud (Ibsen's "Boyg") and Reich's biological father Leon, angst in Norway, the naming of his son Peter after the hero, as Richard Wagner had done with his son Siegfried, and the naming of his dog Troll. Reich was an intensely disciplined thinker who had a poetic sense, the associating, constellating mode of thought that is as essential to psychoanalysis as it is to the experimental scientist.

In Reich's analysis of *Peer Gynt*, the hero's time in the desert represents a descent into the theater of "allegory and caricature." Reich's survey includes the following remark: "Among the interpreters of Peer Gynt, utter confusion reigns as to whether Act IV [the desert scene] was indeed experienced by the hero at all, or whether it is a digression into fantasy on the part of the poet,"[33] meaning Ibsen. It is difficult to avoid seeing Reich prefigured in his own description and analysis. "By breaking through the row of sand dunes which hold back the sea in the west, one could turn the desert into fertile land, cities would arise."[34]

Perhaps the reader will recall from the beginning of this book that the writer characterized Reich's career as one with three phases — three skips on the water, to borrow the flying saucer image — and like a skipping object, each successive phase shorter and, in certain ways, more intense than the last. Wilhelm Reich divided his analysis of Peer Gynt, or the Gyntish self, into three periods also. In Freudian terms, Reich explains the first is that of

fantasy formation, the stage (expressed in terms of libido) in which the individual, as a consequence of an unconscious incestuous fixation, withdraws his libido from the external world leaving a small portion which is directed toward the object of his fantasy. We know from the theory of neurosis that this condition cannot last long due to the increasing stasis of sexual energy, which finds no real outlet in the object of the fantasy and is replaced by a neurosis or psychosis. Neurosis

33 Wilhelm Reich, "Libidinal Conflicts and Delusions in Ibsen's *Peer Gynt,"* in *Early Writings: Volume 1,* trans. Philip Schmitz (New York: Farrar, Straus and Giroux, 1975), 14–15.
34 Ibid., 18.

occurs when the repressed drives are at least partially satis-
fied by symptomatic actions; psychosis, when the libido is
withdrawn from the fantasized objects and directed towards
the self. In the latter stage, a case of regression to the narcissistic stage of sexual development takes place (megalomania;
dementia paranoides).[35]

The transition from first period to the second period of "the
Peer Gyntian madness,"[36] Reich tells us, is ambiguous as compared with the transition from the Gyntian madness to the third
period, the desert and Gynt's asylum imprisonment. At that
third point:

Now we also understand the meaning of Peer's delusions of
being a prophet — and a man of science. First, it was his belief,
or rather his desire, to know everything or even to predict the
future; and second, his desire to continue his infantile sexual
investigations on a pathologically enlarged scale.[37]

There is seduction in the possibility of folding Reich and Gynt
together — particularly in a pejorative sense, that Reich's end
is Freud's *Beyond the Pleasure Principle* and Ibsen's Peer Gynt
on a "pathologically enlarged scale." Rather, I believe that the
Gyntish self was displaced by *The Day the Earth Stood Still,* and
other cinematic narratives, a position supported by material in
the Reich archives.

The Gynt introjection was made explicit by Nathan G. Hale
in his 1974 review of Jerome Greenfield's *Wilhelm Reich Vs
the USA.*[38] Although Hale's 1995 book *The Rise and Crisis of
Psychoanalysis in the United States*[39] devotes little space to Reich,

35 Ibid., 15.
36 Ibid., 16.
37 Ibid., 33.
38 Jerome Greenfield, *Wilhelm Reich vs. the U.S.A.* (New York: W.W.
    Norton & Co., 1974).
39 Nathan G. Hale Jr., *The Rise and Crisis of Psychoanalysis in the
    United States: Freud and the Americans, 1917–1985* (New York: Oxford
    University Press, 1995).

he nevertheless affords him a place of importance and influence. His review of Greenfield's account of the persecution and trials of Reich from 1947–1957 goes further in its analysis of Reich's dispositions.

> Reich strongly identified with Peer Gynt, the subject of his first analytic paper. Reich saw Peer as the unconventional dreamer, bursting with energy, eager to change the world, but certain to get his neck broken because of his darling curiosity. Like Peer, Reich was an inveterate optimist.[40]

Echoing Ferenczi's agreement with Freud that introjection represents autodidactic attempts at self-cure, Hale writes, "By focusing the transcendent Peer, Reich could defend himself against the gothic realities of his early life."[41] Jerome Greenfield's work is the first comprehensive study of Reich's final decade, framed in the lens of his legal conflict with the Federal Drug Administration. Although Greenfield makes several references to Reich's concern with flying saucers, or UFOS, or Ea in Reich's later terminology, and is obviously familiar with the content of *Contact with Space,* he studiously ignores Reich's opening question: the one that opened this book. Greenfield walks up to the silver ramp of introjection but passes it by.

In his paper on Peer Gynt, Reich acknowledges that he is entering the "long-standing inquiry of psychologists concerning the relationship between poetic and psychotic phenomena."[42] Poetic phenomena naturally pass from the dramatic stage to the cinematic screen. In the case of Reich and *The Day the Earth Stood Still,* following Freud and Ferenczi, conscious of the greater part of his introjection, one must find Reich was not neurotic. He recognizes the doppelgänger and the extent to which the narrative is his own, quite reasonably, and he declares it so. Despite

40 Nathan G. Hale Jr., "Wilhelm Reich vs. the U.S.A.: The Discoverer of the Orgone," *The New York Times,* August 11, 1974. https://www.nytimes.com/1974/08/11/archives/wilhelm-reich-vs-the-usa-the-discoverer-of-the-orgone-by-jerome.html.

41 Ibid.

42 Reich, "Libidinal Conflicts," 4.

cinema's mechanism of projection, and the seductive appeal of that term as mirrored in psychoanalysis, this is not that. As another analyst turned UFOlogist might have explained it, "The word 'projection' is not really appropriate, for nothing has been cast out of the psyche; rather the psyche has attained its present complexity by a series of acts of introjection."[43] In cinematic terms, Reich was not responsible for the projection of the image that appeared to mirror him. Ferenczi, Freud, and Jung might together have been compelled to admit that Reich consciously introjected an uncanny synchronicity of unusual complexity, something more inexplicable than the roots of animism. Marie-Louise von Franz develops Jung's acausal connecting principle in *Projection and Re-Collection in Jungian Psychology: Reflections of the Soul.* In a chapter that happens also to analyze a dream of Jung's concerning a UFO, where the "fact that the flying saucer is a 'machine' might indicate symbolically that behind this object is a power that devises and arranges our reality for us,"[44] Von Franz differentiates between projection and reflection, or the mirroring of psyche and matter that occurs in a Jungian description of synchronicity. One thinks here of the reflective surfaces of flying saucer phenomena, particularly in cinema: the reflective fuselage of the UFO, and the silver of the space suit and of the uncanny android. Von Franz is occupied with the question of "whether and how the material world can mirror the objective psyche."[45] This was Jung's problem in the Flying Saucers as he wrestled with synchronicity. Where this is indeed a problem for the natural sciences with which she has been concerned, it is not a problem for cinema or art in general, cinema being material in more than one sense. For *Peer Gynt* or *The Day the Earth Stood Still,* the idea that "material events in the external world would have to be regarded as statements about conditions in the objective

---

43 Carl Jung, *The Archetypes and the Collective Unconscious,* trans. R.F.C. Hull (Princeton: Princeton University Press, 1968), 25.

44 Marie-Louise von Franz, *Projection and Re-Collection in Jungian Psychology: Reflections of the Soul,* trans. William H. Kennedy (La Salle: Open Court Publishing, 1995), 188.

45 Ibid., 190.

psyche"[46] presents us with little difficulty. Interpreting a Chinese Daoist narrative, Von Franz concludes: "Events in nature *mirrored* the psychological state of things at the emperor's court and provided information about psychic processes of which the rulers were not sufficiently conscious."[47] In literary criticism, this is simply an instance of the pathetic fallacy, like the tendency for rain during funerals in art.

James Baldwin discusses escape personalities in his 1976 cinematic memoir *The Devil Finds Work*: "That the movie star is an 'escape' personality indicates one of the irreducible dangers to which the moviegoer is exposed: the danger of surrendering to the corroboration of one's fantasies as they are thrown back from the screen."[48] It seems to me that this describes the danger that presented itself to Reich more than twenty years earlier. Alienated, he found his existence, his theories, his fantasies corroborated repeatedly in cinema. In this, he was not unusual. Baldwin also limns an inverse in the movie star. "One does not go to see them act," he says, "one goes to watch them be. One does not go to see Humphrey Bogart, a*s Sam Spade:* one goes to see Sam Spade *as Humphrey Bogart.*"[49] Which is to say, in Reich's case, that he did not so much see Michael Rennie as the Christlike spaceman, but the Christlike spaceman as Michael Rennie, whom Reich took to have his own likeness. Reich had need of an escape personality, for obvious reasons. In a sense, his personality had always been an escape personality.

Later, Susan Sontag would note that survivors of the attack on the World Trade Center in New York on September 11, 2001 were prone to describing the disaster they had survived in cinematic terms. "After four decades of big-budget Hollywood disaster films, 'It felt like a movie' seems to have displaced the way survivors of a catastrophe used to express the short-term unassimilability of what they had gone through: 'It felt like a

---

46 Ibid. Italics in original.

47 Ibid., 193.

48 James Baldwin, "The Devil Finds Work," in *Collected Essays,* ed. Toni Morrison (New York: Library of America, 1998), 500.

49 Ibid.

dream.'"⁵⁰ The 1950s swarmed with flying saucer movies, most of which — *The Day the Earth Stood Still* as a mystical exception — presented catastrophic destruction and fetishistic disaster porn with one national monument or institution destroyed after another. There is something exhausting in the din of the 1953 adaptation of *The War of the Worlds.* For moviegoers, these films, as Reich observed, were a kind of preparation, anticipating imminent reality. We should not be at all surprised that people comment on reality as something they have experienced in cinematic terms before. Sontag is a more contemporary reflection of the pre-cinematic point Friedrich Nietzsche made in 1872: "Thus the aesthetically sensitive man stands in the same relation to the reality of dreams as the philosopher does to the reality of existence; he is a close and willing observer, for these images afford him an interpretation of life, and by reflecting on these processes he trains himself for life."⁵¹ Cinematic eidola have usurped the phantoms of dreams and arguably of the family in the initiation and training of identity.

50 Susan Sontag, *Regarding the Pain of Others* (New York: Farrar, Straus and Giroux, 2003), 22.
51 Friedrich Nietzsche, *The Birth of Tragedy,* in *Basic Writings of Nietzsche,* ed. and trans. Walter Kaufmann (New York: Random House, 2000), 34.

7

The Planet Is Dying:
From Cloudbuster to Space Gun

We stopped there all Sunday night and all the next day — the day of the panic — in a little island of daylight, cut off by the Black Smoke from the rest of the world. We could do nothing but wait in aching inactivity during those two weary days.

— H.G. Wells[1]

In *CORE* VI, nos. 1–4: *OROP Desert, Part 1: Space Ships, DOR and Drought,*[2] Reich reports that from the late spring of 1952, the effects of the Oranur Experiment prevented "any orderly activity before November 1953."[3] For Reich, the Oranur Emergency of 1951 seemed to have environmental consequences beyond the evacuation of the Observatory in April 1952, and indeed beyond the precincts of Orgonon. The interaction of orgone and nuclear radiation generated sinister clouds. On March 24, 1952, his fifty-fifth birthday, Reich was beset by Oranur sickness. A week later he notes, "Oranur continues — blackening of rocks."[4] The blackening of the rocks was caused, Reich believed,

1   H.G. Wells, *The War of the Worlds* (London: Penguin, 2005), 115.
2   The acronyms are for Cosmic Orgone Engineering (CORE) and Orgone Operations (OROP).
3   Wilhelm Reich, *CORE (Cosmic Orgone Engineering)* VI, nos. 1–4: *OROP Desert, Part 1: Space Ships, DOR and Drought* (Rangeley: Orgone Institute, 1954): 8.
4   Wilhelm Reich, *Where's the Truth? Letters and Journals, 1948–1957,* ed.

by a kind of malevolent energy emanating from these dark DOR clouds. Reich seems to have noticed the first effects on the rocks in his fireplace: a blackening that included disintegration and changes to their form, rendering some of the stone pumice-like, reminiscent of brittle coral, or spongy, riddled with tiny holes. He would name this blackened substance Melanor — the effect of a melancholic perversion of orgone life energy. He said,

> The leaves of the trees and the needles of the evergreens look very 'sad'; they drop, lose turgor and erectility. [...] The trees look black, as though dying. The impression is actually that of *blackness,* or better, *bleakness.* It is not something that "came *into* the landscape." *It is rather, the sparkle of Life* that WENT OUT *of the landscape.* [...] A DOR-cloud is usually surrounded by normal atmospheric OR activity, such as *blueness* of the mountain ranges, sparkling of the sunny atmosphere, greenness of the trees. One cannot help but feel that natural cosmic OR energy retracts from the "evil," "bleak," "black," "lifeless" DOR-cloud and lets it pass. [CO, 28–29]

From a Freudian perspective, Reich was not himself experiencing melancholia, at least not in orthodox form. Out of this bleak sympathy with the environment, projection or otherwise, sickness led to creativity. It was during the late spring of 1952, with the black fallout of Melanor settling "upon everything, rockwalls, apparatus, skin surfaces — doing all kinds of damage" [CO, 8], that Reich developed a new device for the mitigation of DOR-clouds and Melanor: the cloudbuster.

The cloudbuster had its experimental origins more than a decade earlier, in August 1940 on the banks of the Mooselookmeguntic Lake, about six miles to the southwest of the land where Reich would later build Orgonon. Reich was there with Ilse Ollendorff and wrote to their daughter about the idyllic setting, the animals, and the way that the landscape was reminiscent of Norway. It was remote from what Reich called the "emotional plague" of mass humanity. Reich was using metal pipes, as one

Mary Boyd Higgins, trans. Derek Jordan and Inge Jordan (New York: Farrar, Straus and Giroux, 2012), 108.

might a telescope, as a means of narrowing attention on the presence of orgone energy. As Reich and Ollendorff observed the ripples of the lake through the pipes, or along their length, he had the impression that there was some relationship between the tubular metal and some shifting in the movement of the water. The pipes seemed to draw upon the surface. No, Reich resolved that this was too incredible. The idea remained latent until Reich engaged with the problem of removing atmospheric DOR. First, he sought to understand it better. Reich's process is detailed in the *CORE Report,* which was written in late 1953 and details developments during 1952–1953.

"The ORANUR Experiment," Reich determined, "had not *caused* the atmospheric conditions that were responsible for the DOR emergency. The experiment had only *reproduced* and *revealed,* as if under a high power microscope, what had been going on over ages on a lesser scale; it had, furthermore, accentuated effects of various atomic functions" [CO, 13].

Oranur sickness had attacked the weakest point of each of those affected. It revealed biopathic disease, or functionally identical psychic disease; Reich was not a dualist when it came to the so-called mind-body problem, nor did he subscribe to parallelism between somatic and psychic processes. Orgone energy was the common functioning principle of unity between these traditionally antithetical modes; simultaneous identity and antithesis in the superimposition of orgone. This is Reich's specific way of thinking, of orgonomic functionalism encapsulated in OROP — the operations that would soon involve the cloudbuster were to be undertaken in those terms, under the common functioning principle of all-pervasive orgone. Reich's philosophy rendered all things permeable and collapsed the distinction between soma and psyche, and between psyche, biosphere, and cosmos. This should not be confused with any notion that the cosmos is "all-mind," or with animism. Since orgone was the prematerial life energy, the first obstacle to clearing the DOR clouds was within the human animal within the biosphere. As Reich considered the effects of DOR, the sickening of the environment, the drought, he turned toward the image of the wasteland, the desert. Orgonomy pointed Reich toward the superimposition of

the "emotional desert" in man and actual drought, actual desertification. This is one of the earliest findings of the CORE report.

The emotional desert recapitulated the emotional plague.
The "inner" and the "outer" desert were one and the same. *"Man
himself prevents now and prevented over the ages the combat of deserts"* [CO, vii]. On the one hand, Reich's orgonomic theory is
reminiscent of the fertility myths that preoccupied the myth and
ritual school of mythographers and poets — not least Sir James
G. Frazer's *The Golden Bough* (1890), Jessie L. Weston's *From
Ritual to Romance* (1920), and the ancient fertility rites and the
Grail legend bleeding into T. S. Eliot's *The Waste Land* (1921) — a
scholarship and literature that aligned the sexual vitality of the
sovereign with the vitality of the land. The sovereign, brought
low and into impotence by dolorous stroke suffers, in Reich's
terms, from the "immobilization of *biological energy*" [CO, vii].
What is radical here is that Reich relocates the armoring that
holds DOR in the body from the sovereign as figurehead, to the
mass of humanity, replacing the individual icon with the com-
monwealth, fusing *The Golden Bough* with Thomas Hobbes's
Leviathan (1651). Reich's thinking in 1952 presents a potent
image, the mass recapitulation of fertility myth as environmental prescience. The emotional plague afflicting humanity afflicts
the orgone envelope of the Earth; replace the words "orgone
envelope" with climate, or atmosphere, and Reich's view is com-
monplace as I write this fifty years later, after the emergence of
environmentalism and ecopsychology. Not by coincidence does
Reich deploy the same term for the contaminated atmosphere
at Orgonon on March 22, 1952, as he does in his tape recording
of ten days later when describing speculation about his own
personal deterioration, that he had "gone haywire," as quoted
in Chapter 4.

The black material of Melanor, Reich discovered, had its
antithesis in a white powder that he dubbed Orite. Just as he
observed the blackening in disintegration of the rocks under
attack, as it were, the white dust was a product of the defensive
reaction of orgone, as was the presence of the yellowish Orene
which was also an assertion of the life-energy against degrada-
tion. Brown coloration of the blackened rocks was regarded as
evidence of the counterattack that had been observed in the

human organism and in the experimental mice. Melanor had been attracted to Reich's environs by the orgonomic potential of the Oranur Experiment — in orgone physics the lesser charge is drawn to, or accumulates to the greater. Melanor, this cosmic energy lacking in water and oxygen, tended toward this also. Its process "disclosed the riddle of *desert development*" [CO, 18]. Yet, what was seeding the Earth's orgone envelope with Melanor? Reich's thought can be difficult to follow here. There are two simultaneous assertions: that desertification is the sublunary effect of the emotional plague, the emotional desert contingent upon the trapped DOR in the organism from armoring and repression, and the fallout of atomic ambitions; desertification is also caused by a malign fallout called Melanor which is of cosmic origin. These hypotheses would be unified in November of 1953. In the meantime, the problem of the DOR clouds and the presence of Melanor persisted.

In late April 1952, recalling the effect of passing metal pipes over the surface of Lake Mooselookmeguntic with Ollendorff in 1940, Reich arranged a series of pipes, each nine to twelve feet long and one and a half inches in diameter, connected by long, armored or "BX" cable (an abbreviated of Bronx cable, from the General Electric factory which manufactured them), to the well water, deep underground. Reich's intent was to break up or "bust" the DOR clouds over Orgonon by drawing their charge. According to Reich,

> The effect was instantaneous: The black DOR-clouds began to shrink. And when the pipes were pointed *against* the OR energy flow, i.e., toward the west, a breeze west to east would set in after a few minutes "DRAW," as we came to call this operation; fresh, blue-grey or energy moved in where the nauseating DOR-clouds had been a short while before. Soon we learned that rain clouds, too, could be influenced, increased or diminished as well as moved, by operating these pipes in certain well-defined ways. [CO, 32]

At the end of June 1952, Reich sought to patent a new technology, the cloudbuster. As he wrote to the Commissioner of Patents,

It is technically possible, by using the so-called "orgonomic potential" (potential from low to high) in primordial Orgone Energy functioning, to disperse clouds, to concentrate water vapors in the atmosphere to the extent of making rain, and to draw atmospheric energy into lakes and rivers. This also makes it possible to remove the so-called "DOR"—clouds which lately appeared over this region and caused biophysical distress to many people.[5]

Where the orgone accumulator suggested an analog to womblike incubation, the cloudbuster would appear at first glance more like a piece of artillery, a phallic projection with several barrels. Such were the origins of the first pair of cloudbuster units, constructed in September–October in Portland, Maine. If desertification was to be reversed, the cloudbuster was vital to the expansion of operations. "Cloud-busting" (Reich's hyphenation is inconsistent) involved the "destruction as well as the *formation* or clouds of water vapor in the atmosphere and of orgone energy concentrations." The cloudbuster permitted interventions "with all phenomena which are related to or derive from atmospheric changes of climate including weather... the origin of deserts as well as areas of green vegetation, and all similar functions which depend on the presence or absence, on the scarcity or plentifulness of or energy, oxygen, water vapor, rain, sun and wind and their interaction" [CO, 33]. Reich coined the operational name "OROP Desert" on July 7, 1952, by which time the cloudbuster with telescoping pipes could be mounted on the bed of a pick-up truck.

Reich had been in correspondence with Robert McCullough, born in Utah and at this time a biologist and researcher from the University of New Hampshire. McCullough wrote to Reich on July 8 and 11, and in his reply of July 14, Reich conveys, without mentioning the cloudbuster directly, that his experiments will soon take him to the Arizona desert. Suggesting that this will take place before the end of the year, Reich invited McCullough to be part of the expedition [WT, 114]. The journey would not take place until the autumn of 1954, but by then McCullough,

5   Reich, *Where's the Truth?*, 111.

his wife, and his young children would comprise the advance party that would arrive in Tucson ten days ahead of Reich, Eva Reich, William Moise, and Peter Reich. McCullough had read Reich's books *The Function of the Orgasm* and *The Cancer Biopathy* in 1949, and had sought to replicate several of Reich's bion and orgone experiments. By 1952, McCullough, having completed his graduate study with the observation of atmospheric orgone energy and its transit in the desert of northwestern Utah, was deeply immersed in Reich's ideas, but was not without his doubts. Indeed, McCullough accepted the research associate position at the University of New Hampshire precisely due to its proximity to Orgonon and Reich. In the summer of 1951, McCullough made several visits to Orgonon, "to inquire about character restructuralization which was then required for all workers in the field [of orgonomy], to get an accumulator etc. I wanted to get training in this field because all other fields had largely lost their significance to me since I became aware of OR biophysics. I continued with my work in wildlife management, at the same time reporting orgone phenomena wherever I encountered them."[6] McCullough volunteered some research into Melanor, and when Reich offered McCullough a full-time associate researcher position at Orgonon in the spring of 1953, his first assignment was the Melanor problem. McCullough would become a central figure in Reich's late work, but when he began working formally for Reich, he had his doubts. He was still a mechanistic thinker.

> When I first arrived at Orgonon, I was cocky. I would disregard warnings and let myself get overexposed to the radiation. I was somehow trying to prove to myself the actuality of ORANUR. Somewhere inside of me was a little voice that kept saying, "Maybe it's a hoax, a colossal stupendous hoax. Perhaps or doesn't even exist. *Prove that it does.* [...] This continual *proving* to myself in an ORANUR field was extremely

6 Robert A. McCullough, "Rocky Road Toward Functionalism," *CORE (Cosmic Orgone Engineering)* VII, nos. 3–4 (1955): 146.

dangerous; I'd become quite ill, my cervical glands would swell up, and I would suffer from severe anxiety.[7]

Later, and ironically for a man whose inner voice cried hoax, McCullough would be crucial to the mythology of Reich and the flying saucers, adjusting his memories to fit the myth in a way that I will suggest was self-serving.

Reich had his first experience with a "space ship" in August 1952, joining several others who reported similar phenomena to him at Orgonon that year. The extent to which Reich practiced a radical partitioning of his experiences is evidenced in the way he conducted himself during the visit of Kurt Eissler to the Observatory and its library that October. With Eissler, at least as we have it, none of Reich's experimental preoccupations come up, except for a brief explanation of the way in which DOR relates to Freud.

> What he felt with the death instinct, what he tried to catch there, what he felt in the human being was a certain dying quality. We call it DOR today in a physical sense. There is a deadly orgone energy. It is in the atmosphere. You can demonstrate it on devices such as the Geiger counter. It's a swampy quality. You know what swamps are? Stagnant, deadly water which doesn't flow, doesn't metabolize. Cancer, too, is due to a stagnation. *Cancer is due to a stagnation of the flow of life energy in the organism.* So Freud was trying to grasp that quality. I know, today, that *he sensed something in the human organism which was deadly. But he thought in terms of instinct. So he hit upon the term "death instinct." That was wrong. "Death" was right. "Instinct" was wrong.*[8]

There was Reich, holding forth beneath the photographic portrait of Freud, diagnosing the father-genius, making his corrections, like the figure of Carpenter in *The Day the Earth Stood*

7   Ibid., 147.
8   Wilhelm Reich, *Reich Speaks of Freud,* eds. Mary Higgins and Chester M. Raphael, trans. Therese Pol (New York: Farrar, Straus and Giroux, 1967), 89–90.

Still. Perhaps, in holding more of the Oranur Experiment back from Eissler, Reich was insulating himself from the Freudians, whom he had reasons to distrust, even as he struggled to present his findings to the United States government and the disbelieving Robert Oppenheimer. Yet, it is, nevertheless, remarkable that given the nature and extent of the Oranur emergency, the presence of the cloudbuster, and the fact that Reich believed that his bioregion was literally deteriorating as it struggled with DOR/ Melanor fallout, that he was so disciplined. How simple it would have been to draw Eissler's attention to the blackening rock in the structure of the buildings at Orgonon. How simple it would have been for Reich to inform Eissler that the Observatory where he recorded his interview, in the library beneath the portrait of Freud, had been abandoned when Oranur ran amok, and how his family and colleagues had sickened and nearly died. How much ambivalence was in the exception Reich granted to Eissler, in permitting him to be there?

On May 13, 1953, Reich wrote to the office of Burton M. Cross, Governor of Maine, to introduce the cloudbuster. By this time, Reich had commissioned the construction of three of the devices from the Southworth Machine Company in Portland, and these were in operation at Orgonon and in the field. At issue was Reich's concern that his weather control experiments had the potential to "endanger aircraft pilots and also embarrass the weather stations" when his interventions using the cloudbuster undermined regular weather predictions. In July, Reich worked with blueberry growers of Ellsworth Bank to draw rain against the drought. The cloudbuster thus entered the public imagination on July 24 when the Bangor *Daily News* reported on the apparent "rain-making" that Reich had conducted for the growers on July 6. Quoted in Myron Sharaf's biography of Reich:

> A puzzled witness to the "rain-making" process said: "The queerest looking clouds you ever saw began to form soon after they got the thing rolling." And later, the same witness said the scientists were able to change the course of the wind by manipulation of the device.[9]

9   Myron R. Sharaf, *Fury on Earth: A Biography of Wilhelm Reich* (New

Reich's journals describe briefly the cloudbuster drawing for one hour and ten minutes, and five hours of rain that night [WT, 128]. The cloudbuster experiments were known from August 1953 as OROP, after Oranur Weather Control Operation. But for Reich, the instances of rain were accidents, contingent upon the work of using the cloudbuster to remove the nauseating atmospheric DOR from Orgonon and its vicinity, a process he referred to as "dedorization." Of these contingent effects, of rain, of thick dew attending his experiments, Reich was unsure. And yet, there was an ambivalence in Reich that confused his assistants, notably the artist William Moise, who had married Reich's daughter Eva. In his journals of the summer of 1953, Reich refers to his work with Ellsworth Bank as an "assignment to make rain" [ibid.], and on July 19 he notes that he failed in "making rain after 4 attempts" [ibid.]. So, there were at least some occasions when the line between the mitigation of pollution resulting from the Oranur emergency and rainmaking was unclear. Even in his long rebuke to Moise in which he insists "*We are not professional rainmakers, not even experimental professional rainmakers*" [WT, 130], and that "I learned that we do not MAKE rain; we only influence the OR potential in the atmosphere while we trigger the various regions of the OR envelope" [WT, 131], Reich describes his causal effect on the rain at Ellsworth; one can forgive Moise some semantic imprecision, given Reich's own. Yet, as much as Reich insists that he did not make rain, he does identify the cloudbuster operations as causing the Ellsworth rain reported in the *Daily News* and describes "planned rain" [ibid.]. The letter to William Moise ends with a return to the language of contingency and Reich's amusement at "the sudden changes which are pronounced by weather stations... in accordance with our DOR removal operations" [WT, 132]. One can sympathize with Moise's confusion, even as Reich works to clarify his position. Following a storm, Reich and the cloudbuster were televised on Portland's Channel 6 on March 30, 1954. In July 1954, Reich claimed that rain "could be produced or stopped at will during 1952." He described the breaking of droughts at Orgonon in early August 1952, for the

York: Da Capo, 1994), 379–80.

Ellsworth growers in July 1953, and at Orgonon and Hancock, Maine in October that year as "unequivocal successes" [CO, 9].

Reich did not, in 1952 and for most of 1953, associate flying saucers or UFOS with the DOR and Melanor fallout at Orgonon until Donald Keyhoe's work reached him in November of 1953. This marks something of a coda to the sometimes disorderly period marked from the April 1952 evacuation. Reich also received a copy of occultist and hoax-artist George Adamski's *Flying Saucers Have Landed,* published in September of 1952, but Reich does not dwell on its contents. Reich states: "The problem of what was causing the grave distress at Orgonon and in other parts of the USA remained unsolved until the *Keyhoe report* on the so-called *'Flying Saucers'* appeared in autumn 1953, released under the auspices of the US Air Force" [CO, 13]. Those present at Orgonon continued to report sightings into December of 1953. By this time, Reich assimilated the flying saucer reports within his understanding of the fallout from the Oranur emergency, the DOR clouds, Melanor, and the blackening rocks, and this resulted in the evolution of the cloudbuster from a weather-influencing device to one suited to interplanetary defense. Reich's concern with flying saucers and with cloud busting operations overlapped, then, until they merged into a single thesis that one sees emerging in November 1953. On November 20, Reich wrote:

After reading Keyhoe report
Summary: State of affairs
1. The flying saucers are real, to judge from Keyhoe's report.
2. They use OR energy in propelling and lighting: speed, colors, silence
3. Most likely they were stirred into action in far outer space by the atomic explosions: *Oranur effects.*
4. They come to investigate the disturbance of their lives by nuclear Oranur.
5. They are directed by intelligent beings who come peacefully. [WT, 134]

Reich's introjection of *The Day the Earth Stood Still* and Keyhoe's avowedly nonfiction account in *Flying Saucers from*

Outer Space of the same motivations on the part of the flying saucers fused with Reich's belief that not only atomic experiments in the military scientific theater, but also the effects of the Oranur emergency on his part, were drawing the attention of the saucers. Yet, Reich goes further. He summarizes that the flying saucers are able to travel by means of orgone energy, that its galactic stream functions like a river of energy. The affliction of Melanor was "brought down to earth" by the pilots of the flying saucers who he sees as Cosmic Orgone Engineers, CORE people, or CORE men [WT, 134]. The first entry of Reich's published journals for 1954 includes the existential problems: "How to feel comfortable in a spaceship; how to keep a child happily secure for his or her life. How to live well and happily" [WT, 139]. This would have bearing on what followed in the Arizona desert later that year, and the question bears directly upon Reich's son Peter and the nature of their relationship. It was also in January 1954 that Reich initiated his first formal contacts with the United States Air Force concerning UFOS, flying saucers, or, as he would term them, "Ea," or Energy alphas. The first was a letter to US Air Force Intelligence typed on the morning of January 29, following a double sighting at 10 p.m. the previous night from his working room within the Lower House at Orgonon. Reich did not know how to contact the relevant parties, so Ollendorff enlisted the help of a Rangeley State Trooper named Lester Farrar. The letter contains Reich's report and is also signed by Ollendorff, and includes her own corroboration of the sightings, describes a "bright, white-yellowish light" joined minutes later by "a second, similar, lighted object... moving toward the right or the East among the trees in the valley with Spotted Mountain in the background. It was the same appearance and disappearance and the same shining glimmer."[10] Reich received a response to this letter on March 10 from Major John Dunning at Dow Air Force Base, now Bangor International Airport, 120 miles east of Orgonon. Reich and Ollendorff's report was itself sent to Air Force Headquarters in Colorado Springs. At that time, under the Eisenhower administration, the Air Force advocated for a

---

10 Wilhelm Reich, *Contact with Space: Oranur Second Report, 1951–1956* (Haverhill: Haverhill House Publishing, 2018), 50.

military missile satellite program. Colorado Springs required that Dow Air Force Base send Reich and Ollendorff a copy of their USAF Technical Information Sheet, a questionnaire to be completed detailing the sightings. Reich returned the completed document to First Lieutenant Andrew Maytas on March 19. A facsimile of these contacts is published in *Contact with Space: Oranur Second Report, 1951–1956.*

Reich kept his own typed version of his answers to the questionnaire. The first page of these answers is retained within the Archives of the Orgone Institute, and there are subtle differences between what Reich presented to the Air Force and what he recorded for himself. It is located with Reich's hand-corrected draft manuscript for *Contact with Space.*[11] For example, Question 6 asks for the condition of the sky at the time of the sighting. On the form, Reich underlines *No trace of daylight.* The archival document adds that the atmosphere surrounding the Observatory possessed an unusual luminosity due to the agitation of Oranur. Question 16 requests information on the sound and color of the UFO. Of the color of the object, he reports to the Air Force that it was "bright yellow — white, at times toward orange" [CS, 57], but his own unpublished notes describe not only the indefinable nature of the yellow-orange spectrum, but also a whitish intensity. Reich keeps from the Air Force, but includes in his own transcription, that he had seen the same whitish luminosity in flashes of discharge with certain orgonomic phenomena he had observed in vacuum tubes, and references his 1949 article "Further Characteristics of Vacor Lumination," reprinted in *The Oranur Experiment: First Report, 1947–1951.*[12] The Air Force would learn from Reich's answer that the that the atmosphere in the valley was illuminated by the object, reminiscent of a bright star, but significantly larger, whereas his personal notes describe more sharply delineated objects surrounded by an energy field. An object surrounded by a luminous energy field is not the same as an object that emits light. It is not clear why this discrepancy

11 A copy was provided to the author on request, courtesy of the Archives of the Orgone Institute.

12 Wilhelm Reich, *The Oranur Experiment, First Report (1947–1951)* (Rangeley: Orgone Institute Press, 1951), 248 ff.

occurs, although one might say that the questionnaire answer is objective description where the archival document is more speculative. Even if he did not believe it so, Reich seems to have determined that some division was necessary.

On March 17, 1954, Reich presents the early history of his involvement with "the *'flying saucer'* problem" [CS, 68]. The facsimile published in *Contact with Space* is identical to that in the draft maintained in the Archive. It was first published under "Space Ships and Space Problems" in Chapter X of Reich's *CORE: OROP Desert* report of July 1954 [CO, 101–4]. It describes Reich's general lack of disquiet at the idea of alien visitors, including his own relative disinterest in his own experience at Orgonon in August, 1952. Reich reiterates the chronology where it was only after reading Keyhoe's work that he regarded the black presence of Melanor as related to flying saucer activity. From that point in November 1953, Reich is concentrated on the problem. I believe that the flying saucers were analogous to the issue of rainmaking in the removal of atmospheric DOR: the more emotive concept (rainmaking, flying saucers) issued from the less emotive research (removal of atmospheric and environmental Oranur contamination). It was always thus with Reich: in researching Freud's provocative theory of libido, Reich's more provocative application of the orgasm theory attached; from this provocation, the greater provocation of orgone energy emerged; and so forth. This is how it is to be curious, to ask radical questions. It is recognizable as scientific or creative dialectic. In his survey of his interest in the saucer problem, Reich finds himself returning to calculations and equations developed during his early experiments with orgone energy. A full account is given in *The Discovery of the Orgone,* Vol. II: *The Cancer Biopathy,* published in 1948, based on Reich's writing between 1942–1945. Significant among these are Reich's descriptions of the "spinning wave" or *Kreiselwelle* trajectory of the fluorescent bluish and violet impressions of orgone energy observed by Reich and his assistants that led to the construction of the orgone accumulator. From this relatively microcosmic scale of observation, Reich developed a macrocosmic and galactic theory of spinning wave orgone energy in

Cosmic Superimposition (1951).[13] Indeed, Reich was suspicious of the manner in which the saucer problem seemed to align with his work. "Things were fitting well," he says, "even too well for my taste."[14] He thought of the saucers, their spinning harmonious with the galactic orgone streams, and his equation of mass free energy. Reich was also concerned that Orgonon had been infiltrated and his work on an orgone energy motor stolen in the fall of 1948. An assistant, William Washington, had fabricated a background of work with the Atomic Energy Commission and had taken materials, including the motor, from the laboratory; he was due to return to work ahead of the summer of 1949, but did not come back. Reich understood that Washington, an African American Harvard mathematician, had been contacted by investigators about Reich's work in 1947. Reich tried to contact Washington but was unsuccessful until a phone conversation sometime in the summer of 1949. According to Myron Sharaf, Reich asked Washington if he was being coerced, implying the involvement of either the Atomic Energy Commission or of communist agents in his failure to return to Orgonon and the theft of Reich's research. "Washington answered, 'In a way,' but did not elaborate."[15] If apparently disparate ideas were aligning too conveniently, if Reich suspected a set-up toward his downfall, his experience with Washington would have contributed to his caution. Washington had "disappeared in 1949 under mysterious circumstances. He was under suspicion of being a Russian spy" [CS, 71].

On the evening of May 12, 1954, at the observatory at Orgonon, Reich's assistant biologist Robert McCullough set up a projector to replay the television footage from Maine's Channel 6 of the cloudbuster. The audience was Reich, Ollendorf and ten-year-old Peter Reich. The projector was reloaded with footage of

13 Wilhelm Reich, *Ether, God and Devil / Cosmic Superimposition* (New York: Farrar, Straus and Giroux, 1973).

14 Reich, *Contact with* Space, 71, and Reich, *CORE Report,* 104.

15 Wilhelm , *American Odyssey: Letters and Journals, 1940–1947,* ed. Mary Boyd Higgins (New York: Farrar, Straus and Giroux, 1999), Myron R. Sharaf, *Fury on Earth: A Biography of Wilhelm Reich* (New York: Da Capo, 1994), 354–55.

an experimental orgone energy powered motor. When they were finished, it was late in the evening, approaching midnight. As they prepared to leave the observatory, Reich called their attention to a "very bright, orange-yellow oval shaped 'star' to the NW of the Observatory, some 25 to 30 degrees declination" [WT, 164]. Observing the idiosyncrasies of the object, noting the presence of a second, it occurred to Reich to concentrate a cloudbuster upon these strange lights. Reich assumed that "if these were CORE space ships, they would react in some manner to a cloud buster being pointed at them" [ibid.]. Reich and his assistants took action:

> We opened all ten pipes and directed them toward the lower bright object. At first there was no reaction. But when I moved the pipes slightly a reaction occurred. *The bright light dimmed slowly and vanished for a few seconds from sight.* It appeared again, brightened up to the former intensity. But, as I continue moving my machine, it dimmed again staying dark linger this time and returning seemingly with some difficulty to former brightness. Then it dimmed twice more, remaining invisible. In other words it did not reappear in the sky. This was incontrovertible proof to me that we were dealing with a space ship propelled by cosmic energy. [WT, 164]

From this point on, Reich could feel himself "slowly being carried out from the realm of man's affairs" [WT, 165]. Indeed, he sensed that the preceding decades had moved him, sometimes against his will, toward a serious engagement with space. Reich had insisted on taking Freud's libido and its energies seriously and had not abandoned the theory where others had. It was, Reich felt, inevitable that he should find himself at the *center of space problems.* Unlike Carl Jung, Reich did not need to rescue his system of thought from flying saucer phenomena; he concluded that he was uniquely positioned to help others, including his government, comprehend it. In some retrospect, the Oranur Experiment was, with conventional government atomic experiments, within the plexus of radioactive outbursts that attracted the scrutiny suggested by *The Day the Earth Stood Still,* after Keyhoe's pulpy paperbacks. By the time Reich entered the

Arizona desert in the fall of 1954, he had come to believe that his "operations on earth seem to be carefully watched by living beings from outer space" [cs, 31]. Of course, he was not alone in that suspicion in the mid-fifties, and the thought had been articulated in the first lines of H.G. Wells's *The War of the Worlds* at the end of the nineteenth century, and in the opening monologue of the 1953 film version that Reich records having seen in January 1954.

The transformation of the cloudbuster into a spacegun depended upon a return to the materials of the Oranur emergency, specifically the radium needles that had been sequestered in the accidental accumulator environment of the safe in the spring of 1951. The vital events in this progression occurred after Reich concluded the *CORE Report* in July 1954. They are occluded from Reich's published journals. The posthumously published account in *Contact with Space* is obscure. What is clear is that the materials and their safe had been removed from their original location at the end of March 1952. On September 31, 1954, when it would occur to Reich to bring their influence to bear upon the cloudbuster, they were 15 miles away, along Route 17 in what Reich refers to as "an uninhabited area" [cs, 23], which one can estimate is to the south of Rangely Plantation between the highway and Mooselookmeguntic Lake.

Orgonon caretaker Tom Ross was dispatched to retrieve the radium and return it to the Observatory. He arrived at noon. Once more, a malaise descended upon Reich and his assistants. From here, the account of the energetic transformation of the cloudbuster into the "spacegun" is rushed. Water had infiltrated one of the supposedly watertight lead vessels that held the radium needles, and Reich had this lead container placed in contact with the bx cables that connected the cloudbuster to the deep well water. Something inexplicable in this contact alleviated the distress experienced by Reich and McCullough, who records "a general feeling of wellbeing" in himself and Reich, and "a sudden brightening of the rocks and vegetation; distant mountains which had been black, suddenly became blue; the sky cleared and the rest wind started" [cs, 26].

Over the next seven days, Reich and McCullough experimented with the original Oranur materials again. Rather than producing new DOR effects, the post-Oranur radium needles produced effects that were "astonishing" and "incomprehensible. It was unknown and somehow weird" [CS 29–30]. After their extended interaction with orgone in the accidental accumulated mechanism of the safe, the naked unshielded needles showed greatly diminished radioactivity. But when shielded, brought back within their lead containers, the radium needles gave extraordinary CPM readings. This occurred also when the needle and container were brought into close proximity. With the needle brought into subtle, brief interaction with a container in contact with the cloudbuster, Reich observed another operation of orgone, and coined another word to describe the variant form and mechanism: ORUR, its verb to "orurize," and its process of "orurization." This referred to the charging of the atmosphere by means of the cloudbuster augmented by radium that had been weakened by interaction with concentrated orgone. The volatile interaction now resulted in a rapid and potent charging of the atmosphere and the eradication of DOR. The ORUR action was the positive opposite of the negative fallout of the Oranur Experiment. The original mechanism of the cloudbuster, of drawing atmospheric energy, could be supercharged by judicious contact with the weakened Oranur materials. Reich states:

> The idea forced itself upon me: *It will be possible to draw off DOR from the deserts and draw in moisture from the Pacific Ocean.* The orurization effect of September 29th had reached as far as 170 miles toward the coast where my daughter lived. She had witnessed a sudden clearing of DOR and a fresh brilliance in the atmosphere. [CS, 30]

Reich also turned the cloudbuster on what others thought of as flying saucers, the spaceships or Ea, observed from Orgonon, drawing from them, with the result that "their lumination was weakened or even extinguished; they moved conspicuously out of order on several occasions at Orgonon in 1954" [CS, 31]. The "spacegun" was officially invented on September 29, 1954, in the combined use of ORUR and the cloudbuster.

In early October, Reich and three of his assistants observed four UFOS haunting Orgonon. Three of these "large, pulsating, yellow Ea" were recorded low against the horizon to the south of Orgonon, and the fourth to the northwest beyond the Observatory. The sighting was repeated on consecutive nights, with one Ea materializing "as so often out of nowhere, as it were, directly over the Observatory." Reich recorded in his Log Book of October 7 that the "switch-like, sudden sensation of being drawn from or being relieved was reported by many workers" under the auspices of the UFO that acted against their orgastic potency. "There is no doubt," Reich writes, "that I am at war with Ea. What was only a possibility one year ago is certainty now" [CS, 34]. The biopathic drawing, the draining, continued for the next two days, with Reich manning the spacegun, trying to draw from the Ea in return.

8

A Flying Saucer Attack:
Ambivalence and Lies

Early on October 7, 1954, Robert McCullough had been dispatched as an advance party for Operation ORUP Desert Ea to Tucson, Arizona, and to a location north of the city where the expeditionary team of Wilhelm Reich, Eva Reich, Peter Reich, and William Moise would join him at the end of the month. McCullough was not present for Reich's declaration of war with the flying saucers, although it is possible that Reich communicated the events to him by telephone at some point. It is not clear. McCullough's journey put him in Tucson on October 19. His Ford truck was fitted with one of the 1953 telescoping cloudbusters, and loaded with laboratory equipment from the Rangeley laboratory, including two Geiger-Müller survey meters, a refracting telescope, small orgone accumulator devices — a shooter, a funnel of the type that Reich had applied to his heart in 1951 when he had come close to death during the Oranur Experiment, and an orgone blanket — a bottle of Orene, and various photographic and video equipment. Reich had the words "Wilhelm Reich Space Gun / Orgone Institute" painted on the door of the truck that mounted the transformed cloudbuster. Above this was the spiral image that depicted both the "drawing" motion of the device and spinning wave form of orgone. Writing in 1955, an ambivalent McCullough reflects on his time at Orgonon:

I know now how easy it would have been to leave, tell every-one that WR was crazy, unscientific, a charlatan, a mystic, etc. It would have been awfully easy to have done just that. It undoubtedly has occurred in the past. It frightens one to think how grossly his structure can distort the truth, unbe-knownst to him; nay, even with his thinking that he is the exponent of truth. One comes across descriptions of occur-rences like this in the writings of WR, but you really have to experience it yourself to know what a dangerous and deadly thing it is. Subsequently, whenever I become aware of feelings of superiority, I study myself with the greatest suspicion. I have seen my irrational armor and a healthy mistrust has been engendered. One has to be continuously on his guard against such distortions and avoidances caused by his armor. They keep cropping up.[1]

In *Wilhelm Reich vs. the U.S.A.* Jerome Greenfield notes that, in contrast to the rest of his oeuvre, *Contact with Space* shows "evidence of haste and insufficient regard for scientific method in the arrival at conclusions regarding UFOS."[2] On the work's sig-nificant confusion and shortcomings, he writes, "These defects, together with the evidence of his irrationality in dealing with his legal trouble, would seem to make it valid at last to 'psycholo-gize,' to see Reich's work of this period, especially with UFOS, as nothing more than an aspect of his loss of touch with social real-ity. And yet to do so would be to ignore the fact that others were present and witnessed these 'battles.'"[3] I suspect that Greenfield is missing something with regard to forms of ambivalence in the other witnesses and their familial and professional relationships with Reich.

In *The Mass Psychology of Fascism,* Reich had elucidated the relationship between the figurehead and his followers, conclud-ing that "a führer, or the champion of an idea, can be success-

---

1   Robert A. McCullough, "Rocky Road Toward Functionalism," *CORE (Cosmic Orgone Engineering)* VII, nos. 3–4 (1955): 152.

2   Jerome Greenfield, *Wilhelm Reich vs. the U.S.A.* (New York: W.W. Norton, 1974), 140.

3   Ibid., 175

ful... only *if his personal point of view, his ideology, or his program bears a resemblance to the average structure of a broad category of individuals.*[4] He continues, *"Only when the structure of the führer's personality is in harmony with the structures of broad groups can the 'führer' make history"* [MP, 35]. Reich's own explication of the relationship between the emotional plague and the authority figure goes some distance toward explaining why the collaboration between the other witnesses and Reich functioned in the way that it did. Absent the upward libidinal cathexis of the witnesses, Reich's program could not have been what it was.

Out of Orgonon, McCullough drove the dark Ford with the cloudbuster covered with a tarpaulin and its pipes pointed downward, toward the rear of the truck bed. With his wife, daughter, and two-year-old son, he made it 200 miles south, to Hopkinton, south of Concord, New Hampshire, and the next day a similar distance west, through Green Mountain National Forest to Sangerfield, New York. Before entering the forest, from Keene, New Hampshire, McCullough records that the landscape and towns were oppressed by DOR. "Every town was cloaked with it, every valley was filled with it."[5] McCullough describes the journey in Reichian terms, with Reichian concerns, and through Reichian eyes. Erie, Pennsylvania gives way to Mansfield, Ohio, on October 10, and more oppressive DOR.

Eight hundred and fifty miles to the east, back at Orgonon, on the evening of October 10 Reich and Eva confronted two Ea. The first was a prodigious red light they sighted in the west over Bald Mountain. Drawing from it with the spacegun, it faded and seemed to climb, before Eva watched it fall below the horizon. They drew on a second yellow object in what Reich characterized as the "distinct impression of a struggle, fading alternating with strong pulsation, wobbling, moving in various directions." An hour after the struggle with the first red object, four Ea returned, spreading themselves about the horizon. It seems that they arranged themselves in acknowledgment of Reich's

---

4   Wilhelm Reich, *The Mass Psychology of Fascism,* trans. Vincent R. Carfagno (New York: Farrar, Straus and Giroux, 1980), 35.
5   Wilhelm Reich, *Contact with Space: Oranur Second Report, 1951–1956* (Haverhill: Haverhill House Publishing, 2018), 124.

defense before seeming to "remove themselves, growing smaller and fainter, *as if by common command*" [CS, 36]. Rushing to his study, Reich was taking down the evening's events when Eva and William Moise reported that a flare had gone up. Reich suspected that their work was being observed by the US Air Force; again, this seemed to be some signal of recognition, perhaps by the USAF, or perhaps as a signal of distress from the diminished spaceships. Reich was not certain.

Later, two of the Ea returned to a higher position against the star field to the north and south of the Observatory. Reich wrote: *"Tonight for the first time in the history of man, the war waged for ages by living beings from outer space upon this earth (with respect to DOR, Drought and Desert, WR, 1956)* was reciprocated with ORANUR with positive result" [CS, 37]. Curiously, it is as if the events of May 12 — when Reich first turned the cloudbuster upon what he assumed was a spaceship, causing it to flicker and dim — had not occurred. Nevertheless, by the close of October, 1954, as the Cold War escalated, Reich was convinced of the potency of the ORUR-assisted spacegun against the threat environmental retaliations posed by Ea, by the CORE men in their spaceships engineering conditions inimical to life. He would take his battle with the flying saucers to the Arizona desert. What is published of Reich's journals in *Where's the Truth? Letters and Journals, 1948–1957* contains a conspicuous lacuna from September 29 to October 18 when Reich would leave Orgonon to follow McCullough to Tucson. One is left with the tangle of *Contact with Space* to fill in the gaps. Myron Sharaf's biography of Reich, exhaustive in many respects, self-consciously avoids almost all of the operations described in *Contact with Space*. Keeping it at a discrete distance, he refers to it as an "unusual document."

I say "unusual" because the book was submitted as part of Reich's court appeals of his later "Contempt of Injunction" verdict. Only a very limited number of copies of this work were available. The book was also extraordinary because of its content. Written under great pressure and disorganized in its structure, it blended wild speculation about space ships and blasts at the FDA as well as other enemies with remarkably sensitive observations and astute conceptualizations of the relationship between orgone energy and DOR.[6]

Not without his ambivalence toward Reich, not least because Reich had initiated an affair with Sharaf's wife Grethe Hoff in the fall of 1954, Sharaf's biography is presented as if the events that defined Reich in late 1954 through the spring of 1955 never happened or are not worthy of interrogation. One reads the side of Sharaf that remains invested in protecting Reich. Sharaf's avoidance of *Contact with Space* might also be due to the small, unwitting part that Hoff played in what I believe was a deception perpetrated against Reich by one of his assistants. Whatever the rationale, this breach in the narrative, Sharaf's balking is curious.

The morning after Reich's declaration of his war of the worlds, Robert McCullough drove from Mansfield, Ohio to Pendleton, Indiana where he records a break in the saturation of DOR. Now, five days into the journey, McCullough began to suspect that the cloudbuster was acting upon cloud formations that he witnessed breaking up behind the truck. McCullough continued through Missouri and Kansas, each state afflicted with the melancholy of DOR that seemed to come in stripes or bands. McCullough's account of October 13 includes travel from Hannibal, Missouri to Hiawatha, Kansas, a westward drive of approximately 230 miles. Approaching Hiawatha, McCullough noted a violent thunderstorm to the south of the highway, over Atchinson. He makes no mention of the extraordinary events that he would describe occurring at that moment that he would send to Reich six days later from Tucson. The following day, seemingly unperturbed, McCullough describes the journey from Hiawatha until Atwood, Kansas.

We stopped at a restaurant there for supper. It had fluorescent lights. Everything was dead in it: the waitresses looked and acted dead, the service was horrible, tempers all around were short. I had had a few "cold" symptoms the preceding morning: running eyes and nose, ear noises, sore throat, sneezing

6 Myron R. Sharaf, *Fury on Earth: A Biography of Wilhelm Reich* (New York: Da Capo, 1994), 432.

etc. They had left after a few hours and had not reappeared. However, they came on again in that cafe and in 10 minutes were full blown. I got out. I felt that if I had stayed in there 10 minutes longer I would have come down with double pneumonia. Our two year old boy *had* to get out also. He was all right outside. My wife reacted in strong shrinking. [CS, 127]

A twelve-year-old boy at a neighboring table threw up. Perhaps, this was an appalling restaurant. McCullough, from the beginning of the journey, had suffered from contact with the anorgonic and synthetic environment, not least his first touch of chlorinated water in almost 18 months since Orgonon: "It wasn't wet — it left one's skin dry. After a shower with it, one felt scaley — dehydrated. It was not refreshing at all. It was as if the skin couldn't or wouldn't absorb it" [CS, 124]. The cold symptoms exacerbated by the depressing restaurant diminished later that night. It may be that McCullough, exhausted from driving with his family, experienced some psychosomatic hysteria, or that Reichian framing of experience had left McCullough open to something like neurasthenic symptoms when confronted by the dreariness of modernity outside of Orgonon. One cannot know for certain, but what can be said is that orgonomy, now extended to the natural environment and to a cosmic orgone ocean with a galactic orgone stream, had become a totalizing ontology in which all phenomena, from the affect of a waitress to the formation of clouds, the erosion of rock, and the flying saucers that haunted the skies and cinema screens of the 1950s, were implicated and understood.

On October 15, McCullough made for Kit Carson, Colorado. Importantly, as we will see, for Reich's relationship with cinema, the town that seemed to be one of the "worst infested" with DOR and the most "putrid" [CS, 127] town was the railroad town of Hugo, Colorado. Drought and desertification were at work on the cropland. McCullough's itinerary shows that from Kit Carson, he passed through Lamar, and cut through the Oklahoma panhandle, observing some Melanor effects in the landscape, before driving likely through Boise into Texas where he stopped at Dalhart. At Dalhart, McCullough found that his neck was swollen, and his parotid or saliva glands were enlarged.

This is reminiscent of McCullough's previous observation that his exposure to ORANUR had left him with swelling of his cervical lymph nodes. From Dalhart, he turned southwest to Tucumcari, New Mexico, arriving on the evening of October 16.

On the 17th, McCullough continued into the southwest, making for Carrizozo, New Mexico, with its black lava formations, and the vast gypsum fields of White Sands National Monument. To the west, he observed Mesa del Contadero, or Black Mesa, which in the clarity of the desert he perceived as shrouded in DOR, the darkness of Melanor standing out among the red mesas and desertification he had become accustomed to in New Mexico. From the lava fields, McCullough reports that the effects of Melanor are less than he had experienced at Orgonon. McCullough was on what is known as the Jornada del Muerto, the "journey of death" of the conquistadores moving north from Mexico. He was also within the precincts of the missile range where the Trinity atomic bomb test was carried out on July 16, 1945. He gives only one line to this: "There was no overt evidence of any lasting results from the first A-bomb blast which took place in this area." Instead, he describes the compulsion he and his family, and others camping at White Sands experienced to "stand motionless for perhaps hours on the dune crests. One was just moved to do so. It was very noticeable" [CS, 130]. Such are encounters with the sublime. He recounts that he had been there fourteen years earlier. "It had been a lush verdant desert as deserts go — tall Joshua, cholla, yucca, mesquite, creosote bush and grasses. In traveling over it again all this was changed. There was just a plain on which grew a few short tumbleweeds and saltbush — rarely reaching 12 inches high. All the vegetation was gone. Even the desert was dying." As there had been in New Mexico, McCullough saw some evidence of rains, "but the land had not responded. The land was completely dried out — burned" [CS, 131]. McCullough reached eastern Arizona on October 18.

Reich left Orgonon that same day. According to a deletion in the original manuscript, Reich's travelogue and observations as they appear in the published edition of *Contact with Space* were compiled by Eva Reich from... the rest of the annotation — the source — is illegible. McCullough arrived at his

Tucson destination on the following day, October 19. Unlike Robert McCullough, Wilhelm Reich's journey to the deserts of the southwest was agitated by his sustained conflict with the Ea engaged on October 10. Reich might have flown, but decided to drive to observe manifestations of DOR en route. Conditions were such that he observed it almost everywhere he applied the formula "Large cities + chemical offal + decaying nature + Ea + DORized health officials***" [CS, 112]. Outside of the bioenergetic idyll of Orgonon, it was with great concern that Reich discovered,

> From Boston onward, except for a few exceptions, the landscape represented well-known signs of clearcut DOR DESERTS: Brown-black, disintegrating, crumbling rocks, trees dried, branches bent to the ground like rubber hoses, foliage lacking autumnal coloration and turned brown, leaves crumbling to brown powder in one's hand, CPM (on the Geiger Counter) of an erratic nature (anywhere from 50 to 200), square, fuzzy, gray-blackish drought clouds overhead. [ibid.]

Reich's route to Tucson differed from McCullough's, swinging further to the south, passing through New Jersey, Virginia, Tennessee, and Arkansas before entering Texas, New Mexico, and Arizona. Notable among Reich's observations of his journey west are the decaying trees of Hartford and its "bitter taste" reminiscent of Oranur sickness; the "sudden sharp DOR zone" at Warrentown, Virginia and the "total impression: *dying countryside*" [CS, 114]; the "ghost trees" of New Jersey [CS, 115]; the oppressive effects of the anonymous tenements of Baltimore; giving way to the blue clarity experienced approaching and inside Washington, DC on October 21. Basing himself across the Potomac in the new, air-conditioned, red brick drive-in Clarendon Hotel Court at 3824 Wilson Boulevard in Arlington, Virginia, three miles from Capitol Hill, Reich crossed over, describing the capital city as an "Oasis." He added the enigmatic remark that "the impression was 'someone is cloudbusting (deDORizing) here'" [ibid.]. Of course, Reich has been preceded in Washington, DC by Michael Rennie, the spaceman Klaatu disguised as the christlike Carpenter — Reich's presence is DC was anticipated by what James Baldwin might have called his "escape personality." The "someone" who had cleared the city for Reich was Reich himself. The extent to which Orgonon and Washington, DC are oases is determined by the alignment of the introjected spaceman image Reich had of himself suggested by *The Day the Earth Stood Still*. Reich spent two days in the capital, in a kind of stillness, "absorbing its meaningful design" [ibid.]. He visited Arlington National Cemetery, on October 22, as Carpenter had with Bobby. One sees the intent in Reich's decision to route through DC, and to spend two days there — meaningful design, indeed.

Also on October 22, at his motel Reich received a report from McCullough. Again, like McCullough, Reich does not record this in his travelogue, but includes it later, in a separate section of the erratic collage of *Contact with Space*. For the sake of chronology, I will describe it here. Reich says that he received it "at a motel in Washington DC," but this is likely the Clarendon Hotel Court. It was received initially by Hoff in Boston, then relayed to Reich. Without evidence, Reich also alleges that his motel phone call was intercepted by agents of the Air Technical Intelligence Center "in a room beneath my motel room; it was hurried away by car immediately after the phone report was ended" [CS, 138]. Some part of the Clarendon Hotel Court is set on two floors, but Reich's suggestion does sound delusional. But to McCullough's belated report of events on October 13 that he — inexplicably — does not mention in his travel diary, even as he saw fit to include the vomiting of a child in a bad restaurant the next day: he revises his account of the storm that he witnessed to the south as he approached Hiawatha, Kansas. Making a stop in Blair, outside of St. Joseph, McCullough and his family were beset with "a tremendous storm buildup directly overhead." He continues:

Altho [sic] it was dark, the landscape was continuously illuminated by cloud to cloud lightning. I was suddenly *sure* that Ea was building that up against me and the truck. Things happened just then. I saw a yellow moon-like Ea just appear below the cloud edge to the east. It disappeared immediately. Also observed by my daughter. Then a blinking white light was observed moving right to left in the *NW*. There was *NO*

sound — and a plane would not fly into or under that storm
[...] I feel that this was an attack on the truck. [CS, 139]

McCullough's report also informs Reich that he encountered
no further Ea until he was close to Tucson, when a "dumbbell-
shaped light was observed for about 30 seconds at 8pm." Four
hours later, McCullough says, "a B-47 Stratojet bomber made a
practice landing at Tucson, couldn't get up again and crashed and
burned. One killed. Possibly a connection? (October 18, 1954)"
[CS, 140]. The crash occurred at Davis-Monthan Airbase, and
the dead airman was Captain Stanley Lowell Perry. Two other
airmen suffered burns and lacerations. Crashes were not uncom-
mon in the vicinity of the base. Another B-47 had crashed near
the base in the spring of 1953, killing four; two airmen were killed
in August 1954 when their AT-6 training plane crashed to the west
of Tucson; an additional four were killed and eleven injured in a
T-29 crash on November 5, barely two weeks after the B-47 crash
that McCullough suggested might be linked to UFO activity.
Nothing of flying saucer involvement is suggested in the Tucson
news reports.[7] That is not extraordinary. What is extraordinary
is that nothing of this disturbed either McCullough's travelogue
of October 13 when the Ea attack — not only against the truck,
but by extension against his wife, children, and himself — is supposed to have occurred or Reich's travelogue record of October
22 when he received it. How should one take McCullough when
he details his two-year-old son's reaction to an unpleasant restaurant on October 14, but somehow fails to even allude to a flying
saucer attack against him the previous day? Reich's brief published entry for October 22, 1954 in *Where's the Truth?* makes no
reference to any word from McCullough, let alone so dramatic a
report. And yet, for Reich, it was this report from McCullough
"that corroborated our previous experiences at Orgonon: The
war of the planets was truly on" [CS, 138].

In fact, none of this is really inexplicable — not the storm originally reported twenty miles to the south now described as attack-

7   Tucson Fire Department, *Plane Crashes, Start to 1959: Tucson Area,*
    http://www.tucsonfirefoundation.com/wp-content/uploads/2020/01/
    Plane-Crashes-Start-to-1959.pdf.

ing directly over McCullough's truck with the cloudbuster, nor the dramatic appearance of the menacing UFO beneath the lightning clouds. It is my belief that Robert McCullough simply fabricated it all when he reached Tucson to impress Reich.

Sharaf interviewed McCullough in July 1978 during the writing of *Fury on Earth*. McCullough "had already worked for a year in the biology department of the University of New Hampshire, with periodic visits to Reich in Orgonon. Then Reich offered him a full-time position at a better salary than the university provided, an offer McCullough happily accepted."[8] McCullough's place on the payroll seems to me the source of his ambivalence. It might be prudent to read McCullough's essay-memoir "Rocky Road Toward Functionalism" *not* as an account of McCullough overcoming his doubts about orgonomy and his suspicions about Reich as a scientist, or a man, but as something of a "tell," the expression of the ambivalence of a man who has taken a higher salary to do work he does not fully believe in.

> When the work for my Master's thesis took me out on the desert of northwestern Utah, I observed that the orgone energy flow, which was very prominent there, was not west to east as reported by WR, but predominately *southeast to northwest*. I also observed that this direction was constantly changing. I kept exact records of these changes and sent them to WR. [...] I happened to be in a location where I could gather data and thereby help the total work along. I expected no reward; I just wanted to help. The fact that some of my letters weren't answered hurt, but had no gross effect on my attitude.

McCullough had read *The Function of the Orgasm* and *The Cancer Biopathy* in 1949. There is nothing surprising in the fact that orgonomy has no part in McCullough's Master's thesis for Utah State Agricultural College in 1951, "An Ecological Survey of the Muskrat at Locomotive Springs, Box Elder County, Utah, 1950–51." It does show that McCullough is aware of the avant-garde nature of Reich's work, and that inclusion of orgonomic theory would undermine his ability to graduate from

8   Sharaf, *Fury on Earth*, 408.

the Wildlife Management program. However, some readers of "Rocky Road Toward Functionalism" might assume, in the framing of McCullough's observations of orgone energy within the context of his (otherwise not described) thesis, an academic claim. I will leave to the reader whether McCullough's framing is disingenuous.

But McCullough's fabrication of the October 13 attack was a strategy to remain indispensable to Reich, to demonstrate his commitment to the new cause. It was not an isolated incident. If this has been said elsewhere with any force, then I am not aware of it, but one must take seriously the possibility that McCullough's actions are *performative*. Reich's self-identified "Gyntian self" rendered him vulnerable. One must consider the extent to which the charlatanism and hoaxing that is often said to attend Reich actually attended the man in the form of those who were willing to exploit his desires, or as Baldwin put the problem in another context, "the danger of surrendering to the corroboration of one's fantasies,"[9] in ambivalent men like Robert McCullough, who had been wounded by Reich but was dependent upon him. One thinks here of the passages on Lazarus from *The Murder of Christ* that were part of the introduction of this book.

To return to Reich's travelogue: on October 24, Reich's account mistakenly claims that he spoke to people in "Sperryville, Pa.," when surely what he means is Sperryville, Virginia. He describes people "in whose faces despair and listlessness reflected the desperate state of affairs in their environment. They knew the severity of their situation: 'Meadows and fields are burnt up, wells gone dry *** people are sick, slowed down, dying ****" [CS, 116]. Driving through Shenandoah National Forest on Skyline Drive, Reich is struck by what he observes of the Blue Ridge Mountains:

> From the mountain ridge at the "Skyline Drive" we saw for the first time the *"Desert Armor,"* in confirmation of the orgonomic desert theory. It was fresher on the ridge than in the valleys below. On the ridge, vegetation and trees looked

9 James Baldwin, "The Devil Finds Work," in *Collected Essays,* ed. Toni Morrison (New York: Library of America, 1998), 500.

sparkling, healthier, greener than down in the valley, similar to what is true of forested mountain-crests in deserts. Below the ridge, one could see the DOR-*layer* all formed, covering the earth to the distant horizon like a blanket, with a sharply delineated upper edge; beneath it the details of the distant views were hidden in an opaque veil, as it were. [...] As the ridge road rose over the peaks and dipped down into passes, one could subjectively feel the abrupt descent into the DOR layer: a sudden pressure in the head or chest, a sour taste in the mouth. One could also observe that while the trees sparkled and stood erect above the DOR ceiling, they drooped, were withered, and looked dark below it. [...] I observed a north-eastward bending of tree trunks, with Melanor and moss formation on the east side of trees. [CS, 116–17]

Reich also observed strong Melanor reactions in Rogersville and Knoxville, Tennessee. Crossing from Arkansas into Texas at Texarkana, Reich continued another 270 miles west to Wichita Falls where "the drought situation worsened," with Reich and his passengers running "into the beginning of sharp DOR zone, with DOR ceiling" [CS, 118]. Their last night in Texas was spent at the Siesta Motel in Seymour — another red brick motel, yet unkempt compared with Clarendon Hotel Court back in Virginia — where a waitress described the three-year drought as "desperate" [ibid.].

Almost 600 miles due west, Reich passed through Roswell, New Mexico, where instead of shimmering heat haze from the asphalt, Reich observed that "DOR was well marked to the west against purplish, black, barren mountains, in the sky as blinding grayness, and over the horizon as a grayish layer. The caking of formerly good soil was progressively characteristic and eventually the caked soil prevailed over vegetation, which now consisted only of scattered low bushes, while grass disappeared" [CS, 119–20]. The so-called Roswell Incident — the alleged crash and partial recovery of a flying saucer — occurred one month after Kenneth Arnold's account of saucers instigated the first wave of flying saucer contagion. In 1947, debris from the Roswell crash was quickly determined to be silver foil, struts, and rubber materials from a weather balloon. Almost a decade later, when Reich passed through Roswell, the city was still far from the vortex of UFO tourism that it would become after the grifting of the late 1970s subsequent to UFOlogist Stanton Friedman's resuscitation of the case, such as it was. Roswell is similarly afflicted today, but Reich's transit there was coincidental. The Roswell Incident is not included among several references to New Mexico flying saucer stories in Keyhoe's pair of paperbacks. Reich's westward journey coincides with McCullough's at Alamogordo and White Sands, New Mexico. Descending toward the basin,

> We saw the plain covered towards W, SW, and N with a thick layer, several hundred feet high, of a gray, dead, opaque mass of DOR. Overhead the sky was a blue-black, with some droughty, thin, high clouds. One felt a strong salty taste. The white sand dunes showed a clear Orite accumulation. Could it be that White Sands was further attracting DOR? The DOR veil was the most remarkable we had yet seen, hanging thick and opaque, low over the landscape. The mountains edging this plain looked jagged, barren, with deep ravines "as if eaten out." About 20 miles beyond White Sands the air brightened, but DOR still prevailed. I remarked: "DOR *is eating up mountains, as it were.*" This spot was Sahara-like without any vegetation. [CS, 120]

Compare this with McCullough's report of October 17, when he camped at White Sands:

> There was no DOR there then. The shadows were blue. I felt no DOR — only one short period where my pulse speeded up a lot. However, there was something very moving about these many acres of white sandlike matter. [CS, 130]

The difference is stark. How could the most prodigious DOR veil Reich had ever seen not have been manifest to McCullough, who otherwise describes his own exposure to ORANUR and its sickness in such daredevil terms, the DOR affecting his throat? Could it be that, briefly, McCullough's more skeptical persona returned, and that in the sublimity of the pale dunes where he stood motionless and enraptured by nature, he lost something of the Reichian lens through which he perceived the world before and after? Reich reached Tucson on October 29, 1954.

The anachronistic assemblage that is *Contact with Space* is not widely regarded with any great seriousness, because Reich is presumed to have slipped into psychosis at this point. With Reich under the duress of his trial, the material inevitably suffers from accidents and contradictions. Yet, there is also evidence that Reich was consciously or unconsciously manipulated to the extent that it appears that at least one UFO encounter was fabricated to reinforce his introjection or projection of identity. This is not to suggest that Robert McCullough had any idea of the precise psychic constellation that was working on Reich; he could not know. But one is compelled to take seriously the possibility that it in trying to impress Reich, and in events to come, McCullough ushered Reich closer to his final existential crisis.

9

Little Orgonon:
Echoes of Lazarus

On Halloween 1954, Wilhelm Reich, Robert McCullough and his family, Eva Reich, Peter Reich, and William Moise established themselves on the fifty-acre property north of Tucson that they would call Little Orgonon, flanked by the mountain range including Mount Catalina to the northeast and Mount Lemmon beyond that. There had been no rain in the area for more than five years. Reich records that "Many Ea were seen hanging in the sky during the nights of October 31 and November 1."[1] The DOR in the region was worse when the Ea were present at night. The Orur materials — the radium needles — were not yet at Little Orgonon. These did not travel with McCullough or Reich but were to be flown to Tucson later when events on December 7–8 called for their use in augmenting the cloudbusters. They would not arrive until December 14, so Reich's ability to engage with the Ea was limited, except to the extent that the cloudbuster could be used to remove the DOR and mitigate CORE desertification actions. "There was," Reich said, "no doubt whatsoever about the DOR emergency in the desert" [CS, 145]. Peter Reich recalls that Reich painted the spinning wave trajectory of orgone energy, and of flying saucers, on the front door of Little

1   Wilhelm Reich, *Contact with Space: Oranur Second Report, 1951–1956* (Haverhill: Haverhill House Publishing, 2018), 145.

Orgonon, just as it was painted on the door of the truck upon which the space gun was mounted.[2]

Reclining in a chair, Reich watched the skies from Little Orgonon's observation deck, or took to the ragged terrain with his Geiger-Müller counter and made field notes. The combined effects of the emotional plague, the attention of the CORE ships, and the melancholy fall of deadly orgone energy and its action upon the landscape left in Reich the sense that the mountain ranges had been gouged and *"eaten out,' gnawed at by the DOR as if a monster were feeding on the mountain rocks"* [cs, 146]. B-movie imagery aside, Reich was prescient in terms of planetary emergency. Reich's original language of the orgasm had expanded to fill an ecology and a cosmology that is not alien to the 21st century.

> Life is at *present, under the given circumstances,* existing on the razor's edge between kinds of deaths. [...] Life thus holds only a narrow wedge as its own domain in the infinite vastness of the cosmic energy. Organismic Life Energy metabolizes from and into the cosmic energy ocean. Respiration, feeding and direct radiation ("heat") are the basic vehicles of the metabolism of Life Energy between organism and environment. [...] Energy equilibrium between charge and discharge is easily maintained in the healthy organism. During sickness more OR seems to change into DOR, also more DOR seems to be retained in the tissues. Thus, a prevalence of DOR energy would be a *basic* feature of all disease. [...] If emotional pestilent reactions are due to DOR, then the emotional desert does exactly to its host or giver what the tapeworm or DOR in the tissues does: Kill the host, the giver of life in silent destruction by way of sapping its strength [cs, 149–51].

The Ea slipped from view for a week, as Reich made his initial studies of the desert, and worked to refine the theories of July's CORE Report by annotating the specific effects of DOR and Melanor on different types of vegetation, soils, and clays, and in the return of proto-vegetation to affected regions. Reich dif-

2 Peter Reich, *A Book of Dreams* (London: John Blake, 2015), 13.

ferentiated between primal vegetation and secondary vegetation, or those cacti and scrubland plants that subsist, as opposed to thrive, in the DOR saturated desert. But as the work in *Contact with Space* become more florid, it lost some of its coherence, flirting with animism and personification such as in Reich's uncharacteristic use of "mother earth" [CS, 151]. For a week, Reich worked hopefully with the cloudbuster, and on November 7, the expeditionary team felt they had succeed in drawing atmospheric orgone energy to effect the formation of clouds over the drought-stricken region, including the space directly over Little Orgonon. Yet, that night and the following, Reich records the presence and intervention of an antagonist. The clouds that Reich anticipated might break the drought broke up.

"That evening," he says, "a bright, large luminating ball was seen coming up like a star on the northern shoulder of Mt. Catalina." The DOR they had drawn off during the day returned. Reich was quick to conclude that it was the arrival of the Ea that thwarted his rain operation. "There was no escape from the fact that we were at war with a power unknown to man on earth" [CS, 162–63]. Suffering from the effects of DOR sickness until the following day, Reich was able to restate his previous theses on the 10th, describing the desert-forming and mountain-consuming properties of DOR, and adding that,

3. Ea causes strong DOR and dissolves clouds, prevents cloud formation.
4. Ea can be weakened or even extinguished by drawing off energy with the Spacegun.
5. Ea has caused the deserts of the planet, supported by earthman's emotional desert. [CS, 165][3]

Another obstacle to the formation of rainclouds was the propensity of the expedition members to become "dorized," that is, they had to learn "to integrate malignant human reactions with outer, atmospheric DOR situations. *'You are dorized today,'* became a standing phrase to describe a behavior of confusion,

---

3   The original manuscript does not use the science fiction term "earth-man" where this material appears, on page 94.

crisscross activities ('pranking') and discomfort, clearly due to DOR" [CS, 166]. This is really nothing but a cover for the ambivalence in the expedition team, a loss of patience with Reich's most extravagant claims, perhaps, as they waged their battles in this American Sahara.

> The Tucson basin, the hottest spot in the U.S. southwestern desert, may for 25,000 years have been submitted to Ea attacks without man having been aware of it. Were the Ea which we saw in the sky possibly space machines which had been keeping deserts going for ages, preventing rain all along the times? No one could tell. But it was very much within the limits of reasonable possibilities. It could not and should not be ignored. [CS, 168]

No one could tell, Reich said. No one was prepared to argue, at least. How much of the cooperation, with its outbreaks of pranking and discomfort, was performative only those present could really tell. McCullough was — in my view — almost certainly pretending an interest at this point. Moise, the painter who was in love with Reich's daughter — what should he have done? Eva Reich, and Peter — what could be said? Peter was a child. It was profoundly exciting for him, at the time. For several days, Reich's writing on the sinister presence of his extension of flying saucer phenomena is thin, distracted by the arrival of government officials at Orgonon proper in Rangeley, and Reich's grandiose claims that the Eisenhower administration's Atoms for Peace initiative was "somehow connected" [CS, 171] to his work, and yet no sooner could this be observed in the DC scene than it was classified, and the evidence vanished. Einstein returns to Reich's attention, also.

> About the same time Einstein was reported to have said it would have better if he had become a plumber rather than a scientist. We wondered whether he had finally found about about the deceit perpetrated upon him by a Stalinite mastermind in 1940. His age was dying; so much we knew from the practical aspects of Oranur. But the memory of meeting with

Einstein in January 1941 was to be retained with great pleasure. [ibid.][4]

Here is Reich, having drifted away from the affairs of man, compounding the dramatized cuckolding of the Einstein figure by the Reichian/Spaceman/Christ figure in *The Day the Earth Stood Still*. Reich wants to believe — is unable to believe otherwise at this moment — that Einstein's regrets refer specifically to his rejection of Reich. Reich's desires or resentments are apparently corroborated. Routine observations of, and drawings from Ea continued on until November 28, 1954, when Reich made his most explicit analysis to that point. It was not yet dawn. Reich was using the 3.5-inch refractor that had come to Little Orgonon on Robert McCullough's truck. What Reich observed this time, McCullough offered some resistance to, but not a definitive refutation; McCullough suggested that the object observed might be Saturn. According to Reich's account:

> Venus stood already as a sickle high in the sky. To the north of Venus I noticed a small star. Viewed with 60x magnification it presented the following shape and structure: It had two dark symmetrically located black points looking like portholes of a ship. The object had the clear-cut cigar shape of a spaceship. [...] I refused to accept the notion, but its being father away from Venus in a direction opposite to the ecliptic path stuck in mind. [CS, 175–76]

This dramatic observation does not appear in *Where's the Truth?* Except for the overcast night of November 30, the "spaceship" was observed in the proximity of Venus until December 17. Reich could not explain its trajectory with respect to Venus. He struggled to reconcile what suggested itself to him. "In the face of a rigid, doctrinaire, self-appointed, ready-to-kill hierarchy of scientific censorship it appears foolish to publish such thoughts." And here Reich senses danger. "Anyone malignant enough could do anything with them. Still the right to be wrong has to

4   This last sentence and the preceding designation "Stalinite master-mind" are hand-corrected additions to the original typescript.

be maintained" [CS, 178–79]. And Reich had been reluctant to accept his observations and their implications. Another incident, evolving over December 6–8, and again involving McCullough would fix the idea in Reich's consciousness.

Reich records an episode at Little Orgonon as "The Breakdown of a Spacegun Operator." On the morning of the 6th, McCullough was using the cloudbuster to remove DOR from the atmosphere. The inconsistent appearance and dissipation of a jet plane's vapor trail seemed to suggest some other presence, that DOR was being distributed, affecting the moisture in the air. Eva Reich, who was regarded as acutely sensitive, held out her fingers, and seemed to catch some signs of the energy coming down. Between Reich, McCullough, and Eva Reich, it was determined that the energy field, the sensation of DOR fallout, was coming from the location on the ecliptic where Venus would be at that time. Geiger counter readings of the background radiation rendered anomalously high measurements of 400–800 CPM. Although it could not be seen in the daylight, Reich believed, *"An Ea was doubtlessly in the sky high up in the region above"* [CS, 180]. As Reich ordered both cloudbusters trained toward the source, McCullough corroborated, "DOR is coming down strong." He complained of a "very bitter taste, much stronger than usual and *tasting like offal.* We apparently got the exhausts or whatever else it might have been right down on us." The following day, at around 11 a.m., McCullough said once more that the DOR was "coming strong and 'sour.'" Suddenly, McCullough experienced a "crippling sensation in his right leg," followed immediately by paralysis of his right side. The symptoms were temporary, and McCullough recovered fully. On December 8, at 8:30 a.m., McCullough was drawing from the unseen Ea once more, he was stricken with paralysis of his right side for the second time. "He came into the quarters sick, purple in is [SIC] face, sadly able to move his right leg, limping and with little motility in right arm and hand" [ibid.]. The treatment of McCullough's condition was reminiscent of that provided to Eva when she had injured herself with the accumulator. That the affected spacegun operator was McCullough is confirmed by Eva Reich's examination protocol which refers to "RMC" [CS, 182]. Of McCullough, in her father's words,

Warm tea and Southern Comfort liqueur removed the paralysis to a great extent. However, I knew it was serious. The operator had developed a progressive paralytic anorgonia of the
right side, under the stream of DOR, still in a functional state,
but certainly in the direction of a possibly lasting structural
paralysis and nerve atrophy. [CS, 180]

Whatever happened to McCullough — if anything beyond performance — he did not receive conventional medical treatment.
Although it was Reich who told McCullough not to go hospital
for a neurological assessment, this would have suited McCullough
if there was, indeed, nothing wrong with him. Instead, he earned
a reprieve from desert operations. It was at this time that Reich
determined that the operation, with so much ranged against it,
required the presence of the Orur radium needles. They would
arrive a week later, on December 14.

To say that the Orur materials were flown from Lewiston,
Maine to Gilpin Airport, Tucson, elides much of the physical
situation. The Orgone Institute's treasurer Michael Silvert char-
tered a private plane from the Tucson Hudgin Air Service owned
by Alfred "AL" Hudgin; according to Reich's account, AL's
brother Henry was the pilot, and his copilot was Frank Bolman.
They were accompanied on the flight by Silvert. Orgonon caretaker Tom Ross was charged with transporting the Orur materials to the airfield. A bizarre scene ensued. Concerns regarding the
danger of bringing the Orur material on board the plane meant
that it was placed inside a pair of plastic containers, wadded with
cotton, within an egg-shaped vessel made of wood — there could
be no metal involved. The container was secured inside a canvas sack. This was taped and laced and attached to the charter
plane by 100 feet of nylon rope. The Orur materials were literally
dragged behind the plane during the flight. During take-off and
landing, through a mechanism of garden hose, it could be reeled
in and its slack adjusted by Silvert inside the aircraft. A chapter
of *Contact with Space* is taken up with this protocol and Silvert's
report of the flight. Reich had significant concerns about the
potential effects of the Orur materials and the propellor plane's
navigation instruments, and a "possible plane disaster" [CS, 188].

Subsequently, in early January 1955, the flight with its dangerous materials made local news, but with Al Hudgin credited as the pilot [CS, 195]. Ironically, although the Orur flight met with no disaster, during the early evening of June 30, 1956, the other two Hudgin brothers, Henry and Palen, would be the first to discover the wreckage of what was then the worst domestic air disaster in the United States, the collision of two commercial passenger flights over the Grand Canyon and their fall into the vast trench.[5] Hundreds of lives were lost.

But the flight with the Orur materials that landed in Tucson in the early hours of December 14, 1954, was relatively uneventful. Except that retrospectively, Reich would claim that the landing was accompanied by the "dropping of about 30 flares around the region" [CS, 199] that Reich would come to associate with Air Force responses to rumors of flying saucers or Ea operations. It might be that this reflects merely Reich and his colleagues' inexperience with the southwest, where fireworks were common during all manner of festivities, formal and informal. It might be that if there were flares, there was some training exercise underway. Later that morning, Moise drove to the airfield to collect the football sized vessel and the radium needles. The materials were significantly agitated from their transport. "It appeared," Reich says, "that the transport through the OR ocean and the atmosphere at 250 miles per hour over 3000 miles had had an exciting effect upon it." Geiger-Müller measurements recorded a staggering 100,000 CPM. "Its field stretched upon arrival at Tucson to several hundred feet. It behaved, as should be expected of life energy, like an excited animal that calms down after a while. After nine hours the field of excitation had shrunk from 300 to 5 feet" [CS, 198]. Reich had not anticipated that the presence of the Orur materials would be a provocation to the Ea. What is described in Contact with Space as "The Ea Battle of Tucson" is precisely the kind of material from which Myron Sharaf demurred. It is curious also that Jerome Greenfield, in *Wilhelm Reich vs. the USA,* says that Reich describes this battle

5   Bonnie Henry, "Sacred Ground," *Tucson.com,* June 22, 2006, https://tucson.com/lifestyles/bonnie-henry-sacred-ground/article_1de89819-bb19-5ac8-958c-af4198e49bf9.html.

in "extensive detail," when truly, he does not. The entire incident is described in four terse paragraphs comprising a little over two hundred and fifty words. Reich begins:

> On December 14, about 16:30 hours, a full scale interplanetary battle came off; [...] The *"Ea Battle of Tucson"* fitted without difficulty into the pattern of our past experiences from previous encounters with Ea. It demonstrated in a concentrated form, as it were, what had gone on before and what we could expect, roughly, of future encounters with our uninvited visitors from outer space. [CS, 199]

Excised with pencil and red crayon from the original manuscript are Reich's concerns that the emotional plague is leading to conscious and unconscious resistance to the planetary emergency. Reich advocates that force of law should work against those who might undermine orgonomy or seek to provide other prosaic explanations for the apparent manifestation of UFO phenomena. Under the red deletion is the notion that polite presentations of alternative explanations — hallucinations, light effects, etc. — represent treasons against the species analogous to the harassment or interruption of a messenger in this war between the planets.[6] It is an angry passage, in keeping with other deleted sections of the original manuscript where Reich warns against the dissemination of information regarding Ea to the masses, who would — in their narcissism, or from the emotional plague, each demand their personal involvement.[7] There *should* be full disclosure of the extent of the Ea problem, but only subsequent to orgonomic, counter-pathological efforts to prepare the public.[8]

Earlier, Moise had returned to Little Orgonon with Silvert and the Orur material. It is not at all surprising, given the demands of the 3000-mile flight, that Silvert would be exhausted, and then experience some car sickness. Yet, Reich suspected DOR sickness in the men. This was confirmed for Reich when his assistants

---

6   Original Manuscript, 130 / Equivalent of *Contact with Space,* 199.
7   Original Manuscript, 40 / Equivalent of *Contact with Space,* 48.
8   Original Manuscript, 41 / Equivalent of *Contact with Space,* 78.

returned from a visit to a hardware store with a description of an enervated clerk, as sick as them, straight out of B-movie science fiction. "One operator was of the opinion that we were dealing with a special kind of DOR attack" [CS, 199]. It is important to note, again, that this is not Reich's speculation alone; his assistants are participants in the construction of this narrative.

Reich describes a malevolent dark cloud hanging over Tucson as if a section of the city is aflame, extending like a blood bruise, pushing the Geiger–Müller readings to 100,000 CPM once more. Soon, Reich dismissed the explanation that fire could be the cause of the cloud, deciding that it must be symptomatic of an attack on the city by low-flying Ea. Suddenly, Little Orgonon seemed to be at the center of a plexus of flights by a dozen or more USAF planes, their vapor trails dissipating quickly in the DOR-saturated atmosphere. "We all suffered from nausea, quivering, pain in the upper abdomen and discoordination of movements" [CS, 200]. Scrambling his spacegun operators, Reich discovered that his voice was weak. Peter Reich took up a megaphone, and by this method the father relayed orders to those at the controls, probably Eva Reich and Moise, since McCullough had been relieved after his incident of paralysis in the conflict of December 7–8. Peter Reich's megaphone issued orders to draw using both devices, their tubes aimed over Tucson and toward the zenith respectively, to diminish the black cloud and to remove energy from any spaceship involved in the assault. As he swung the megaphone, Peter pointed to another object over Tucson. A little over half an hour later, at 17:18, "a single jet plane circled Little Orgonon. Four big B-56 jet bombers gathering from over Tuscon flew toward Little Orgonon and passed low overhead and slowly in closed formation at 17:30 hrs. I had the impression that they saluted our base. There was in the situation an emotion of deep concern, determinations and gratitude." Reich reports that "Peter also discovered a *silvery disk moving from the region over the city, where the purple clouds had developed, toward the west*" [ibid.]. In the aftermath, the speechless expedition team at Little Orgonon "all took stiff drinks" [CS, 201]. Reich's hypothesis was that the Ea had attacked the airfield, mistakenly believing that the Orur materials had been stored there, but he understood that this was unknowable. Emotionally drained, Reich reports that "Even seasoned operators refused to admit fully what had happened. However we all knew that something extraordinary and dangerous had happened" [cs 200–201]. Reich closes with a melancholy thought: "I cannot tell how many people had died during that hour from heart attack and similar reactions to a sudden DOR attack as severe as the one just experienced" [cs, 201].

What should one make of this? What to make of the speechless party, taking their drinks, in denial? Were Eva Reich and William Moise speechless because they had seen something in Reich that, go along with it as they did, left them disturbed? Was it simply that in the excitement between father and son, that no one wanted to deny Reich and Peter that closeness that came from the excitement and the discovery of the silvery disk in the night sky? Was it that, coming down from the drama, they could only reflect upon it with remorse, these "seasoned operators" in their "refusal to admit fully what had happened" — is there some tragic, dramatic irony in this? One can imagine various states of stunned silence attending this so-called "Ea Battle of Tucson."

In a further irony, the next day, a small section of the front page of the *Tucson Daily Citizen* for December 15 is headed "Saucers Not from Outer Space," following a news conference by Eisenhower given in Washington, DC. The terse clipping reports, "President Eisenhower said today that an air force official told him some time ago that so-called flying saucers do not come from outer space.... He did not, however, say whether there are any such things. Or, if so, where they do come from."[9] There are no reports in the newspaper of either a large fire, flares, maneuvers, or dramatic weather. The only reference to a fire on December 14 is to the accidental burning of a seven-year-old girl's chenille robe, catching too close to a gas heater, resulting in her death. There is, however, an article on page 5 concerning the 50ft parabolic mirror antenna at the University of Arizona — then the largest of its kind — laconically headlined "Radio 'Static' May Only Be Galaxy-To-Galaxy Broadcast." Reich might have been amused by the newsman John Riddick's observation, "the

9   "Saucers Not from Outer Space," *Tucson Daily Citizen Evening Edition*, December 15, 1954, 1.

fact is that the universe makes a terrific racket."[10] Yet, whatever activity Reich and his assistants observed and engaged, nothing of it is recorded in the Tucson press.

From December 21, 1954, into the new year, and until January 20, 1955, Reich and his space gun operators worked on drawing from a single Ea (now known as an Ea-CM, the CM standing for Core Machine), with Eva Reich keeping a log of their effect upon it. On January 11, she records that between 9:30 p.m. and 1 a.m., catching the machine in the crossfire between both spaceguns, it was "extinguished 4 times" [CS, 211]. It was not observed for the next week, and rainfall occurred in its absence. It would seem that the Ea attempted a return on January 17th, and on the 18th a preemptive crossfire drawing prevented all but the weakest presence. It was absent again on the 19th, before Eva Reich's record concludes with the image of the Ea apparently in retreat [ibid.].

Later, Reich himself would make an extraordinary declaration. "During the tug of war of January 12th, Ea seemed to have surrounded the Tucson valley en masse; I conceived of the idea that this may be a routine measure on the part of spacemen to attack a certain region" [CS, 217]. Reich's new hypothesis was that the limits of the desert were delineated by a barrier created by the CORE machines. It is possible that the shielding, reminiscent of a bell jar, that protected the Martians in the film of *The War of the Worlds* which Reich had seen in 1954 was on his mind at this point.

On February 10, 1955, Reich telegrammed William Steig. Steig is described in *Contact with Space* as heading the DOR Emergency Financial Committee from 1954–1956. Steig was also the artist who had illustrated Reich's *Listen, Little Man!* (1945) which had been published in an English edition in 1948, and was entrusted as the eventual publisher of the *Contact with Space* manuscript under Reich's CORE Pilot imprint. Reich followed his telegram with a letter to Steig, urgent in its tone. The letter reflects Reich's concerns that would be deleted from the published *Contact with Space* — his anxieties about the preparedness of the public to

10 John Riddick, "Radio 'Static' May Only Be Galaxy-to-Galaxy Broadcast," *Tucson Daily Citizen Evening Edition*, December 14, 1954, 5.

receive his research on the flying saucer phenomenon. Reich says, "I have just sent the telegram asking you not to publish any facts or claims regarding my desert work. It is *too much, too new, too incredible for average people to swallow.*" He suggests that Steig use financial reasons as a cover for the lack of publication of findings. "We are all happy about the great success, but with the success more and tougher responsibilities emerge, esp. with regard to the spaceship problem."[11]

On March 1, Reich resolved to discover the barrier by driving one of the spacegun trucks west, a journey that would terminate in Jacumba, in southern California along the border with Mexico. On March 3, at Gila Bend, Arizona — where the Gila River takes a hard westward turn, Reich observed fertility, but attributed this to OROP Desert operations reaching west, rather than the natural greening that attends the presence of a river valley. As he proceeded, he became increasingly attuned to the presence of black rocks — Melanor — and vacant stretches of sand. For Reich, locating and breaking down the barrier were imperative if there was to be a possibility of bringing more rains than they already had to the stricken desert areas of the southwest. Reich records arriving at "the tower" early on Friday, March 4. The tower he refers to is the Desert View Tower, built in the 1920s, close to Jacumba and Boulder Park, immediately to the western side of the barrier, where Geiger-Müller counts "indicated the presence of Ea." Reich asserts, "there could be no doubts that Ea effects were present over the sharply delineated divide" [CS, 242]. Still, Reich continued to San Diego and Los Angeles before doubling back to Boulder Park to attack the barrier, bringing the truck with its mounted spacegun into position and beginning operations on the afternoon of March 6. Three operators kept the draw pipes in continuous motion against the zenith where DOR broke up any gathering of cloud and vapor.

During the afternoon of the following day, Reich observed that "the barrier seemed to fall apart. Melanor appeared on the rocks, ranges, boulders en masse. The white sands darkened. Around our truck, greening began to appear. We all had the

11 Wilhelm Reich, *Where's the Truth? Letters and Journals, 1948–1957,* ed. Mary Boyd Higgins (New York: Farrar, Straus and Giroux, 2012), 191.

impression that the white had absorbed the Melanor eagerly."
Once more, an Orur needle was flown in, to augment the spacegun, arriving on the morning of March 8. Something of a breakthrough came on March 9, in the afternoon. The morning had
yielded a successful draw, against a dark and "flat" atmosphere,
"with winds coming up from the southwest, always an indica-
tion of possible rain. Blueness began to stream into the valleys
from the west, the flatness decreased and the atmosphere began
to sparkle" [CS, 244–45]. As much as Reich was encouraged by
the strength of the orgone flow across the barrier, he was disappointed to find that the clouds could not hold. The bluish atmosphere intensified and more clouds formed in the afternoon, and
there was good contact between the cloudbuster operator and
the OR stream. Again, the clouds were dissipated, but the following day — March 10 — Reich felt the barrier breaking up.

> Strange cloud formations appeared to the west and moved
> eastward. These were at first wavy, black lines against the white
> overcast. They extended down into streamers, apparently
> attracted by the still existent DOR ceiling. Then they grew into
> fat clouds and turned yellow-brown. They continued to grow
> and then became dark blue and heavy like thick rain clouds.
> At 20:00 the first sprinkle of rain occurred at Jacumba. [...]
> Light rain began to fall and continued throughout the night
> where the barrier was breaking up. [CS, 246]

Jacumba's central conflict ended on Saturday March 12 with the
presence of heavy dew and greening in the vicinity, the barrier
apparently broken down and rain falling on the desert. "It rained
neatly on March 21, 1955," Reich says. "I concluded our operations on March 24th, 1955. We established a base at Jacumba,
equipped with two Cloudbusters, a truck and sufficient laboratory equipment. We wound up our affairs during April and
stared on the way home to Orgonon again at the end of April,
1955. Our job in Arizona was done" [CS, 259].

10

Box 31:
Black Rock, Melanor, and Movies

Large stretches of "Black Rock," i.e., Melanor, are impressive as witness to the deadly force of DOR. This is true for both the outer desert like the Sahara and the Emotional Desert as presented together in the excellent film, "Bad Day at BLACK ROCK," 1955, with Spencer Tracy in the master role.

— Wilhelm Reich[1]

Box 31 of the Archives of the Orgone Institute at the Wilhelm Reich Museum contains a typed and hand-annotated sheet of paper originally titled "Film." The title has a handwritten "s" added to it, and the explanation "WR considers directly related + originating in his own work" in black ink.[2] Based on the release dates of the films listed — all but three of the eighteen films are from the 1950s — it must have been compiled or finished in 1956. The first film that Reich lists is *The Day the Earth Stood Still.* Reich is careless with titles, and this and the second film's title are typed incorrectly. The second film is *Walk East on Beacon!* (1952),[3] the Cold War FBI anti-communist propaganda-noir based on J.

---

1 Wilhelm Reich, *Contact with Space: Oranur Second Report, 1951–1956* (Haverhill: Haverhill House Publishing, 2018), 154.

2 A copy was provided to the author on request, courtesy of the Archives of the Orgone Institute.

3 Alfred L. Werker, dir., *Walk East on Beacon!* (Columbia Pictures, 1952).

Edgar Hoover's account of "The Crime of the Century: The Case of the A-Bomb Spies" published by *Readers Digest* in May 1951. The expeditious appearance of this docudrama thriller one year later, and Hoover's cameo in it, underlines the coordination between Hoover and producer Louis de Rochemont whose production company also gave cover to the CIA's funding of the animated adaptation of George Orwell's *Animal Farm* (1954). Hoover's "Crime of the Century" and de Rochemont's *Walk East on Beacon* are based on the espionage of Klaus Emil Julius Fuchs, the German physicist who had worked on the Manhattan Project and provided the Soviet Union with atomic secrets stolen during his tenure at Los Alamos National Laboratory from 1944. Fuchs was arrested in 1950. Nevertheless, there is sufficient license in the adaptation of Hoover's account to allow Reich to perceive himself in the place of Klaus Fuchs.

In *Walk East on Beacon,* Fuchs is transformed from an agent of the Soviet Union under Joseph Stalin to a loyal immigrant scientist and Buchenwald survivor named Albert Kafer. It is true that Albert Kafer's name alludes to Einstein, but his features and build are closer to Reich's in the 1950s. As he saw his younger self in Michael Rennie's Klaatu, Reich saw something of himself in (William) Finlay Currie's portrayal of Kafer. The film is set in New England and Washington. Soviet agents have abducted the scientist's son and have him hostage in East Berlin. Thus, they plan to extort Kafer, and to obtain his work related to a secret US military project codenamed Falcon. *Walk East on Beacon* takes a further liberty with Hoover's Fuchs narrative: the full title of the Falcon project is "Inter-Stellar Space: Falcon-86 K." The equations Kafer is working on are for a space station of the Wernher von Braun Wheel type (the iconic design style associated since 1968 with Stanley Kubrick and Arthur C. Clarke's *2001: A Space Odyssey*), which was conveniently the focus of a lavish article in the March 1952 issue of *Collier's* magazine with text by Von Braun. It is not at all unreasonable to believe that Reich might have been put in mind of the William Washington intrigue of 1949 and the anxiety Reich noted in *Contact with Space* about his equations being stolen by Russian espionage agents. In an accent not unlike Reich's, Kafer reads for a tape recording of his work:

BOX 31

From this equation, man now conquers distance and space. By overcoming the force of gravity he may build mansions or fortresses in space itself. The heavens now serve as highways over which he may direct his caravans in peace or in war with unerring accuracy to ant point on the Earth below. I hope this new knowledge will be used for the advancement of mankind.[4]

Albert Kafer resists the communists in almost Reichian terms. One imagines Reich's reaction to Kafer's dialogue: "When men's bodies are enslaved, so are their minds. This is why you have no men of genius. Their talents are in chains. So now, you have to steal the creations of free men."[5] Kafer is himself abducted by the communist spies when they discover that he has given them incomplete and worthless equations. Before his rescue by the FBI, the film's voiceover declares the immigrant scientist to be "a man whose courage and achievement entitled him to the full protection of the United States."[6] Certainly, Reich perceived himself this way. Interviewed by Christopher Turner for *Adventures in the Orgasmatron*, Peter Reich recalled,

He thought these movies were about him, and maybe they were, you see. It's hard to know where the circle starts. For example, *High Noon,* he was really into *High Noon,* and *Bad Day at Black Rock.* And this is why he wore a cowboy hat: he was Gary Cooper. And when the *FDA* came up to see him at Orgonon, he was just like Spencer Tracy. He'd say 'Listen, Mister' — he used that language. That was really part of his American persona, the movie person. He didn't make a distinction between that and real life.[7]

4   Werker, *Walk East on Beacon!,* 1:11:58.
5   Ibid., 1:37:40.
6   Ibid., 1:31:14.
7   Christopher Turner, *Adventures in the Orgasmatron: How the Sexual Revolution Came to America* (New York: Farrar, Straus and Giroux, 2011), 375.

Bad Day at Black Rock[8] is one of two movies from 1955 that Reich lists among those that he regarded as alluding to or directly originating from his theories, the other being *The Court-Martial of Billy Mitchell*[9] (Reich misses the hyphen) released on December 31, 1955. It is the second Gary Cooper film on Reich's list, the other being *High Noon* (1952). It is unlikely that Reich saw *The Court-Martial...* until sometime in 1956. In terms of Reich's presence or the presence of ideas and imagery that he could call his own, the more important film is *Bad Day at Black Rock*.

Less cryptically aligned with Reich and his work than *The Day the Earth Stood Still*, *Bad Day at Black Rock* is uncanny, nonetheless. The resemblance between Reich and Spencer Tracy in the lead role is arguably more striking than between Reich and Michael Rennie as Klaatu/Carpenter, and certainly more than Finlay Currie as Professor Albert Kafer. In *Bad Day at Black Rock*, it is no wild speculation to say that Reich would have recognized another potential cinematic doppelgänger. Seeing Reich seeing himself, one watches *Bad Day at Black Rock* imagining Reich's own self-analysis, aware of his post-Oranur sense of himself and his environment. From this perspective, the uncanny experience Reich had as he watched the film is not only understandable, but inevitable.

The film is set in the American Southwest, not Arizona where Reich was based primarily in 1954, but in California where he traveled. The desert setting is quite consistent with the environment in which Reich had worked. Tracy plays John J. Macreedy, a veteran of WWII conflict in Italy who lost his left arm during the fighting. This outsider has come to Black Rock to locate a Japanese-American named Komoko, whose son saved Macreedy's life during combat. Ostensibly, except for the action seen in Italy in the later conflict, general plot synopses of *Bad Day at Black Rock* do not suggest a Reichian film. So, *Adventures in the Orgasmatron* contents itself with the idea that Reich enjoyed westerns and noir and offers little in the way of analysis

8   John Sturges, dir., *Bad Day at Black Rock* (Metro-Goldwyn-Mayer, 1955).

9   Otto Preminger, dir., *The Court-Martial of Billy Mitchell* (Warner Bros, 1955).

BOX 31

of the content of the films and the reasons for the impression they made on Reich. Turner ignores the content and context provided to him and instead decides to invent a film analogy to attack Reich: "I imagine Reich as the Burt Lancaster character in *The Rain Maker,* a naïve showman and energetic charlatan who charms a sexless old maid and then actually drums up a storm."[10]

When Tracy's Macreedy arrives at Black Rock he confronts an almost unified front of hostility from the inhabitants, all in thrall to the powerful, malevolent rancher Reno Smith, played by Robert Ryan. Again, if one has empathy for Reich as a subject, then details of the film break out and form the plexus of introjection that makes a film experience personal, those moments where the projected scenes contain something of our own story. Reich had already recognized something of his resemblance to the role when Tracy's character steps from the train into the desert town. Was it not in a railroad town that Reich had encountered the most malevolent DOR, that putrescence of energy? So, Macreedy encounters hostility at Black Rock's hotel. After cleaning up, Macreedy steps from the hotel and watches from the porch as Reno Smith pulls up in his car with a dead stag tied to the hood — the buck of the Gyntish self, and perhaps the one that would appear in the dreams of Reich's son.

The suspicious townspeople urge Reno Smith to engage with him and discover his identity and his motives. Initially skeptical, the rancher replies, "What do I talk to him about — the birds, the bees, the uh, the crops, the weather?"[11] One imagines Reich, watching and listening as Reno Smith imagines talking to the Reich doppelgänger about Reichian preoccupations. Observing his exploration of Black Rock, Doc Velie, played by Walter Brennan, notes, "Mr. Macreedy seems to be heading for the jail."[12] Indeed, defiant as he was, even unconsciously Reich understood that this was a possibility; the words would have pinched at him. The point of these gathering allusions were likely driven home when Black Rock's alcoholic sheriff Tim Horn (Dean Jagger) asks Reno Smith, "Do you think he'll kick

10 Turner, *Adventures in the Orgasmatron,* 375.
11 Sturges, *Bad Day at Black Rock,* 0:14:45.
12 Ibid., 0:15:05.

up a storm?"[13] I believe Reich enjoyed this accumulation of subtle, ironic personal allusions. Watching *Bad Day at Black Rock,*
one feels a personal allegory taking shape for Reich. Macreedy's
missing left arm becomes a metaphor for the heart attack that
Reich suffered, the pain in that side. The subtext of the film is
the conflict between the Big Man and the Little Man, with Reno
Smith as an archetype of fascist power that Reich would have
recognized, otherwise — to reiterate — he would have been a very
poor analyst. Reich would have noticed threats in Smith's monologue as he plots with the little men who surround him:

> A nobody like Macreedy can cause a pretty big stink. The
> point is: who'd miss a nobody like Macreedy if he just, uh, say,
> disappeared? [...] I know those maimed guys. Their minds get
> twisted. They put on hairshirts and act like martyrs. All of
> them are do-gooders, freaks, troublemakers. [...] This guy's
> like a carrier of smallpox. Since he arrived this town has a
> fever, an infection. And it's spreading.[14]

Macreedy rents a jeep from Liz Wirth, played by Anne Francis,
the slightly too-glamorous tomboy who runs Black Rock's ram-
shackle gas station, and sets out alone for Adobe Flat, the region
where he understands Komoko Sr. settled. When he arrives, he
finds that Komoko's home has been destroyed, burned to the
ground. The only part of the structure that stands is the blackened stone of the fireplace.[15] Were he not already intrigued by
the film's use of "Black Rock," so reminiscent of his experience
with Melanor, Reich would have felt the film touching him now;
recall that the Reich had first noticed the effects of Melanor on
his own fireplace, where the rocks deteriorated and blackened
in the wake of the Oranur emergency. The weathervane turns
over Macreedy's head: the arrival of the Reichian — at least to
Reich — figure brings a subtle shift in the weather. Then, he
would have watched Tracy's Macreedy — this maimed, yet
heroic outsider, bringing with him so much unease and sus-

13 Ibid., 0:22:01.
14 Ibid., 0:25:01–0:25:50.
15 Ibid., 0:29:30.

BOX 31

picion — finding a source of water, and wildflowers growing against the desert.

During his return to the town, one of Reno Smith's henchmen, Coley Trimble, played by Ernest Borgnine, attempts to intimidate Macreedy by forcing him from the dirt road. Macreedy makes it back to Black Rock, understanding that Smith and his henchmen intend to kill him before he can leave on the morning train. Macreedy's few allies include the laconic, apathetic Doc Velie. As we approach the apocalypse of the film, Doc Velie begins to shake at the consciences of the others, the emasculated Sheriff Horn, and Pete Wirth, the hotel clerk played by John Ericson. "Four years ago," Velie says, "something terrible happened here. And we did nothing about it, nothing! The whole town fell into a sort of settled melancholy and all the people in it closed their eyes and held their tongues and failed the test with a whimper."[16] *Melancholy* — part of the neologism of Melanor; and had not the people around Reich always failed him? Four years earlier, from the time of Reich seeing *Bad Day at Black Rock,* would have been 1951: Oranur, the heart attack, the emergency. *Bad Day at Black Rock* is set four years after the Japanese attack on Pearl Harbor and the inception of internment of Japanese-Americans in Californian camps. This is the guilt at the heart of the film, and the ways in which fascist instincts and murderous impulses are present in the "good" subject is subject of Macreedy's investigation — the film is a psychoanalytic disclosure of repressed material that Reich would have recognized in these terms also. And of course, Reich had himself been detained as an enemy alien in the United States in December 1941, after the Japanese attack on Pearl Harbor. Tracy/Macreedy's words before the end of the film, when he has reckoned with the residue of his self-pity for his biopsychic maiming, would have had obvious and forceful resonance for Reich in post-Oranur, post-OROP, post-spaceship 1955:

> I was bewildered when I came here, full of self-pity. [...] It's strange the way a man will cling to the Earth when he feels he isn't going to see it again. [...] I was washed-up when I got off

16 Ibid., 1:02:39.

that train... I had one last duty to perform before I resigned from the human race. [...] I guess I was just looking for some place to get lost. [...] Because I was afraid I couldn't function any longer. [...] You'd like me to die quickly, wouldn't you? Without wasting too much of your time. Or quietly, so I won't embarrass you too much. Or even thankfully, so your memory of the occasion won't be too unpleasant.[17]

I believe the point has been made that the dismissal of, or an incurious approach to elements that Reich was explicit about being either about him or that he identified with his life and work, represents a kind of neglect, or dehumanization, of Reich by critics. Works of art do not occupy important positions in the psyche arbitrarily; a first rule of criticism is that we may learn from analyzing their presence and their contents. Each of us has, at some time, had the feeling that something ineffable, something uncanny, coincidental, or perhaps God, or the Universe is trying to tell us something. It is the unconscious or preconscious selecting information, signs, and symbols pertinent to the psyche and the tenets it has developed. In this way, signs have personal meaning for us, and yet the same signs may be meaningless to others. We do not all share the same tenets, the same instincts, if you will. Our unconsciously selective perceptions are founded on tenets that have no intrinsic requirement to be meaningful, reasonable, or rational to others. It is the psyche for itself, for its own authenticity, to establish an existence of meaning, however solitary or communal. This is the basis of association, of active imagination, of art, of psychoanalysis; it is the pattern recognition that suggests genius.

17 Ibid., 1:03:12–1:05:12.

11

Wilhelm Reich versus the Bohemians: Including the Strange Case of Mildred Brady

We do not construct our identities alone. We do not control them. This is one of the ambivalent lessons of existentialism, and the sentiment behind Jean-Paul Sartre's "L'enfer, c'est les autres" or "Hell is other people," a dramatic aphorism from his 1944 play *No Exit* that has undergone its own reconstructions in the imaginations of hosts of those other people. There is, Sartre said, after Martin Heidegger, no exit from this locked-room predicament of the psyche. The first subtitle that Reich uses in *The Murder of Christ* in his opening chapter "The Trap" is "Where is the Exit?" The question cries out from the pages: "The nature of the trap has no interest whatsoever beyond this one crucial point: WHERE IS THE EXIT OUT OF THE TRAP?"[1]

Before Sartre, D.H. Lawrence, in his final tubercular and apocalyptic winter of 1929, understood it when he said that — all aspirations to the contrary — Jesus was only a man when he was alone; in the company of others, he was always the aristocratic Christ.[2] And Lawrence in his own mythic self was no stranger

1   Wilhelm Reich, *The Murder of Christ* (New York: Farrar, Straus and Giroux, 1971), 3.
2   D.H. Lawrence, *Apocalypse and the Writings on Revelation,* ed. Mara

to projection. Before Lawrence, Arthur Rimbaud, who had his own season in Hell, understood it when he declared in one of his ecstatic letters of 1871 that "I is another." One could go on, and we will attend to the effects of this crisis on the eidola of Wilhelm Reich. But what Rimbaud the teenage poet comprehended was the nature of intersubjective being: one might have a detailed, examined, and well-reasoned idea of oneself, but one cannot — indeed, one has no right to — demand that anyone else agree with our assessment and its expression. This existential crisis, youth knows well. Erik Erikson nailed the matter when he said that teenagers "seem much concerned with faddish attempts at establishing an adolescent subculture with what looks like a final rather than a transitory or, in fact initial identity formation. They are sometimes morbidly, often curiously, preoccupied with what they appear to be in the eyes of others compared with what they feel they are."[3] In the melancholia of western postmodernism, youth has made its libidinal inward turn toward the body, to *fix* — in multiple senses of the word — and to *insist* on such finalities by making increasingly definitive and defiant modifications that are, finally, forms of resistant asceticism. The extension of adolescence is a threshold mistaken for an endpoint. In the form of a smart phone screen, contemporary youth carries always the pool of Narcissus in its pocket. Yet, even in adulthood, define ourselves as we might, all of this falls apart the moment we come to the attention of anyone else, of other people — narcissism versus resentment. If you are fortunate, others will meet you halfway, agree with or indulge a good part of whom, after skeptical introspection, you believe yourself to be. Subcultures, to the extent that they persist, have always provided reinforcement, a sense of identity without contradiction within their cool and arbitrary precincts, and an armoring against those without, whence come defamation's transfers of prurience. To this end, all subcultures require their visionary archetypes, sometimes at the cost of significant transference distortions of the person required to accomplish the archetypal passion. The archetype

Kalnins (London, Penguin, 1995), 68.

3   Erik H. Erikson, *Identity: Youth and Crisis* (New York: W.W. Norton, 1994), 128.

does not need to to be involved with, or contemporaneous with the subculture that invokes it, but to be an existential precursor — indeed it is more authentic to have preceded and anticipated the moment of crisis. Bohemia has seen Wilhelm Reich through lenses of transference, an unwitting and misconstrued heroic archetype of various subcultures. Indeed, many have come to Reich through his posthumous irruptions in culture and his influence on artists who have articulated versions of his life and theories, waxing the Reich myth.

On the American scene, outside of bohemia, Reich's name came to greater mainstream attention in an article for *Harper's* entitled "The New Cult of Sex and Anarchy," published in April 1947 by Mildred Brady.[4] Perhaps one can read Gay Talese's account of the use of Reich by the 1970s bourgeoisie in *Thy Neighbor's Wife* to represent a nominally square counterpoint.[5] Brady wrote two articles invoking Reich in 1947, but it was only the second article, "The Strange Case of Wilhelm Reich,"[6] that took Reich aggressively to task. Colin Wilson's assertion in *The Quest for Wilhelm Reich* that the two are "equally astringent"[7] only goes to suggest — with some force — that Wilson had read neither. Brady's first article to include Reich is an analysis of one section of the counterculture developing in California, and takes as its core, not Reich whose name is mentioned only seven times and then not always distinctly but within a plexus including D. H. Lawrence, but Henry Miller, who is invoked twenty-seven times across the piece's eleven pages. No, Reich's theories are taken as a nebulous background to some, not all, of the emergence of this Californian scene around Big Sur. Certainly, Brady's appraisal of the counterculture, with Reich's work informing many of its poets, is skeptical and conservative, but it contains little to sug-

4   Mildred E. Brady, "The New Cult of Sex and Anarchy," *Harper's Magazine,* April 1947, 313–22.
5   Gay Talese, *Thy Neighbor's Wife* (New York: Harper Perennial, 2009), 183–201.
6   Mildred E. Brady, "The Strange Case of Wilhelm Reich," *The New Republic,* May 26, 1947.
7   Colin Wilson, *The Quest for Wilhelm Reich: A Critical Biography* (New York: Anchor Press/Doubleday, 1981), 200.

gest that it was written in specific retaliation against Reich for his denial of an interview with Brady in 1946.

Yet, something changed between the innocuous April *Harper's* article and the publication of Brady's "The Strange Case of Wilhelm Reich" in *The New Republic* on May 26, 1947, before it was reprinted in the *Bulletin of the Menninger Clinic* in March 1948. The second Brady article critiques Reich's work and uses orgonomy to critique what she regards as an absence of coherent legal standards of practice across the diverse branches of psychoanalysis. It was written on the occasion of the American Psychiatric Association's annual conference in New York. Reich is certainly the lightning rod, but it is also clear that Brady's objection is to insufficient control of psychoanalysis. Strangely, both Brady and the editors at the Menninger Clinic acknowledge that Reich had left or been exiled from the field of psychoanalysis and the International Psychoanalytic Association since 1934, and that he had never belonged to the American Psychoanalytic Association. The association of Reich in 1947 with the APA is bizarre. This has led to speculation that the attack on Reich from Brady was one element in a concerted communist move against Reich. In *Wilhelm Reich, Biologist,* James E. Strick calls Brady "a muckraking journalist with Stalinist ties."[8] Reich's response to Brady in his journals, that she is "sex hungry" and that it was "obvious that I am the only man who could help her achieve an orgasm, which she so desperately needs,"[9] though he means it in theoretical terms, suggests an unfortunate misogyny, Reich knowing nothing about Brady's sexual life. Myron Sharaf would come to regret the attacks on Brady:

The idea was growing in [Reich's] mind that Brady was more than a fellow traveller; she was a Stalinist, and may well have been acting on instructions from the Communist Party. Brady's Stalinism became a firm conviction. The evidence about Brady was scant — the tone of her article, its appearance

8   James E. Strick, *Wilhelm Reich, Biologist* (Cambridge: Harvard University Press, 2015), 3.

9   Wilhelm Reich, *American Odyssey: Letters and Journals, 1940–1947,* ed. Mary Boyd Higgins (New York: Farrar, Straus and Giroux, 1999), 392.

in *The New Republic* under [Henry] Wallace's editorship, and some hearsay about her politics. A friend of Reich's wrote him that in 1936 Brady was "in sympathy" with the Communist Party, but later information was not available. Regrettably I, too, contributed to the loose political characterization of Brady by repeating to Reich a statement heard from Dwight Macdonald. Macdonald had casually mentioned something about the fellow-traveling or Stalinist sympathies of Mildred and her husband, and Reich exaggerated the significance of this vague remark.[10]

The problem for this view that Brady was involved in a Stalinist smear of, in Reich's words, "red fascist origin" [AO, 403] is that if that characterization of Brady was correct, then "The New Cult of Sex and Anarchy" would not have been written. No serious literary critic could call the *Harper's* story Stalinist. To this writer the piece is quaint anthropology. If anything, it is quite conservative in its skepticism of the Californian bohemians. Epistemologically, its ambivalence toward Henry Miller follows, to an extent, a course laid down in 1940 by George Orwell in "Inside the Whale," and anticipates something of Joan Didion's tone regarding subsequent counterculture iterations of the 1960s. No Stalinists, they. Or could it be that Brady carried such a wound from Reich's refusal of an interview after she had made her way to his office in 1946 that she felt compelled to begin, as Jerome Greenfield has it, "the attack on Reich"[11]? Journalists tend to have thicker skins, but one cannot say for certain, unlikely as it seems that some grudge was engendered the previous year. Now, there is no argument that Brady's use of Reich in the subsequent article is a disingenuous conflation of two subjects. But her reasons for resenting Reich might have been less conspiratorial. Christopher Turner writes:

10 Myron R. Sharaf, *Fury on Earth: A Biography of Wilhelm Reich* (New York: Da Capo, 1994), 366.
11 Jerome Greenfield, *Wilhelm Reich vs. the U.S.A.* (New York: W.W. Norton, 1974), 42.

Brady had first come across Reich when a friend of hers who had been diagnosed with cancer obtained an orgone box and begun to sit in it, hoping for a cure. When Brady, who considered this to be "crack-pot nonsense," made inquiries about Reich and his device, she was astonished to discover that many of the psychoanalysts she spoke to on the West Coast agreed with his theory of the orgasm and the psychic origins of cancer.[12]

Sometimes, doubt is merely doubt. Is it conceivable that Mildred Brady's initial motivation was just that, not Stalinism, not the emotional plague, not armoring, not anorgonia or a lack of orgastic potency, but concern for her friend? In his introduction to Reich ahead of his play *Wilhelm Reich in Hell,* Robert Anton Wilson makes the point:

If some of Reich's critics were motivate day [*sic*] the Emotional Plague, and if Emotional Plague is the most widespread illness on the planet, then it is an easy step to the conclusion that all dissent from Reichian dogma is the result of Emotional Plague. Reich took that step increasingly, as hostility toward him and his work accelerated; and many "orthodox" Reichians are still thinking that framework. [...] The orthodox Reichians, thus, have become the mirror image of the New Inquisition which destroyed Reich.[13]

Wilson co-authored the influential cult books collectively known as *The Illuminatus! Trilogy* (1975). *Wilhelm Reich in Hell* is certainly less well-known; it is not referenced in Turner's *Adventures in the Orgasmatron,* nor in Olivia Laing's more recent *Everybody: A Book About Freedom* (2021), which is founded upon the author's relationship with Reich's theories and the counterculture, not least Kathy Acker with whom there is some avant-garde

---

12 Christopher Turner, *Adventures in the Orgasmatron: How the Sexual Revolution Came to America* (New York: Farrar, Straus and Giroux, 2011), 273.
13 Robert Anton Wilson, *Wilhelm Reich in Hell* (Phoenix: Falcon Press, 1987), 27–28.

overlap. For Wilson, the "Hell" in question is a hybrid of Sartre's, the Tibetan Bardos, and a satirical, burlesque reconstruction of Reich's trial. In addition to the enchained figure of Reich, characters include Sade and Sacher-Masoch incarnating their respective libidinal energies, Marilyn Monroe (one of the more successful characters) a parody of Eichmann as a cabbage, *Playboy* bunnies (Wilson was an editor for the magazine in the 1970s), a lesbian communist member of the Orwellian "Anti-Sex League," a punk chorus of the American Medical Association, and Prince Peter Ouspensky. Wilson is critical, again in his introduction, of the attempts by orthodox Reichians to "obtain an injunction banning a film about Reich because they found Heresy in it."[14] I believe this refers to the Makavejev film. Wilson's play owes something to that film. Wilson is convinced by Reich — to a point. In particular, he is indebted to *The Mass Psychology of Fascism*, the first Reich book he encountered. Even before reading him, Wilson came to an intuitive defense of Reich after learning of the incineration of Reich's work in 1957. The play, written thirty years later, is, Wilson says, "my attempt to make dramatic art out of my dispute with myself about the ambiguities and unsolved enigmas of the life and persecution of Dr. Reich."[15] In terms of theory, *Wilhelm Reich in Hell* confines itself to the issues of character armor, and the emotional plague.

> On Reich's general theory of Character Armor and/or muscular armor, I rate this at about 8 going on 9 [of 10]. The most successful therapies I know anything about all use variations on the muscular armor model to communicate what they are doing.
> The Emotional Plague *as metaphor, I rate at around 9...* The Emotional Plague as a *concrete* illness I rate at around 2 or 3. Most of what Reich considers a species-wide "illness," I think can be better called the natural evolutionary resultant of our temporary condition midway between ape and our future destiny — the free, rational beings we imagine we already are.

14 Ibid., 28.
15 Ibid., 4.

Reich's cosmology I would rate around 3 or 4.[16]

Thus, there is no discussion of orgonomy, and merely a glancing reference, through the circus trial's Ringmaster, to Reich's "being through with UFOS and Illuminati plots and all other fantasies of your last days before First Death."[17] Of course, Wilson is aware that Reich never referenced the Illuminati, it is simply that one possible Hell in which the trial is staged is "In the Mind of the Author of the Play."[18] Much of the opening of the first act is unsuccessful, too literal, irritating, but the character of Reich grows in persuasiveness before his breakdown or breaking down into the everyman and the psychopathology of everyday life. Certainly, something of Reich's appeal to bohemia, to artists, lies in his creativity. For better or worse, Reich is an enviable figure in terms of his facility with, initially, the Freudian unconscious, Marxist dialectic and social analysis, character armor, fascism, and — reject this characterization as some orthodox Reichians may — his fatal commitment to an alternate reality, a fantasy, a creative ontology for which he seemed prepared to die, to be martyred; these are all Romantic imperatives. Mildred Brady wrote that the bohemians who seemed to be enthralled by Reich were "philosophical improvisors, who also toss into their pot... D. H. Lawrence, Emma Goldman, Madame Blavatsky, Henri Bergson, William Blake, and even Ouspenski (sic) of *Tertium Organum*, to name just a few."[19] All but one of these would appear in Colin Wilson's epic study *The Occult* (1971), where Wilhelm Reich occupies not inconsiderable space — something that would have appalled him. Such are the injuries...

When Wilhelm Reich died of heart failure in Lewisburg Penitentiary, Pennsylvania, on November 3, 1957, it was ten years after the Brady articles. Ten years later again, on the night of Saturday, October 21, 1967, novelist and journalist Norman Mailer and poet and performance artist Tuli Kupferberg were forty-four years old (as was Eissler when he taped Reich, and the

16 Ibid., 42.
17 Ibid., 59.
18 Ibid.
19 Brady, "The New Cult of Sex and Anarchy," 316.

age when Nietzsche lost himself). Mailer was born in January and Kupferberg in September of 1923. They were both called Norman; Kupferberg's name was Napthali, but he went by Norman for a time, including in some correspondence with Reich. That night in 1967, Mailer and Kupferberg were imprisoned, subsequent to their arrests during the march on the Pentagon, protesting the Vietnam war that afternoon.

Prowling, Mailer found Kupferberg hunched among long rows of bunks in the hanger-like confines of Occoquan minimum security prison. Kupferberg was, with Allen Ginsberg protégée Ed Saunders, a member of the madcap underground rock band The Fugs, the name taken from the distortion of the word fuck that was forced on Mailer's first novel *The Naked and the Dead* (1948). Kupferberg appears in Ginsberg's Beat lyric poem *Howl*, failing to commit suicide by throwing himself from the Brooklyn Bridge. Now, The Fugs were behind the attempt to levitate the Pentagon as the climax of the protest, which in a tricksterish, occult, quasi-Reichian sense was to be known as The Exorgasm. It is not obvious that the assembled hippies, witches, and dadaists succeeded in anything but a 'pataphysical sense in raising the building from its foundations. And yet, for a moment at least, the Pentagon was recast as a spaceship, hovering over Arlington and the Potomac.

Tuli Kupferberg had corresponded with Reich from the early fifties and acquired one of the limited number of the orgone accumulators Reich's Orgone Institute ever produced. Mailer had constructed his own version at his apartment on New York's Fifty-Fifth Street, although its carpet-lined interior seems to have functioned as a somewhat soundproof booth for primal ecstasy and despair in Mailer's case. As Mary Dearborn says in her excellent biography of Mailer, Reich's imprisonment was "for defying an injunction not to produce this device, a fact that contributed greatly to his cult status in the late 1950s."[20] Though not detailed on the subject, J. Michael Lennon writes that Mailer's "infatuation with Reich would grow throughout the 1950s."[21] Mailer's

20 Mary V. Dearborn, *Mailer: A Biography* (Boston: Houghton Mifflin, 1999), 116.
21 J. Michael Lennon, *Norman Mailer: A Double Life* (New York: Simon

essay "The White Negro: Superficial Reflections on the Hipster," published in the summer 1957 issue of *Dissent,* owes much to his idiosyncratic reading of Reich at the time of Reich's imprisonment.

Then, as ever, Mailer was concerned with the pathologies of the zeitgeist and how one should live under terminal conditions. No doubt, Mailer had a sense of what Reich called the emotional plague. Therefore, just weeks before Reich's death, Mailer's essay claimed, "the intellectual antecedents of this generation can be traced to such separate influences as Henry Miller, D. H. Lawrence, and Wilhelm Reich."[22] Mailer invoked Reich's theories in his projection of the hipster, a novel existential hero whose vitalism is radically embodied in orgasm, the pleasures of drugs, and the subcultural ecstasies of both criminal violence and avant-grade jazz. It is doubtful that any copies of *Dissent* found their way into the penitentiary, but Reich would have almost certainly balked at Mailer's vision of Reich's contribution to the hipster's status as "philosophical psychopath." Ironically, Reich had used the term "hip" in his 1943 essay "The Emotional Plague" that was added to the third edition of *Character Analysis* in 1948. Reich used the term to characterize "cultivated Bohemians" of a superficial, snobbish type. "They are clever," Reich says, but "their intelligence is devoted to a kind of sterile artistic activity. Their acquaintance with the magnitude and seriousness of the problems probed by a Goethe or a Nietzsche is less than superficial, but they take a great pleasure in quoting classical literature. At the same time, they are full of cynicism. They regard themselves as modern, liberal, free of any conventions. Incapable of serious experience, they look upon sexual love as a kind of child's play."[23]

Mailer's preoccupations with totalitarianism, cancer, and orgasm in "The White Negro" are distinctly Reichian, yet the hipster's embrace of violence and orgasm as equivalents is closer

& Schuster, 2013), 164.

22 Norman Mailer, "The White Negro: Superficial Reflections on the Hipster," in *Advertisements for Myself* (New York: The New American Library, 1960), 305.

23 Wilhelm Reich, *Character Analysis,* trans. Vincent R. Carfagno (New York: Farrar, Straus and Giroux, 1972), 524.

to Reich's definition of the sick, or biopathic individual suffering from the emotional plague.

> But to be with it is to have grace, is to be closer to the secrets of that inner unconscious life which will nourish you if you can hear it, for you are then nearer to that God which every hipster believes is located in the senses of his body, that trapped, mutilated and nonetheless megalomaniacal God who is It, who is energy, life, sex, force, the Yoga's prana, the Reichian's orgone, Lawrence's "blood," Hemingway's "good," the Shavian life-force; "It"; God; not the God of the churches but the unachievable whisper of mystery within the sex, the paradise of limitless energy and perception just beyond the next wave of the next orgasm.[24]

In the same fall of 1957, Jack Kerouac's *On the Road* described William S. Burroughs's use of a Reichian orgone accumulator;[25] Kerouac's manuscript dates from 1951. Kerouac's next novel *The Subterraneans* finds his alter-ego struck by the "sudden, glad, wondrous discovery of Wilhelm Reich, his book *The Function of the Orgasm*" and intuiting a form of ecstatic naturalism with "the lovers going to and fro beneath the boughs in the Forest of Arden of the World."[26] Burroughs had built an accumulator in November 1949, and his involvement with Reichian theory is even more extensive than Mailer's. Indeed, Eric Mottram's (1977) definitive critical work on Burroughs states that "Burroughs' work may usefully be seen as a fictional dramatization of Wilhelm Reich's definitions of 'emotional plague,'" which began as early as his reading of *The Cancer Biopathy* "after he left college 1948-9."[27] References to Reich, orgone, and Deadly Orgone Radiation as an environmental catastrophe permeate

---

24 Mailer, "The White Negro," 316.
25 Jack Kerouac, *On the Road*, in *The Road Novels, 1957–1960*, ed. Douglas Brinkley (New York: Library of America, 2007), 136–37.
26 Jack Kerouac, *The Subterraneans* (New York: Grove Press, 1958), 46–48.
27 Eric Mottram, *William Burroughs: The Algebra of Need* (London: M. Boyars, 1977), 119.

almost all of Burroughs's oeuvre, perhaps most vividly in *The Ticket That Exploded* (1962) and in the interviews with Daniel Odier collected in *The Job* (1969), but they continue to his elegiac final novel *The Western Lands* where "Orgone balked at the post. Christ bled. Time ran out."[28]

Burroughs's use of Reich's theories is accurate in the sense of planetary crisis, but Burroughs's use of orgasm reflex suggested a radical *dis*embodiment and the transmigration of psyche is a misreading. The mid-fifties counterculture defined by the Beats and Mailer's codification of hip has its counterpart in the emergence of the "angry young men" and Colin Wilson's *The Outsider* (1956). This was the prelude to Wilson's *The New Existentialism* (1966), and his correspondence with humanist and later transpersonal psychologist Abraham Maslow. When Theodore Roszak published *The Making of a Counter Culture* (1969), the undermining of the "alienated attitude toward the natural environment" adopted by the society he observed was in progress, reclaiming affinities familiar to Romanticism. The sense that the "flora, fauna, landscape, and increasingly the climate of the earth lie practically helpless at the feet of technological man, tragically vulnerable in his arrogance"[29] was developing toward an ecopsychology that would draw on vitalism, animism, and a post-Beat existentialism. The transpersonal, peak experience psychology of both Wilson and Maslow follow Nietzsche to Reich. According to Maslow, "peakers" are "Yea-sayers rather than Nay-sayers, life-positive rather than life negative (in Reich's sense), eager for life rather than nauseated or irritated by it,"[30] aligned then with Mailer's sense of Reich. Mailer's account of the 1967 protest and march on the Pentagon was awarded the Pulitzer Prize. Wilhelm Reich's books had been burned. Unfortunately, Roszak missed the fact that Reich's orgasm formula was not a

---

28 William S. Burroughs, *The Western Lands* (London: Penguin, 2010), 222.

29 Theodore Roszak, *The Making of a Counter Culture: Reflections on the Technocratic Society and Its Youthful Opposition* (New York: Anchor, 1969), 226.

30 Abraham H. Maslow, *The Farther Reaches of Human Nature* (New York: Penguin Compass, 1993), 271.

merely sexual formula, and Rozsak's view is the opposite of this writer's. Roszak situates Reich with "D. H. Lawrence, Henry Miller, Norman Mailer, as well as every pornographer on the scene,"[31] purely — mistakenly — in sexual terms.

Peter Reich writes in his 1989 preface to *A Book of Dreams*, "This book wrote itself in the summer of 1970. Dušan Makavejev had just left Rangeley, Maine, leaving me suspended between the reality of his film *WR: Mysteries of the Organism* and an inexpressible haze of troubling memories."[32] Peter Reich was twenty-five and living in Staten Island when he first met Dušan Makavejev in the fall of 1969. Ironically, before radically distorting Reich's work, Makavajev would remind the son how people related to their memories or experience of the father: "It is as if they have blind spot" [BD, 161]. As much as Peter discussed ideas for the film with Makavejev, none of that prospective material was filmed or appeared in the finished film.

WR: Mysteries of the Organism[33] is Makavejev's "personal response"[34] to Reich's life and work. It introduces him through voiceover as "the revolutionary doctor and communist, Wilhelm Reich."[35] The film has three strands: one a pseudo-documentary about Reich, another an art-film set in Yugoslavia, and another employing New York bohemia in various set-pieces and improvisations. The film opens with the image of two dogs roped to a hydrant on a dirty street, the voiceover of Tuli Kupferberg reciting variations of one of the inquiries of Juvenal's sixth Satire *Quis custodiet ipsos custodes?*, beginning, "Who will protect us from our protectors?"[36] Gradually, he begins to intone, dressed in a ragged orange paramilitary flightsuit, alluding to incarceration, and takes up an m-16 rifle and a helmet from a box of junk Americana and begins prowling the streets. The first significant

31 Theodore Roszak, *The Voice of the Earth: An Exploration of Ecopsychology* (Grand Rapids: Phanes, 2001), 285.

32 Peter Reich, *A Book of Dreams* (London: John Blake, 2015), xv.

33 Dušan Makavejev, dir., *WR: Mysteries of the Organism* (Neoplanta Film, 1971).

34 Ibid., 0:00:45.

35 Ibid., 0:04:43.

36 Ibid., 0:01:45.

problem with Makavejev's film is that its pastiche of Reichian ideas, not least the anachronistic Sex-Pol voiceovers, are presented as, or so readily accepted as, direct quotation from Reich's work. The first Sex-Pol pastiche ends with the image of Mildred Brady's second article, and Reich's handwritten annotation, "The Smear."

In the film, Myron Sharaf, pointedly reading from *Pinocchio,* emerges from an orgone accumulator, and provides an ambivalent explanation of its mechanism: "It mystifies me, in part, because it is very simple. It's just uh, organic material on the outside, metal material on the inside. And it, uh, the organic thing operates like a nylon material and collects what's called 'static electricity,' or what Reich called 'orgone energy.'"[37] One feels that Sharaf's heart is not in it. Eva Reich (credited as Dr. Eva Reich Moise) describes Reich's suppressed work and evidence, his "judicial murder, which resembles that which he outlines in his book *The Murder of Christ,*" and that "the world went the wrong way at the time of his death, 1957."[38] Footage of the penitentiary follows, then the public incinerator in which the FDA burned Reich's works. Eva Reich's tells Makavejev directly, "Because you came from behind the Iron Curtain, and because... if you really said in your own country what you really think, you wouldn't be alive there. *You* don't think so, but I believe that children are manufactured into 'good state beings' in the communist nations. In other words, real creative individuality is *the* crime."[39] It is a prebuttal to what Eva Reich knows, or seems to suspect will be the mangling of Reich's work into a determinedly Marxist film. Concurrently, she declares that the American Dream is also dead. Thence to the quiet streets of Rangeley, accompanied by a Coca Cola jingle. Peter Reich recalls — or does he? — a standoff between Reich and a mob of local residents, led by a "local storekeeper," who came to Orgonon to denounce the "Orgies" and communist activity. Peter doubts his memories of seeing Reich with his .45 caliber pistol pressed into the back of

37 Ibid., 0:08:56.
38 Ibid., 0:09:52 - 0:10:35.
39 Ibid., 0:12:59 – 0:13:30.

a protestor.[40] Through the awkward accounts of residents of Rangeley, the film describes Reich's novel presence in the town. With something lost in translation, Makavejev *almost* quotes Reich in his next female voiceover. Strangely, the voiceover gets the date wrong. The voiceover is from various paragraphs in the first chapter of *Contact with Space*. The voiceover says:

> On March 10th, 1956, at 10 o'clock at night, this almost incredible idea came to me: Am I really a spaceman? Do I belong to a new race of earthlings sired by beings from outer space who had intercourse with Earth women? Are my children the first offspring of an interplanetary race? Is this thought in some way related to what is yet to happen in the future? I claim the privilege of asking these and similar questions without fear of being imprisoned for it by any authority whatsoever. I hate the irrational. However. I believe that even the most flagrant irrationality must contain something of rational truth. There is nothing in this human world of ours that is not in some way right however distorted it may be.[41]

The film cuts to an image of Brady's "The New Cult of Sex and Anarchy," and narration of salacious rumors of abuses at Orgonon. A recording of Reich describes his encounter with the anti-communist protestors introduced by Peter Reich, but it is introduced with narration describing Reich shooting at FBI agents concealing themselves around the grounds of Orgonon. Reich describes meeting with the protestors, denouncing communism, and stating that he voted for Eisenhower. Perhaps this is a trivial edit in a nonlinear film. More salacious is the subsequent footage of Dr. Alexander Lowen's practice. Lowen attended Reich's seminars at The New School in 1940–1941 and practiced Reichian therapies for a period from 1944 to 1948, when Reich recommended that Lowen attend medical school in Switzerland. "On his return to New York in the early 1950s he launched his career in bio-energetics, an offshoot and popularization of

40 Ibid., 0:14:20 – 0:15:37.
41 Ibid., 0:17:36.

175

Reich's therapy."[42] With two other students, Lowen broke from Reich and orgonomy in 1953. In 1956, Lowen, John Pierrakos, and William Walling founded the Institute of Bioenergetic Analysis. Makavejev's film elides this, intercutting footage of Sharaf discussing his own sessions with Reich to imply that Lowen is working as a Reichian, leering camerawork that cuts into a moment of an interview with painter Betty Dodson describing portraiture of masturbating subjects, and, returning to Lowen's practice for something resembling Esalen primal scream therapy. Robert Ollendorff, brother of Ilse Ollendorff Reich, appears briefly to state that "If any sane man or woman were to be produced by a doctor, suddenly, what would be the consequences? This is very simple. He, very likely, would commit suicide."[43]

Cut to Tuli Kupferberg stalking the streets of New York with his M-16, ripped orange flight suit, and oversized helmet. Kupferberg goes largely unseen, unacknowledged, for he represents the unconscious military-capitalist psychopathology of American life; he is the inverse of Karl Marx's specter. It's not obvious that Kupferberg is particularly aware that he is in a film about Reich, but he had been seeking connection with Reich for some time. After approximately 25 minutes, the film alternates between the Marxist sexual revolutionary narrative of its Yugoslavian protagonists, and a dislocated cinéma vérité that introduces the affair between Warhol "Superstars" Jackie Curtis and Eric Emerson, and their cuckolding of conventional marriage. Betty Dobson returns. In Yugoslavia, comrades have sex beneath a photograph of a smiling Reich, and our heroine "Milena" (Milena Dravic) ducks into an orgone accumulator in her kitchen, then declaims from her apartment balcony, "The October Revolution was ruined when it rejected free love."[44] Later, Kupferberg will hustle around the financial district to The Fugs's "Kill for Peace." Later yet, Milena points to a photograph of Reich, beside a photograph of Freud from which three darts protrude, and declares "His name is World Revolution. He died in a U.S. jail, convinced that Moscow agents had put

---

42 Sharaf, *Fury on Earth*, 266n.
43 WR, 0:25:32.
44 Ibid., 0:35:12.

him there. [...] What I wonder is whether they were the same people who went to Mexico and drove a pickax into the skull of Trotsky, comrade-in-arms of Lenin and Stalin."[45] She continues, "[Reich] teaches that every nice person like you and me hides behind his facade a great explosive charge, a great reservoir of energy that can be released only by war and revolution." Milena's lover, the Stalinist ice-skater who will later behead her with one of his skates, is skeptical: "I am charmed by your enthusiasm, so forgive me if I'm a bit ironic, but doesn't your — I mean, his theory — turn Trotsky's concept of a permanent revolution into one — God forbid! — of permanent orgasm?"[46] Curtis improvises a tale of thwarted sex. Nancy Godfrey makes a plaster casting of the erection of Screw magazine editor Jim Buckley. Kupferberg imitates masturbation with the barrel of his rifle, and the film abruptly cuts to footage of one of Reich's cloudbusters, and so on through the decapitation of Milena...The film is not without its virtuosity nor its energy and subversive power. The present writer is the last to deny the abstract its abstraction, but as it regards Reich, *WR: Mysteries of the Organism* is incoherent, anachronistic, and misleading. Blind spots, indeed.

Kupferberg began corresponding with Wilhelm Reich and his offices at the Orgone Institute in Forest Hills, New York, in 1949.[47] In response to a letter of April 9th, mistaking the sex of his correspondent, Reich replied on the 13th to Miss Tuli Kupferberg, and sent copies of *The Sexual Revolution* and *the Function of the Orgasm* separately.

> I cannot, of course, answer all of your statements and arguments, but let me say only this: It requires complete and thorough study of orgonomy and our type of mass psychology, to understand that work democracy is an *actual* bio-social

45 Ibid., 0:58:25.
46 Ibid., 0:59:57.
47 This correspondence is archived at the Fales Library at New York University as the Tuli Kupferberg and Sylvia Topp Papers MSS.385, and I refer in most of the following to materials found in Box 44, Folder 39, "Reich, William / Foundation (Re: Purchase and Use of Orgone Energy Accumulator, Newsletters, and Index) 1950–1957."

process and not a political program. Furthermore, that it is the universal biopathy in men of all professions and all classes which complicates the merely economic problems so tremendously. The main thing is that our present-day education renders the mass individual, without his fault, incapable or less capable to assume responsibility for his special and general social situation.

In early January 1950, Kupferberg wrote to Reich again. The type is very difficult to read but *seems* to open: "I enclose my article on your theory of work that has just appeared in Freedom, London, Dec. 10 [24? unclear] 1949. The article had been rejected by the first journal to which I had submitted it, a paper of revolutionary syndicalism." The article which corresponds to the one referenced in Kupferberg's letter, "The Theory of Work of Wilhelm Reich," was published over the December 10 and December 24 issues of *Freedom: Anarchist Fortnightly,*[48] under what I believe is a pseudonym for Tuli Kupferberg "Jack Gallego" (unless I am misreading the words "my article" and "I had submitted" which seem to claim ownership of it; and I think Kupferberg would have credited another author if that's what he meant, but the writer admits some possibility that he may be mistaken). Of course, the article concludes above another on "D.H. Lawrence and Education." The Reich article is definitely written by an American. Also, in the course of the first article, there is reference to a manual of *Infantry Drill and (sic) Regulations,* quoting "His (the soldier's) loyalty to his country should be like that of a dog to its master." One recalls the opening shot of the first Kupferberg scene in *WR: Mysteries of the Organism,* beginning with two dogs tied to a hydrant. It also references *The Sexual Revolution* which Reich had sent to Kupferberg in April 1949. In the letter's bleary type, Kupferberg reminds Reich,

48 Jack Gallego, "The Theory of Work of Wilhelm Reich," *Freedom: Anarchist Fortnightly,* December 10, 1949, https://freedomnews.org.uk/wp-content/uploads/2020/04/Freedom-1949-12-10.pdf, and Jack Gallego, "The Theory of Work of Wilhelm Reich – 2," *Freedom: Anarchist Fortnightly,* December 24, 1949, https://freedomnews.org.uk/wp-content/uploads/2020/04/Freedom-1949-12-24.pdf.

As you may remember this article (really a general review of a good part of your work) was made possible by the fact that you were good enough to give me two of your books, without which my work would have been quite handicapped. I do find it hard to studying the Great Reading Room of the N.Y. Public Library. My present financial situation is lousy.

He requests a copy of *Character Analysis,* an issue of the *Annals of the Institute for Orgonomic Science* that includes an article on work democracy, and the latest *Orgone Energy Bulletin,* none of which, he insists, are to be found at the Library. The letter closes with Kupferberg's appeal, "Many of my students and otherwise financially embarrassed friends while having real interest in your work, find the cost of the books, rational as the reasons may be, prohibitive. [...] I am considering psychotherapy for myself. Are there any free or reasonable places one could go?"[49]

On January 27, 1950, Ilse Ollendorff replied, "We regret to inform you that is is impossible for the Orgone Institute Press to give away any books," and re-directs Kupferberg to the New York Public Library, where she suggests copies of the *Orgone Energy Bulletin* might be delayed by up to ten months, but forthcoming. "Regarding medical orgone therapy: If you are interested in an initial examination here at the Orgone Institute, please call or write for an appointment."[50] Kupferberg did pursue an appointment and on February 2, 1950, Ilse Ollendorff replied again with available appointment times; examinations were only scheduled for "Wednesday afternoons between 12:00 and 3:00 o'clock."[51] There is a hand annotation beneath Ollendorff's signature: "1st Mar. 2:30." This, a Wednesday, might have been Kupferberg's first appointment.

On March 17, 1950, Kupferberg sent his manuscript *Machine Technic and Compulsive Character* to Reich, "which I would like to submit for publishing in the *Orgone Energy Bulletin."* Kupferberg explains, "I know it is an ambitious attempt," which "ends on a pessimistic note," and he offers some suggestions of

49 Tuli Kupferberg and Sylvia Topp Papers MSS.385.
50 Ibid.
51 Ibid.

where the text might be cut if if were to prove too long for the Bulletin.

> I am also appending (not part of the article) 2 pages, 1 suggested further studies, and the second an outline of an article on THE SALESMAN AS AN ARCHETYPE article on job analysis. If you would care to give any criticisms or suggestions, I would appreciate them. Frankly, I need a little encouragement to keep on with the work. I also feel the lack of more thoroughgoing psychoanalytic and sex-economic understanding. Thus the suggestions for the salesman article are ideals. perhaps some sort of teamwork is more ideal than myself working alone. That of course may also be impractical, and really a large task. If you reject the article, could you kinly (sic) let me know by return mail, and i will pick it up at the Institute.

Reich replied to Kupferberg on March 24, 1950, rejecting the manuscript. He writes:

> This does not mean that your effort was not worthwhile, or that your statements are wrong. However, your exposition fails to search for the root of the evil in the daily and basic behavior of the average man, woman, worker, adolescent, etc. You only add a good description to other descriptions of the misery. But this is no longer sufficient. What is necessary to an ever increasing degree is to make people en masse aware of their terrific responsibility for the processes in society. I hope you will be able to expand in this direction.[52]

None of these disappointments ultimately deterred Kupferberg from subscribing and earnestly following Reich. Correspondence with the Wilhelm Reich Foundation Accumulator Department at Orgonon indicates that Kupferberg took possession of an orgone accumulator, second and, from one Jack Tatarsky of Cherry Street, New York, shortly after August 10, 1952. In the spring of 1956, Kupferberg obtained a Reich Medical DOR-Buster from the Orgone Institute Research Laboratories (OIRL), and

52 Ibid.

apparently went into almost immediate default on payments for the device. On March 26, the OIRL issued a terse note requesting immediate return of the DOR-Buster. Michael Silvert reminded him of this on April 4. Another undated invoice states, "We plan to terminate the loan of the Reich Medical DOR-Buster by June 30, 1956, and ask that you prepare to purchase or return it before then. The price is $75." Silvert wrote to Kupferberg on April 23, with a Certificate of Ownership, transferring the device to him.

The Kupferberg archive contains an intriguing range of ephemera, including yet another iteration of the "Strange Case of...." This article saved by Kupferberg, which seems to have escaped the literature on Reich, is Irwin Ross's writing for the *New York Post* of September 5, 1954, "The Strange Case of Dr. Wilhelm Reich."[53] Ross repeats Mildred Brady's initial appraisal that Reich's prose is "turgid," but is otherwise not wholly unsympathetic to Reich's plight with the FDA, arguing that "citizens who by no means hold with Reich may well be disturbed by the case," which he finds disproportionate, and in which the "wording of the injunction is ambiguous; it is not clear whether the books are to be destroyed or merely withheld from distribution, but in any event they have been banned." Further,

> Included among them are two items of which many of Reich's detractors think highly — 'Character Analysis,' and 'The Mass Psychology of Fascism.' [...] The case of Wilhelm Reich is complicated by more than the freedom of the press. Not only has he made substantial contributions in the past, but his present psychiatric views are hardly subject to simple condemnation. While the FDA is prepared to prove in court that the orgone accumulator is valueless, there is no proof that Reich's psychotherapy cannot produce results. [...] One cannot fairly dispute the Reichians' claim that they effect cures. The point is that there are many conflicting approaches in psychiatry and psychoanalysis, and doubtless all disciplines produce some results — for one reason because the personal

---

53 Tuli Kupferberg and Sylvia Topp Papers MSS.385, Box 44, Folder 40.

skill, sympathy, intuitive understanding of the therapist is often more important than his formal method.[54]

He defends Reich against "A common impression... that a patient merely sat in the box, in quick order was divested of impotence or frigidity, and acquired vast sexual prowess. This is not at all the case; it is much harder for the orgastically impotent to achieve full gratification, through it can be done; and Reich is understandably aggrieved at such blatant caricature of his therapy."[55] And yet, Ross concedes, "The caricature, however, has only added to his fame." The article also covers the Oranur Experiment, cloudbusting, and Reich's 1930s exile from communism and orthodox psychoanalysis.

> After his arrival here in 1939, he served for two years as an associate professor at the New School for Social Research. He built the first orgone accumulator in 1940, established Orgonon in 1942, and in the clear, heady air of Maine began to expand his Orgonomic researches in every direction. At 57, he is still an eager and restless figure and has yet to discover the joys of interplanetary travel.[56]

Kupferberg was aware of Reich's interest in flying saucers, and that the version of Reich to whom he had attached himself was a figure of the past, that Reich's concerns had passed beyond any fusion of Marxist sociology and psychoanalysis. On interplanetary travel, from the month prior, Kupferberg kept "Some Notes on Desert (From a Talk by Reich at Orgonon, August 1954)."

> DOR has always existed. The great increase in atmospheric DOR over the last several years is a result of the atomic blasts and other atomic activities and also, apparently, is due to cosmic orgone engineering by the people who have been visiting our planet in spaceships from other words. (Those who are

54 Irwin Ross "The Strange Case of Dr. Wilhelm Reich," *New York Post*, September 5, 1954.

55 Ibid.

56 Ibid.

still skeptical about the presence our skies of "flying saucers" should realize that our government has not been employing over 2000 people for several years merely to keep track of optical illusions.)

Exactly what the intentions of the "CORE men" are is a matter for conjecture. Obviously they are concerned about the far-reaching effects of our periodic explosions. They could stop these harmful explosions by either destroying us through DOR illness and desert development in our world or by pushing us towards health and good sense. Since the CORE Men are in touch with the orgone functions and undoubtedly unarmored, it is easier to believe their intentions toward us are benign. But the possibility cannot be ignored that they are waging a new kind of war on a dangerous planet.[57]

What might Norman Mailer and Tuli Kupferberg have discussed that October night in 1967, confined at Occoquan, the Pentagon having neither risen nor fallen? Kupferberg's involvement with Makavejev's film was not yet on the horizon. Mailer would continue to write about libidinal forces and psychopathology, and his later masterpiece *The Executioner's Song,* while not directly Reichian, can be read in Reichian terms. Might they have discussed their variations of Reich, their respective orgone accumulators, *The Function of the Orgasm,* or *The Mass Psychology of Fascism?* The intrigue of that conversation, if it took place, is lost. Perhaps it should be the subject of a play.

---

57 Tuli Kupferberg and Sylvia Topp Papers MSS.385, Box 44, Folder 39.

12

Unidentified Flying Object-Relations: Peter Reich's Tale

Half a deer walked up to my house and rattled the door. When I didn't answer, the deer went away and I watched him turn into a whole deer.

— Peter Reich[1]

This penultimate chapter concerns the second conclusion that I have been working with. What is at stake here is not only Reich's identity as scientific martyr, as a man who fell to earth, but also, his existential sense of fatherhood, of how spaceman and father were inseparable and more reasonable than unreasonable in their mutual desperation. In the desert with his son, it was inevitable that Reich's strong cinematic self, compelled into being by *The Day the Earth Stood Still* and *Bad Day at Black Rock* in particular would undergo a final revision to include him. As Oranur before it, the "spaceship" intrigue required recasting.

Peter Reich was eleven years old when his father took him to the desert with the cloudbuster to engage with flying saucers, not least the silver disk the youth observed over Tucson, Arizona. Peter Reich's memoir *A Book of Dreams,* first published in 1974, is profound in the formation of the countercultural Reich myth. It acted most immediately on Patti Smith who draws from it in

1 Peter Reich, *A Book of Dreams* (London: John Blake, 2015), 5.

her science fiction *Sprechgesang* "Birdland," appearing on one of the defining albums of what would become early punk rock, *Horses*, released in November 1975. Smith intones,

> He saw his daddy behind the control board / And he was very different tonight / 'Cause he was not human / [...] Moving in like black ships, they were moving in, streams of them / And he put up his hands and he said: "It's me, it's me, I'll give you my eyes, take me up / Oh, now, please take me up, I'm helium raven / Waiting for you, please take me up, don't leave me here!"[2]

More commercially, Peter Reich's memoir would inspire Kate Bush's "Cloudbusting" from *Hounds of Love*, almost precisely a decade after Smith's take was released in September of 1985. Of the cloudbuster and the Oranur Experiment that inspired it, she sings in the persona of Peter Reich:

> I still dream of Orgonon / I wake up crying / You're making rain / And you're just in reach / When you and sleep escape me / You're like my yo-yo that glowed in the dark / What made it special / Made it dangerous / So I bury it / and forget.[3]

In the accompanying promo video, Bush plays Peter Reich and Donald Sutherland plays a strangely steampunk version of Reich, testing a more voluptuous cloudbuster (even as it appears in silhouette on some covers of Peter Reich's memoir), while menaced and arrested by sinister agents. "You look too small / in their big black car / to be a threat to the men in power."[4]

Peter Reich is the lens through which Patti Smith and Kate Bush approach Wilhelm Reich. "Birdland" and "Cloudbusting" are important works of art, and at the same time, they approach Reich mediated by the emotional tone of his son. These are far superior, however to Hawkwind's earlier yet disastrous psych-

2 Patti Smith, "Birdland," *Horses* (Arista, 1975).
3 Kate Bush, "Cloudbusting," *Hounds of Love* (EMI, 1985).
4 Ibid.

boogie take on the orgone accumulator: "It's a back brain stimulator / A cerebral vibrator."[5] Skipping over that misreading of Reich, the present writer is drawn to return to the question of Wilhelm Reich's Gyntian consciousness and the extent to which the melancholy charm of *A Book of Dreams* depends upon the adoption of that Gyntish self by Peer/Peter Reich. Peter Reich's dreams spin about the image of the flying saucer, and about his father's relationship to them.

I recall Reich's admiration for, and wrestling with, Otto Weininger's interpretation of *Peer Gynt*. Working toward the unconscious of the play, Weininger conceived the father-son relationship in opposing forms: the misanthropic and the philanthropic character types in the father. According to Reich, who was not yet a father, but who of course had his own father as a point of constellation, "He defines a philanthropic type as a person who sees his goal in the 'affirmation' of life, the strong and persistent eroticist, of which fathers and teachers are extreme examples." He quotes Weininger: "He who feels himself to be a son can only hate himself; in other words, a son was *driven* to become a son, to allow himself to be engendered and to emerge as an empirically limited subordinate."[6] Born in 1880 to a Jewish father in Vienna, Otto Weininger could certainly be regarded as self-hating[7] and committed suicide by shooting himself when he was twenty-three, in the former home and place of death of Ludwig van Beethoven.[8] He had, perhaps not incidentally, sought unsuccessfully to impress Freud.[9] Elements of his 1903 book *Geschlecht und Charakter* (*Sex and Character*) also bear aggressively Moreau-esque tendencies; see his pages on "organo-

---

5   Hawkwind, "Orgone Accumulator," *The Space Ritual Alive in Liverpool and London* (United Artists, 1972).

6   Wilhelm Reich, "Libidinal Conflicts and Delusions in Ibsen's Peer Gynt," in *Early Writings: Volume 1*, trans. Philip Schmitz (New York: Farrar, Straus and Giroux, 1975), 8.

7   Weininger expressed this through explicit anti-Semitic statements such as seen in Otto Weininger, *Sex and Character* (New York: A.L. Burt, 1906), 325.

8   Chandak Sengoopta, *Otto Weininger: Sex, Science, and Self in Imperial Vienna* (Chicago: University of Chicago Press, 2000), 2.

9   Ibid., 16.

therapy" and transplantation of or relocation of genital glands and organs, and my allusion to Wells's fictional vivisectionist resolve.[10]

Recall that Wilhelm Reich was twelve years old at the time of the Catastrophe in 1909, when he observed his mother's intercourse with his tutor. Reich's knowledge of the affair, and his Oedipal desire to replace both his father and the tutor and make love to his mother, the *drive(n)* qualities of that moment, impressed upon him the morally, sexually, and "empirically limited" subordinate position of "son." The affair was also "empirically limited" to Reich, the unseen witness who kept it, for a time, as a secret from his father, torn between subordination and insubordination. Weininger, Reich quotes, believed that the self-loathing son "feels he will be forever unfree"[11] of the father. Figuratively and mortally, Reich's decision — the necessity of telling his father about the affair — freed the son from both parents, although not of the attendant guilt. This is *not* to make the argument that Peter Reich was self-hating. It is to suggest the extent to which he too was *driven* to be a son to the "strong and persistent eroticist" in his father who perceived "his goal in the 'affirmation' of life." The more interesting point here than Weininger's self-loathing is that of subordination to the myth of the father.

As the Henrik Ibsen play which began Wilhelm Reich's psychoanalytic career opens with a buck, so Peter Reich's memoir opens with the spectral and severed image of a deer. As the deer becomes whole and moves into the shadows of trees, the child hears disembodied and watery voices discussing it. Perhaps Peter Reich remembers something of the dead deer roped to the hood of Reno Smith's car in *Bad Day at Black Rock,* also. The lake outside the child's house has swollen, as if the watery voices are flooding it, gathering high across the lawn before him. Coming to the water, the child sees first the severed image of a man's feet breaking the surface, and then the body, head down beneath the surface. The image recapitulates in inverted pose, something of

---

10 Weininger, *Sex and Character,* 20–21.
11 Reich, "Libidinal Conflicts," 8.

Leon Reich's slow-suicide alleged by Ilse Ollendorff Reich, part of the Catastrophe described in Chapter 2.

So, the first of Peter Reich's dreams is a dislocated image of both death and parturition. He was, however waking up from a motorcycle accident in a Paris hospital in 1963, returning to consciousness from anesthetic, caught in the pain of having his dislocated shoulder forced back into its socket. He was nineteen years old, on a scholarship. Under the physician's gas, Peter's dream of the deer might have been a misapprehension of the stag — the father — after losing control of his motorcycle as the dreamer after whom he is named lost control of the stag, before Peter finds in it the drowned — unconscious — presence or intimation of his father's death; or it might be that the two images, of a more "feminine" deer — pointedly not referred to as a stag — and the drowned father reflects something of the father's psyche. As Wilhelm Reich put it, as Peer Gynt approaches redemption:

> We have come to know Peer as the victim of his own incestuous mother fixation and of the identification with his father, which resulted in the failure to progress from the pleasure principle to reality principle. [...] We were able to see the death of the mother as a loss of objective reality, and finally to recognize how the guilt feelings resulting from the Oedipus complex [...] were responsible for the lapse into psychosis.[12]

It is thus that, without stating it explicitly as such, Peter Reich's memoir opens with a recapitulation of the Gyntian "Buck Fantasy" and an intuition of this potent stage of his father's tragedy. There is in the risen waters of the lake, or the unconscious, the inundation of Peter's psyche by his father. The boy named after the Ibsen character is "a son *driven* to be a son" of a certain kind. But it is not in the outworn archetype of the Gyntish self that the father and son would most profoundly collaborate, but in the science fiction image of the spaceman, the idealized "father and son" relationship of *The Day the Earth Stood Still,* and of Wilhelm Reich's *becoming.*

12 Ibid., 37.

Also recall Wilhelm Reich's resolutions of January 1, 1952: "I must not ever abandon Peter who needs me. I would suffer from it more than he would, but to guide this boy through puberty, though the pitfalls of a crazy world is crucial to me and to him."[13] It is not insignificant that Peter's time in the desert with his father battling UFOS coincides with the period where his father experienced his formative pubertal catastrophe; as if Wilhelm Reich is substituting science fiction adventure for that primal Oedipal scene.

At least some of the collapse of Reich's scientific methodology is explained here: I believe that Reich never intended the desert scene to be "scientific," as much as he intended it — unconsciously perhaps — to be existential. To the general agreement that Peter Reich's memoir is poignant, I believe that the delirium of *Contact with Space,* and the unconscious material below the scattershot nature of the text, flow in the same manner, in the opposite direction *toward the son,* except that the father is still tangled in the remains of a scientific method inadequate to the task of expressing that what he really needs is not contact with space, but contact with Peter, before the scapegoat ritual can remove the father.

In *A Book of Dreams,* Peter Reich's primary memory of engaging flying saucers with the spacegun and the breakthrough in how to defeat them seems to conflate elements of "The Breakdown of a Spacegun Operator," "The Ea Battle of Tucson, December 14," and allusions to the drawing against the Southern Ea logged by Eva Reich from December 21, 1954, until January 20, 1955. Early in *A Book of Dreams,* Peter Reich recounts the burial and unearthing of his radium painted yo-yo during the Arizona expedition. Aside from its direct lyrical influence on Kate Bush's "Cloudbusting," one notes the recapitulation of form in the yo-yo and the flying saucer. The following accounts are from Chapter One of *A Book of Dreams.*

Daddy said I had to bury the glow-in-the-dark yo-yo because the glow stuff was deadly, just like fluorescent light. Glow-in-

---

13 Wilhelm Reich, *Where's the Truth? Letters and Journals, 1948–1957,* ed. Mary Boyd Higgins (New York: Farrar, Straus and Giroux, 2012), 106.

the-dark light was bad energy and didn't mix with Orgone Energy, which was good energy. Daddy was trying to kill the bad energy in the atmosphere. Bad energy came from flying saucers and bombs. The cloudbuster cleaned the atmosphere of the deadly orgone — we called it DOR — and fought the flying saucers. [BD, 14]

Some days later, returned to Little Orgonon after a father-son dinner at a diner where a waitress flirted with him, Peter broke from his math studies to watch for flying saucers from the observation deck. Using binoculars and a telescope, he observed an Ea that he believed might be the one the expedition had named the "Southern Belle." Peter hastened to alert his father. After making his confirmatory observations through his own binoculars, Reich urged his son to fetch William Moise and Eva. As Peter Reich remembers it, "When I got back upstairs, Daddy was looking through the telescope. 'Here, look through. See if you can see. I can make out a thin cigar shape with little windows'" [BD, 27]. Peter saw the Ea but could not discern anything like windows. This description of the spaceship aligns with Wilhelm Reich's sighting of November 28th, 1954, watching with his 3.5-inch refractor telescope the cigar-shaped spaceship with its pair of portholes. Of course, it would be reasonable for Reich to point out on another occasion, this time with Peter, what he had observed before.

Reich instructed Peter: "Run to the cloudbuster and make ready. Unplug all the pipes and pull them out to full length. I'll be right there." This Peter accomplished before Eva Reich and Moise arrived beside the truck. They watched the Ea through binoculars. "I knew it would come," Eva said, "I felt bad all day and said to Bill that I thought there was something in the atmosphere" [ibid.]. The operators awaited Reich, who at last strode toward them, "with his big gray Stetson soft in the starlight" [BD, 28]. Moise changed places with Peter on the truck. Reich ordered Moise to direct the pipes of the spacegun directly at the Ea.

We waited. It didn't do anything. Sometimes they went from side to side when we started drawing, other times they'd just get fainter and fainter as if they were on the end of some long yo-yo string being pulled back into the sky. Bill usually did the drawing but I did it too.

"I feel terrible," said Eva. "I can feel it reacting already. I get that salty taste in my mouth."

"Ja, I feel it too," said Daddy. "Do you feel anything, Moise?"

"Mmhmm," said Bill, "I can feel it starting in my stomach a bit."

"I've got a kind of choking in my throat," I said.

Ahem. ahem ahem. Daddy took off his hat and pushed his hand through his long silvery hair. "I wish I knew if this was an attack or if they are just observing the Earth and don't know what they are doing."

We all watched the EA, sparkling blue, glowing brighter, then dimmer, then bright again.

After a while, Daddy said, "Pete."

"Yes."

"You know where the Orur needle is kept, ja? Go and get it. Make sure you carry it very carefully. There is a flashlight the truck." [BD, 28–29]

The presence of the Orur material in Peter Reich's memory places this scene at December 14, 1954, at the earliest. Peter recalls making his way, anxiously in the dark, to the dry arroyo where the Orur needle in its lead container was concealed beneath a small pile of stones. The needle could be withdrawn by a length of string that protruded from the vessel. When Peter returned to the cloudbuster, with Moise still at the controls, he transferred the needle to another lead vessel at the place where the cables met the telescoping pipes. There was no appreciable effect on the Ea. Peter asked his father if he might replace Moise at the controls — it was considered unsafe to spend too much time drawing from the Ea. Peter experimented with another drawing action, while Moise retrieved a Geiger counter.

I figured that if the cloudbuster could sort of take the energy away or weaken it, I could make the Ea sort of fall by drawing underneath it and to the side of it, weakening the energy around it. So I moved the cloudbuster slowly from one side of the EA to the other. I let it draw on the right side for a while and then dipped slowly under it like a baby's cradle or a yo-yo and rubbed back and forth at the sky beneath it before going up the other side. I let the cloudbuster Orurize on either side. [BD, 30]

Reich was astounded by the readings when Moise returned with the Geiger counter. "'Such a high count cannot come only from the Orur. It can only come from the Ea or the atmosphere. It is almost as if we are directly in the path of the exhaust from the Ea. Maybe it is the exhaust which is causing the desert, sucking away all the moisture'" [ibid.]. Reich's statement about being beneath the exhaust of the Ea aligns with the earlier McCullough breakdown narrative of December 6, where "We apparently got the exhaust or whatever else it might have been right down on us."[14] In Peter Reich's account, his father and Moise engaged in some expository dialogue regarding the nature of DOR, and the cloudbuster's potential to work against desertification. When they returned their attention to Peter at the controls of the cloudbuster, Moise could no longer trace the Ea with his binoculars. Peter's innovation worked. This was the breakthrough.

When it was gone and we were putting the pipes back together, Daddy said, "That was very good, Peeps, very good. You are a real good little soldier because you have discovered a new way to disable the EAS. I am very proud of you."

After I put the needle away in the dry riverbed and Bill had finished putting all the rubber stoppers the cloudbuster, we all walked back to the house together. I walked between Bill and Daddy. Daddy had his hand around my shoulder.

"Yes," he said, "we are really engaged in a cosmic war. Peeps, you must be very brave and very proud, for we are the first human beings to engage in a battle to the death with spaceships. [...] Here, at the age of eleven, you have already disabled a flying saucer using cosmic Orgone Energy. Quite a feat." [BD, 31–32]

14 Wilhelm Reich, *Contact with Space: Oranur Second Report, 1951–1956* (Haverhill: Haverhill House Publishing, 2018), 180.

All of this, you will recall, took place after the waitress had flirted with Peter at the diner. The events represent a kind of phallic displacement of Peter's confused libidinal energy. Reich had explained to Peter that the waitress was flirting with him because, actually, she wanted to make love with his father. "But," Peter remembered, "I couldn't figure out why the waitress was flirting with me, unless it was because she liked me" [BD, 26]. He did not quite believe or could not accept his father's explanation. The engagements with both the waitress and the flying saucer were rites of passage, earning Peter a promotion. "It felt good. I was proud and happy. I had disabled a flying saucer and was in the Cosmic Engineers" [BD, 32].

Later, Peter was with his father in his study, listening to Beethoven's 9th — echoes of Weininger — where they discussed plans for an Army of Cosmic Engineers with Peter now as Lieutenant, and their silk flag with the spinning wave design in white against its orgonomic blue-green.

> I closed my eyes and my mind was joined with Daddy's and Beethoven's and we were all seeing the same thing: a great plain with bold white clouds climbing the sky like mighty stallions, and coming through the clouds on beams of sunlight was the Army of Cosmic Engineers marching straight, forward, and proud beneath tall flags snapping in the wind, marching proudly in smart blue uniforms with hats with shiny brims and shiny white belts. First Daddy — the General — and then Bill and Eva and me, and Tom and the others.... [BD, 33]

In this communion, the CORE men are transposed from the pilots of the hostile spaceships to Reich and his son, and their immediate family and loyal intimates. Peter Reich establishes a cosmic identity for himself and his father. It is more important than which episode of spacegun-Ea battle Peter Reich's memoir refers to, or if it conflates a series of episodes in the preceding, that he begins the process of identification of his father as Cosmic Engineer some time — at least one year — before Reich himself would suggest that identification on March 20, 1956. It is the identity the son needs of the father. It is this transference projection of the father as scientist to spaceman and a melancholy sense of loss that pervades *A Book of Dreams,* an elegiac quality. Peter Reich also partakes in his father's cinematic sense of identity, regarding himself as Gary Cooper, John Agar, his life flickering with Looney Tunes, Federico Fellini, and Jean Cocteau — and later, in Dušan Makavejev's film.

Peter Reich's seminal dream, the one that Patti Smith would draw upon for "Birdland," closes the first part of *A Book of Dreams.* Peter Reich seemingly remembered it as he awoke from treatment on his shoulder, six years after the loss of his father. The dream itself occurred close in the wake of his father's death in November 1957. At boarding school, the son dreamt the night sky was riddled with Eas descending toward him. For some time, he had been developing the fantasy that Reich might be at the controls of any of the flying saucers that he had envisioned. "What if Daddy is in the spaceship?" [BD, 99]. Peter made hand gestures that he felt would generate an energy field visible to its viewing scope.

> *Daddy looked through the scope and he could see me. He wasn't wearing his khaki pants and red-and-black checked shirt. They were in mothballs at Bill and Eva's house in Maine. He was wearing a new uniform made of silky blue, with the spinning wave symbol across his chest. On his shoulders were general's stars, only these were real stars, five on each side, glowing and sparkling. His face was pink and looked calm and serene as he looked through the scope.* [ibid.]

Running across the lacrosse field below the spaceship, Peter pleaded, "Please come and take me away please please. Please here are my eyes, here I am sending them far out to you" [BD, 100]. The giving of eyes was Reich's vernacular for giving full concentration, full commitment to communication.

> *Daddy's eyes were soft and smiling. He was happy because he was going to come and take me way with him to another planet where we would be happy and free. The world wasn't ready for him. In a new language without words, the navigator looked at Daddy. Daddy went over to the Orgone Radar Screen that glowed with red and blue specks of light.* [ibid.]

At first Reich saw only the radar signals of the other three space-ships present in the sky above the school. Yet, almost immediately as Peter had envisioned this moment, Air Force jets screamed in from the south. "The jets were going to chase them away! Oh my God, didn't they understand that these flying saucers weren't enemies now? That they had Him? O God, please don't let them chase him away" [ibid.]. But as he ran across the field toward the flying saucer with his father at the scope, the jets closed in. Telepathically, the CORE captain warned Reich that they would be destroyed if they did not leave. In turn, Peter received a tele-pathic message from his father:

> *Daddy thought at me in the screen. 'Peter, we cannot come and save you. You must be brave and stay here on Earth.' His tears, when they hit the soft blue screen, made little soft noises. 'I'm sorry, Peeps, sonny. We have to go. They still don't believe it, but we won. We won. Goodbye, Peeps, goodbye. I will always love you.' He looked at the captain and nodded.* [BD, 101]

The religious imagery of victory in death, transfiguration, and ascension — the capitalization of Him — require no belaboring. It is the imagery not only of the "murder of Christ," but of *The Day the Earth Stood Still*, also. The surrogate family of the space-man in whom Reich saw himself, not least the boy Bobby with whom he has shared his secrets in Washington, DC must yield their affections to the transcendence of the cosmic mission. Is Reich's shift from antagonist to protagonist in the flying saucer drama really so strange? The hero usurps the role of the "danger-ous enemy alien," as Reich was once supposed to be by the FBI on his first arrest in 1941. Recall Myron Sharaf's observation of the Oranur emergency once more: "What was and remains most impressive is the rapid and profound way Reich conceptualized the many observations he made."[15] Reich's experience demanded ongoing reconceptualization. It was ever thus, and that is one sign of an examined life. Is this not another rapid and profound revision of his hypothesis in the direction of his son, who he

15 Myron R. Sharaf, *Fury on Earth: A Biography of Wilhelm Reich* (New York: Da Capo, 1994), 376.

had dedicated himself to after his Oranur-period heart attack? As Reich had said, "I must not ever abandon Peter who needs me. I would suffer from it more than he would, but to guide this boy through puberty, through all the pitfalls of a crazy world is crucial to me and to him."[16]

A curious thought occurs to me when considering the recasting of the "flying saucers," the "spaceships," or Ea of the CORE men, their once malevolent machines: Reich was born on March 24, 1897, just as the first serialized chapter of H.G. Wells's *The War of the Worlds* was going to print for the April editions of *Pearson's Magazine* (UK) and *Cosmopolitan* (US).[17] As Wells revised the serial manuscript for publication as a novel, he was compelled to add to it. One of the revisions Wells made was the introduction of the artilleryman whose monologue on adaptation and survival under the Martians occurs in Book Two, Chapter 7 of the novel. The artilleryman fantasizes a reversal that anticipates Reich's, that men will take control of the Martian fighting machines. "For a while," the narrator says, "the imaginative daring of the artilleryman, and the tone of assurance and courage he assumed, completely dominated my mind."[18] This coincidence is not to say that Reich modeled himself consciously on the artilleryman of Wells's novel, arguably the greatest of all "invasion from outer space" and catastrophe novels. It is to say that I find myself intrigued by the "imaginative daring" and "tone of assurance and courage" of Reich — the artilleryman with his cloudbuster and space gun recasting his spaceship hypothesis in terms that, resist as one might, have such a powerful precedent. The zeitgeist is not exorcized without a struggle, and in my analysis, such an exorcism should not be attempted.

If one may be permitted some license with Donald W. Winnicott's theory,[19] what occurs with Reich, the flying sau-

---

16 Reich, *Where's the Truth?*.

17 Peter J. Beck, *The War of the Worlds from H. G. Wells to Orson Welles, Jeff Wayne, Steven Spielberg & Beyond* (New York: Bloomsbury, 2016), 139.

18 H.G. Wells, *The War of the Worlds* (London: Penguin, 2005), 158.

19 D.W. Winnicott, "The Use of an Object and Relating through Identifications," in *Playing and Reality* (London: Routledge, 2005),

cers, and the spacemen identity can be brought into focus; and one might triangulate Peter Reich here, also. The transitional relationship is one in which the object changes from an object of *relation* to one of usage. The writer is tempted to warp Winnicott's terminology toward "unidentified flying object" relations. "Between relating and use is the subject's placing the object outside the area of the subject's omnipotent control; that is, the subject's perception of the object as an external phenomenon, not as a projective entity, in fact recognition of it as an entity in its own right."[20] In Wilhelm Reich's case, this means his recognition that his projection — since his introjection of the flying saucer and the spaceman became one of usage after the uncanny effect of *The Day the Earth Stood Still* — has always been himself. In Winnicott, the paradox is that the object is "destroyed" in the transition, yet persists.

> After "subject relates to object" comes "subject destroys object" (as it becomes external); and then may become "*object survives* destruction by the subject." But there may or may not be survival. A new feature thus arrives in the theory of object-relating. The subject says to the [unidentified flying] object: "I destroyed you," and the object is there to receive communication. From now on the subject says: "Hullo object!" "I destroyed you." "I love you." "You have value for me because of your survival of my destruction of you." "While I am loving you I am all the time destroying you in (unconscious) *fantasy*." Here fantasy begins for the individual. The subject can now use the object that has survived. [...] In other words, because of the survival of the object, the subject may now have started to live in a world of objects, and so the subject stands to gain immeasurably; but the price has to be paid in acceptance of the ongoing destruction in unconscious fantasy relative to object-relating.[21]

115–27.

20 Ibid., 120.

21 Ibid., 120–21, addition of "[unidentified flying]" mine.

One recalls the ways in which the flying saucers, the Ea, the Unidentified Flying Object-relations in Reich's battles tended to fade out — they were both "destroyed" and retained. Reich's agon was with himself, with his depression, as subject to persecution, even as one driven to be a son in an Oedipal struggle. Eventually, and in relation to Peter Reich's subjectivity, the writer believes that Reich came to understand this, and the projection of the spaceman (relation) gave way and became the usable fantasy-identification that both father and son required. He would no longer project, he would embody the spaceman. Peter Reich observed the physical destruction of his father — and something of his psychic destruction also in the burning of his books — and yet the image of the father as spaceman at the controls of a flying saucer was caught in the persistence of memory; it is not difficult to perceive the passion narrative here, nor the mechanisms of mourning. To the extent that the father cannot take the son away in his spaceship, the son can come into being as a subject in "relation" as son to the dead father; at least, he might. Another passage from Winnicott serves us here:

> The object has become meaningful. Projection mechanisms and identifications have been operating, and the subject is depleted to the extent that something of the subject is found in the object, though enriched by feeling. Accompanying these changes is some degree of physical involvement (however slight) towards excitement, in the direction of the functional climax of an orgasm.[22]

22 Ibid., 118.

13

Unidentified Flying Objects of Desire: A Brief Coda

The fact remains that Reich, in the name of desire, caused a song of life to pass into psychoanalysis. He denounced, in the final resignation of Freudianism, a fear of life, a resurgence of the ascetic ideal, a cultural broth of bad consciousness. Better to depart in search of the Orgone, he said to himself, in search of the vital and cosmic element of desire, than to continue being a psychoanalyst under those conditions. No one forgave him this...Reich was the first to attempt to make the analytic machine and the revolutionary machine function together. In the end, he only had his own desiring-machines, his paranoiac, miraculous, and celibate boxes, with metallic inner walls lined with cotton and wool.

— Gilles Deleuze and Félix Guattari[1]

In *Anti-Oedipus: Capitalism and Schizophrenia* (1977), Gilles Deleuze and Félix Guattari found in Wilhelm Reich a culture hero, with D.H. Lawrence and Henry Miller. Following Deleuze and Guattari, one might regard the irruption of the flying saucer as a response to forms of totalitarianism and the Oedipus complex, as a manifestation of irrational desiring-production. Their

1   Gilles Deleuze and Félix Guattari, *Anti-Oedipus: Capitalism and Schizophrenia,* trans. Robert Hurley, Mark Seem, and Helen R. Lane (London: Penguin, 2009), 119.

phantasmal or eidetic presence are precisely desire, or lack, and yet still they are still the *unidentified* flying objects of desire, where experiments on the body are performed — penetration, castration, impregnation — where speech is impossible — the loss of the subject, the death of the speaking "I." Here, they are the machines of unconscious or Oedipal desire produced by desiring-machines.

Where, on the radar scope, do these unidentified flying objects of desire, or these unidentified flying object-relations appear in constellation with desire, and with mourning? Whence this interest in performing autopsies on their occupants, ourselves? The flying saucer is — the uterus, the führer, the surgical theater, the family romance, the tomb, the projection, the introjection — the perfect object of psychoanalysis. And whatever his experiments, Wilhelm Reich never truly left psychoanalysis, as certain as it abandoned him. In consideration of the preceding, the writer finds Reich — the man who died, and died again — as sane as himself, as sane as you reader who have come to this end.

Wilhelm Reich was a man, yes, of "monumental disproportions," and he was, in the terms Lawrence's *Apocalypse* — that great Nietzschean cry transumed by *The Murder of Christ* — "aristocratic." This is to say that his originality, the force of his personality, pressed hierarchization and danger into his relationships. Lawrence declares, "As soon as he is with other men, Jesus is an aristocrat, a master."[2] One recalls the unusual way Reich had described the version of himself he witnessed in *Bad Day at Black Rock,* with "Spencer Tracy in the master role."[3] As Lawrence said of the passion of the scapegoat, "And just as inevitably as Jesus had to have a Judas Iscariot among his disciples, so did there have to be a Revelation in the New Testament. Why? Because the nature of man demands it and will always demand it."[4] The Apocalypse, Lawrence writes, hard upon the edge of his life, "has been running for two thousand years: [...]

2   D.H. Lawrence, *Apocalypse and the Writings on Revelation,* ed. Mara Kalnins (London: Penguin, 1995), 68.

3   Wilhelm Reich, *Contact with Space: Oranur Second Report, 1951–1956* (Haverhill: Haverhill House Publishing, 2018), 152. Italics mine.

4   Lawrence, *Apocalypse,* 67.

It wants to murder the powerful, to seize power for itself, the weakling."[5] And perhaps at another time one could make the case that the apocalyptic appearance of flying saucers conceals an ineffectuality. Their appearance and their methods of waging this interplanetary war are vague, ineffable, and furtive, such that they are vulnerable to a father and son with an improvised weapon, dreaming together in the desert, each fighting for the love of the other as their relationship began to flicker and fade out, threatened by time and government. I called it a tragedy, this story of Wilhelm Reich. In *The War of the Worlds,* H.G. Wells writes of pathology at the microscopic and macrocosmic scale, and of the observing Martians:

> No one would have believed, in the last years of the nineteenth century, that this world was being watched keenly and closely by intelligences grester than man's and yet as mortal as his own; that as men busied themselves about their various concerns they were scrutinized and studied, perhaps as narrowly as a man with a microscope might scrutinize the transient creatures that swarm and multiply in a drop of water. With infinite complacency men to and fro over this globe about their little affairs, serene in their assurance of their empire over matter. It is possible that the infusoria under the microscope do the same.[6]

The present writer sees the alienated Reich at his microscope, observing the pulse of life that would convince him of the orgasm formula, of the presence of orgone energy. In his experiments of the 1930s and 1940s, Reich studied his infusoria as keenly as the Martians studied the inhabitants of Earth, and what Wells imagined allegorically Reich made a tenable ontology, founded at the biopsychic threshold where psychoanalysis had hesitated. There are those, arguably a majority, who believe that Reich was, as it were, abducted by alien ideas; yet I maintain that Reich found himself inside the numinous, unconscious, immanent, and nightmare preoccupations of his time. To the

5   Ibid., 69.
6   H.G. Wells, *The War of the Worlds* (London: Penguin, 2005), 7.

first words of this book, Reich's statement of 1938, "I am neither a 'fanatic' nor a 'madman.' Simply happen to be involved
in work that is destroying me slowly but surely,"[7] one could add
much concerning the tendency of the abyss to gaze back. There
is inevitability in Reich's tale; in his agon with Sigmund Freud;
in his own Oedipal catastrophe that would lead to imaginative
attempts at resolution, of, as Sándor Ferenczi put it, "self-taught
attempts on the patient's part to cure himself"[8] of its fallout; and
in how in the process the novel cinematic unconscious would
snatch up the man who loved Peer Gynt in the metapsychologi-
cal triangulation of Freud, Albert Einstein, and Wilhelm Reich
forced home by *The Day the Earth Stood Still*. Perhaps you will
recall my early invocation of Philip Marlowe: "There is no trap
so deadly as the trap you set for yourself."[9] And as Reich said in
The Murder of Christ: *"The trap is man's emotional structure, his
character structure."*[10]

From this trap, there was — and is — no exit.

7 Wilhelm Reich, *Beyond Psychology: Letters and Journals, 1934–1939,* ed.
   Mary Boyd Higgins (New York: Farrar, Straus and Giroux, 1994), 181.

8 Sándor Ferenczi, "Introjection and Transference," in *First
   Contributions to Psycho-analysis,* ed. and trans. Ernest Jones (London:
   Routledge, 2018), 57.

9 Raymond Chandler, *The Long Goodbye* (New York: Vintage, 1992), 86.

10 Wilhelm Reich, *The Murder of Christ* (New York: Farrar, Straus and
   Giroux, 1971), 3.

Bibliography

Anonymous23Skidoo. "Wilhelm Reich – Alone (10 min. home recording) (03.04.1952)." *YouTube,* March 23, 2012. https://www.youtube.com/watch?v=4t5h-93bxOY.

Baldwin, James. "The Devil Finds Work." In *Collected Essays,* edited by Toni Morrison, 479–572. New York: Library of America, 1998.

Beck, Peter J. *The War of the Worlds from H.G. Wells to Orson Welles, Jeff Wayne, Steven Spielberg & Beyond.* New York: Bloomsbury, 2016.

Bloom, Harold. *Take Arms Against a Sea of Troubles: The Power of the Reader's Mind Over a Universe of Death.* New Haven: Yale University Press, 2020.

Brady, Mildred E. "The New Cult of Sex and Anarchy." *Harper's Magazine,* April 1947, 313–22.

———. "The Strange Case of Wilhelm Reich." *The New Republic,* May 26, 1947, 20–23.

Burroughs, William S. *The Ticket That Exploded.* New York: Grove Press, 1987.

———. *The Western Lands.* London: Penguin, 2010.

Burroughs, William S., and Daniel Odier. *The Job: Interviews with William S, Burroughs.* London: Penguin, 2008.

Bush, Kate. "Cloudbusting." *Hounds of Love.* EMI, 1985.

Chandler, Raymond. *The Long Goodbye.* New York: Vintage, 1992.

Conger, John P. *Jung & Reich: The Body as Shadow.* Berkeley: North Atlantic Books, 2005.

Dearborn, Mary V. *Mailer: A Biography.* Boston: Houghton Mifflin, 1999.

Deleuze, Gilles, and Félix Guattari. *Anti-Oedipus: Capitalism and Schizophrenia.* Translated by Robert Hurley, Mark Seem, and Helen R. Lane. London: Penguin, 2009.

Eliade, Mircea. *Journal I, 1945–1955.* Translated by Mac Linscott Ricketts. Chicago: University of Chicago Press, 1990.

Erikson, Erik H. *Identity: Youth and Crisis.* New York: W.W. Norton, 1994.

Elliot, T.S. *The Waste Land and Other Writings.* New York: Random House, 2002.

Ferenczi, Sándor. "Introjection and Transference." In *First Contributions to Psycho-analysis,* edited and translated by Ernest Jones, 35–93. London: Routledge, 2018.

———. "On the Definition of Introjection." In *Final Contributions to the Problems and Methods of Psychoanalysis,* edited by Michael Balint, translated by Eric Mosbacher and others, 316–18. London: Routledge, 2018.

Fitzgerald, F. Scott. *The Crack-Up.* New York: New Directions, 1993.

Frazer, James G. *The Golden Bough: A Study in Magic and Religion.* Oxford: Oxford University Press, 2009.

Freud, Sigmund. "Beyond the Pleasure Principle." In *Beyond the Pleasure Principle and Other Writings,* translated by John Reddick, 43–102. London: Penguin, 2003.

———. "Instincts and Their Vicissitudes." In *On the History of the Psycho-Analytic Movement: Papers on Metapsychology and Other Works,* trans. James Strachey, 190–40. London: Vintage, 2001.

———. *The Psychopathology of Everyday Life.* Translated by Anthea Bell. London: Penguin, 2003.

———. *Totem and Taboo: Some Points of Agreement between the Mental Lives of Savages and Neurotics.* Translated by James Strachey. New York: W.W. Norton, 1950.

Garber, Megan. "The Man Who Introduced the World to Flying Saucers." *The Atlantic,* June 15, 2014. https://www. theatlantic.com/technology/archive/2014/06/the-man-who-introduced-the-world-to-flying-saucers/372732/.

Gay, Peter. *Freud: A Life for Our Time.* New York: W.W. Norton, 1998.

Greenfield, Jerome. *Wilhelm Reich vs. the U.S.A.* New York: W.W. Norton, 1974.

Hale Jr., Nathan G. *The Rise and Crisis of Psychoanalysis in the United States: Freud and the Americans, 1917–1985.* New York: Oxford University Press, 1995.

———. "Wilhelm Reich vs. the U.S.A.: The Discoverer of the Orgone." *The New York Times,* August 11, 1974. https://www.nytimes.com/1974/08/11/archives/wilhelm-reich-vs-the-usa-the-discoverer-of-the-orgone-by-jerome.html.

Haskin, Byron, dir. *H.G. Wells' The War of the Worlds.* Paramount, 1953.

Hawkwind. "Orgone Accumulator." *The Space Ritual Alive in Liverpool and London.* United Artists, 1972.

Henry, Bonnie. "Sacred Ground." *Tucson.com,* June 22, 2006. https://tucson.com/lifestyles/bonnie-henry-sacred-ground/article_1de89819-bb19-5ac8-958c-af4198e49bf9.html.

Hobbes, Thomas. *Leviathan.* London: Penguin, 2017.

Jung, Carl. *Aion: Researches into the Phenomenology of the Self.* Translated by R.F.C. Hull. Princeton: Princeton University Press, 1979.

———. *Flying Saucers: A Modern Myth of Things Seen in the Sky.* Translated by R.F.C. Hull. London: Routledge, 2002.

———. *Memories, Dreams, Reflections.* Edited by Aniela Jaffé. Translated by Richard Winston and Clara Winston. New York, Vintage, 1989.

———. *The Archetypes and the Collective Unconscious.* Translated by R.F.C. Hull. Princeton: Princeton University Press, 1968.

Kerouac, Jack. *On the Road.* In *The Road Novels, 1957–1960,* edited by Douglas Brinkley, 1–278. New York: Library of America, 2007.

———. *The Flying Saucers Are Real.* Illustrated by Frank Tinsley. New York: Fawcett Publications, 1950.

———. *The Subterraneans.* New York: Grove Press, 1958.

Keyhoe, Donald E. *Flying Saucers from Outer Space.* Hutchinson: Doubleday, 1954.

Lawrence, D.H. *Apocalypse and the Writings on Revelation.*
Edited by Mara Kalnins. London, Penguin, 1995.

———. *Psychoanalysis and the Unconscious; and, Fantasia of the Unconscious.* Edited by Bruce Steele. Cambridge: Cambridge University Press, 2014.

———. *The Man Who Died.* New York: Ecco, 2002.

Lennon, Michael. *Norman Mailer: A Double Life.* New York: Simon & Schuster, 2013.

Leonard, Jonathan N. "Flying Sky-High." *The New York Times Book Review,* November 22, 1953.

Mailer, Norman. "The White Negro: Superficial Reflections on the Hipster." In *Advertisements for Myself,* 302–22. New York: The New American Library, 1960.

Makavejev, Dušan, dir. *WR: Mysteries of the Organism.* Neoplanta Film, 1971.

Malcolm, Janet. *In the Freud Archives.* New York: New York Review of Books, 2002.

Marcuse, Herbert. *Eros and Civilization: A Philosophical Inquiry into Freud.* Boston: Beacon Press, 1974.

Maslow, Abraham H. *The Farther Reaches of Human Nature.* New York: Penguin Compass, 1993.

McCullough, Robert A. "Rocky Road Toward Functionalism." *CORE (Cosmic Orgone Engineering)* VII, nos. 3–4 (1955): 144–54.

Mottram, Eric. *William Burroughs: The Algebra of Need.* London: M. Boyars, 1977.

Nietzsche, Friedrich. *The Birth of Tragedy.* In *Basic Writings of Nietzsche,* edited and translated by Walter Kaufmann, 16–144. New York: Random House, 2000.

Ollendorff Reich, Ilse. *Wilhelm Reich: A Personal Biography.* New York: Avon Books, 1970.

Preminger, Otto, dir. *The Court-Martial of Billy Mitchell.* Warner Bros., 1955.

Reich, Peter. *A Book of Dreams.* London: John Blake, 2015.

Reich, Wilhelm. "A Case of Pubertal Breaching of the Incest Taboo." In *Early Writings: Volume 1,* translated by Philip Schmitz, 65–72. New York: Farrar, Straus and Giroux, 1975.

———. *American Odyssey: Letters and Journals, 1940–1947.* Edited by Mary Boyd Higgins. Translated by Derek Jordan,

Inge Jordan, and Philip Schmitz. New York: Farrar, Straus and Giroux, 1999.

———. *Beyond Psychology: Letters and Journals, 1934–1939.* Edited by Mary Boyd Higgins. Translated by Derek and Inge Jordan and Philip Schmitz. New York: Farrar, Straus and Giroux, 1994.

———. *Character Analysis.* Translated by Vincent R. Carfagno. New York: Farrar, Straus and Giroux, 1972.

———. *Contact with Space: Oranur Second Report, 1951–1956.* Haverhill: Haverhill House Publishing, 2018.

———. *CORE (Cosmic Orgone Engineering)* VI, nos. 1–4: *OROP Desert, Part 1: Space Ships, DOR and Drought.* Rangeley: Orgone Institute, 1954.

———. *Ether, God and Devil / Cosmic Superimposition.* New York: Farrar, Straus and Giroux, 1973.

———. *History of the Discovery of the Life Energy (American Period, 1939–1952): The Einstein Affair.* Rangeley: Orgone Institute Press, 1953.

———. "Libidinal Conflicts and Delusions in Ibsen's Peer Gynt." In *Early Writings: Volume 1,* translated by Philip Schmitz, 3–64. New York: Farrar, Straus and Giroux, 1975.

———. *Passion of Youth: An Autobiography, 1897–1922.* Edited by Mary Boyd Higgins. Translated by Philip Schmitz and Jerri Tompkins. New York: Farrar, Straus and Giroux, 1988.

———. *Reich Speaks of Freud.* Edited by Mary Higgins and Chester M. Raphael. Translated by Therese Pol. New York: Farrar, Straus and Giroux, 1967.

———. *The Bion Experiments on the Origin of Life.* Edited by Mary Boyd Higgins. Translated by Derek Jordan and Inge Jordan. New York: Farrar, Straus and Giroux, 1979.

———. *The Discovery of the Orgone,* Vol. I: *The Function of the Orgasm: Sex-Economic Problems of Biological Energy.* Translated by Vincent R. Carfango. New York: Farrar, Straus and Giroux, 1973.

———. *The Discovery of the Orgone,* Vol. II: *The Cancer Biopathy.* Translated by Andrew White, Mary Higgins, and Chester M. Raphael. New York: Farrar, Straus and Giroux, 1973.

———. *The Mass Psychology of Fascism.* Translated by Vincent R. Carfagno. New York: Farrar, Straus and Giroux, 1980.

———. *The Murder of Christ.* New York: Farrar, Straus and Giroux, 1971.

———. *The Oranur Experiment, First Report (1947–1951).* Rangeley: Orgone Institute Press, 1951.

———. *Where's the Truth? Letters and Journals, 1948–1957.* Edited by Mary Boyd Higgins. Translated by Derek Jordan and Inge Jordan. New York: Farrar, Straus and Giroux, 2012.

Renan, Ernest. *The Life of Jesus.* London: Trübner & Co., 1871.

Rickels, Laurence A. *I Think I Am Philip K. Dick.* Minneapolis: University of Minnesota Press, 2010.

Riddick, John. "Radio 'Static' May Only Be Galaxy-To-Galaxy Broadcast." *Tucson Daily Citizen Evening Edition,* December 14, 1954.

Robinson, Paul A. *The Freudian Left: Wilhelm Reich, Geza Roheim, Herbert Marcuse.* New York: Harper, 1969.

Ross, Irwin. "The Strange Case of Dr. Wilhelm Reich." *New York Post,* September 5, 1954.

Roszak, Theodore. *The Making of a Counter Culture: Reflections on the Technocratic Society and Its Youthful Opposition.* New York: Anchor, 1969.

———. *The Voice of the Earth: An Exploration of Ecopsychology.* Grand Rapids: Phanes, 2001.

"Saucers Not from Outer Space." *Tucson Daily Citizen Evening Edition,* December 15, 1954.

Self, Will. "Chernobyl." In *Why Read: Selected Writings, 2001–2021,* 52–74. New York: Grove Atlantic, 2023.

Sengoopta, Chandak. *Otto Weininger: Sex, Science, and Self in Imperial Vienna.* Chicago: University of Chicago Press, 2000.

Sharaf, Myron R. *Fury on Earth: A Biography of Wilhelm Reich.* New York: Da Capo, 1994.

Smith, Patti. "Birdland." *Horses.* Arista, 1975.

Sontag, Susan. *Regarding the Pain of Others.* New York: Farrar, Straus and Giroux, 2003

Strick, James E. *Wilhelm Reich, Biologist.* Cambridge: Harvard University Press, 2015.

Sturges, John, dir. *Bad Day at Black Rock*. Metro-Goldwyn-Mayer, 1955.

Talese, Gay. *Thy Neighbor's Wife*. New York: Harper Perennial, 2009.

Tevis, Walter. *The Man Who Fell to Earth*. London: Bloomsbury, 1999.

Torok, Maria. "The Illness of Mourning and the Fantasy of the Exquisite Corpse." In Maria Torok and Nicholas Abraham, *The Shell and the Kernel: Renewals of Psychoanalysis,* Vol. 1, edited and translated by Nicholas T. Rand, 107–24. Chicago: University of Chicago Press, 1994.

Tucson Fire Department. *Plane Crashes, Start to 1959: Tucson Area,* http://www.tucsonfirefoundation.com/wp-content/uploads/2020/01/Plane-Crashes-Start-to-1959.pdf.

Turner, Christopher. *Adventures in the Orgasmatron: How the Sexual Revolution Came to America*. New York: Farrar, Straus and Giroux, 2011.

Tynan, Kenneth. *The Diaries of Kenneth Tynan*. Edited by John Lahr. New York: Bloomsbury, 2001.

von Franz, Marie-Louise. *Projection and Re-Collection in Jungian Psychology: Reflections of the Soul*. Translated by William H. Kennedy. La Salle: Open Court Publishing, 1995.

Weininger, Otto. *Sex and Character*. New York: A.L. Burt, 1906.

Wells, H.G. *The War of the Worlds*. London: Penguin, 2005.

Werker, Alfred L., dir. *Walk East on Beacon!* Columbia Pictures, 1952.

Weston, Jessie L. *From Ritual to Romance*. Mineola: Dover, 1997.

Wilson, Colin. *Introduction to the New Existentialism*. London: Aristeia Press, 2019.

———. *The Occult: The Ultimate Guide for Those Who Would Walk with the Gods*. London: Watkins, 2015.

———. *The Outsider*. New York: Tarcher Perigee, 2016

———. *The Quest for Wilhelm Reich: A Critical Biography*. New York: Anchor Press/Doubleday, 1981.

Wilson, Robert Anton. *Wilhelm Reich in Hell*. Phoenix: Falcon Press, 1987.

Winnicott, D.W. "The Use of an Object and Relating Through Identifications." In *Playing and Reality,* 115–27. London: Routledge, 2005.

Wise, Robert, dir. *The Day the Earth Stood Still.* 20th Century Fox, 1951.